Tennessee
MUSIC
Its People and Places
Nashville • Memphis • East Tennessee
Blues • Country • Soul • Gospel • Bluegrass • Old-Time • New Acoustic

PETER COATS ZIMMERMAN

**COMISSIONED PHOTOGRAPHY
BY JAMES PERRY WALKER**

MF Miller
Freeman
Books

First published in the United States
by Miller Freeman Books
600 Harrison Street
San Francisco, CA 94107

E-mail: mfbooks@mfi.com
Web: www.books.mfi.com

Miller Freeman Inc., is a United News & Media Company.

Edited by Andrew Coe
Designed by David Hurst
Photograph and illustration procurer: Pauli Galin
Maps by Chris Folks and Mike Morgenfield

Distributed to the book trade in the U.S. and Canada by
Publishers Group West, 1700 Fourth St., Berkeley, CA 94710

Distributed to the music trade in the U.S. and Canada by
Hal Leonard Publishing, P.O. Box 13819, Milwaukee, WI 53213

Library of Congress Catalog Card Number has been requested.

ISBN: 0-87930-533-9

Printed by Twin Age

Odyssey Productions Limited
1004 Kowloon Centre, Ashley Road, Kowloon, Hong Kong
Tel: (852) 2856 3896 Fax: (852) 2565 8004
E-mail: odyssey@asiaonline.net

Printed in Hong Kong
98 99 00 01 02   5 4 3 2 1

opposite: Primitive wood carving from West
Tennessee, circa mid-19th century. Courtesy
of Ellis Truett Jr., photo by Perry Walker.

Contents

Essays

Excerpts

Maps

Acknowledgments

I WOULD LIKE TO THANK the musicians for sharing their time and insights: Earl Banks, Nancy and Norman Blake, Alison Brown, Felice Bryant, Janette Carter, Jessi Colter, Steve Cropper, Jim Crosthwait, Stephen Allen Davis, Jim Dickinson, Jerry Douglas, Tav Falco, Ed Finney, Al Green, John Hartford, Teenie Hodges, Harlan Howard, Waylon Jennings, Bill Keith, Doyle Lawson, Larry Lee, Claire Lynch, Del McCoury, Edgar Meyer, Rob and Amy Nicar, Mark O'Connor, Carl Perkins, David Rawlings, Kristi Rose, Sid Selvidge, Tim Stafford, Carlock Stooksbury, Marty Stuart, Doc Watson, Gillian Welch, and Victor Wooten.

The following also helped in various ways: Tom Adkinson, Stephen Betts, Alison Black, Roger Brashears, Will Campbell, Robie Cogswell, Corinna Cornejo, Ray Crabtree, Douglas Day, Alex deLaszlo, Margarita Delgado, Alexa Duncan, Katharine England, Colin Escott, Janet and Dick Flowers, Wes Flowers, Tommy Foster, Ray Fox, John Fry, Bob Fulcher, Pauli Galin, Albert Gore, Kevin Grogan, Barbara Harnack, Christine Havelock, Katharine Herndon, Laura Helper, Sarah Hollister, Bill Ivey, Matt Kelsey, Amy Kurland, Penelope Lane, Bernard Lansky, Ken Levitan, Kip Lornell, Jack May, Jody and Dan McCall, Fred McClellan, Wendy McDaris, Roddy Moore, Joe Morrell, Bud Phillips, Douglas Pote, Ronnie Pugh, Jim Ramer, Gil Reavill, John Seigenthaler, Jim Sherraden, Frank Stewart, Happy Traum, Perry and Mary Walker, Charles K. Wolfe, Blake White, Tim White, James Wolfe Jr., and Jean Zimmerman.

May and Herb Shayne provided safe haven and encouragement in Nashville, and Jim Cole served as point man in Memphis. Magnus Bartlett nurtured the project and David Hurst put the pieces together; Alfred von Krusenstiern, Walter Carter, and John Hartford read the book and made invaluable suggestions. My parents, Betty and Steve Zimmerman, kept the faith through its gestation.

Please send comments and corrections to Peter Zimmerman, 7269 via del Reposo, Scottsdale, AZ 85258, USA.

Tennessee is a lucky state because it's a façade. You would think that all the music world comes from Tennessee, but if you really think about it, what's poured into Tennessee is the talent of the Carolinas, Georgia, Alabama, Mississippi, Texas . . . from all over the place, you know? And that makes up Tennessee music. And that's not just today; it's been that way for a lot of years. So Tennessee's a very fortunate state, musically.

~ Marty Stuart of Philadelphia, Mississippi

Introduction

THIS BOOK IS ABOUT MUSIC in Tennessee past and present, and covers seven related and somewhat arbitrarily defined genres. For the most part, I have focused on music of the 20th century, which, due to the advent of records and radio, is better documented than that of earlier times. Over the years, Tennessee music has been created not just by native Tennesseans. Rather, the state has served as a crossroads for transplants from throughout the mid-South region and beyond.

It is arguable that no other state in the Union has contributed so many great musicians, singers, and songwriters — natives and transplants — and nowhere else has so much good music been recorded, and such a diverse range of it. Most people associate Tennessee with Nashville's country music or the Memphis blues, but the state has also made important contributions to rockabilly, jazz, bluegrass, old-time, gospel, soul, new acoustic, even classical, rock, and rap. The Queens of Rock and Soul, Tina Turner and Aretha Franklin, were born in Tennessee, and its King, Elvis Presley, lived and died there. Likewise, both Roy Acuff and Kitty Wells — country's King and Queen — came from Tennessee. So did Bessie Smith, the Empress of the Blues (the Queen, Koko Taylor, hails from Memphis), as well as rockabilly legend Carl Perkins and Jimmy Blanton, who revolutionized the jazz bass.

Music is, to borrow from Shakespeare, "boundless as the sea." Its scope, according to Duke Ellington, is "immense and infinite." Trying to categorize it makes for a thankless task at best. The different types of music that have developed in Tennessee are in fact a hodgepodge of interrelated and cross-influencing styles. For instance, gospel is said to be the mother of the blues, which in turn serves as the foundation for rock and roll; bluegrass combines elements of blues, old-time, and jazz. All music has roots: blues in Africa, old-time in Britain, and so forth. While race often plays a big role in shaping the various genres, music transcends color lines as well.

Neither encyclopedic nor technical, the following guide is meant to be a sampler for those who want to learn more about this amazingly rich and diverse microcosm of American music. I have relied on interviews with musicians conducted across the state, including the famous, such as Waylon Jennings, as well as those who, for various reasons, never made it big — like Memphis blues guitarist Earl "the Pearl" Banks. Others, like Bristol's Rob Nicar, don't *want* to make it big. He pounds nails by day to support his amateur fiddling habit.

The genre chapters are followed by a destinations section that provides information on the state's music-related sites and venues, as well as giving an impressionistic, scattershot overview of the three "grand divisions" of East, Middle, and West Tennessee, with special attention to Nashville and Memphis. At the end is a select list of books and records, and information on how to order them.

My hope is that this book will be both useful to those visiting Tennessee — which is at once beautiful, centrally located, and quirky — and an interesting read for those armchair travelers content to explore it from afar.

MY GRANDMOTHER, VIRGINIA WHITE COATS, who passed away a few years ago at age 81 in Scottsdale, Arizona, spent the first 75 years of her life as a farmer and housewife in Greenfield, a small town in northwestern Tennessee's Weakley County. My mother's side of the family has lived in the area since the 1820s, when William Hillis built a cabin near the Obion River, making him a contemporary of Davy Crockett's, the bearhunter and three-time congressman who lived in the county's southwestern corner.

In his evocative 1834 autobiography, Crockett described a reunion with his family after a hard week's commerce along the Obion. "They seemed mighty glad to see me, however little the quality folks might suppose it," he wrote. "For I do reckon we love as hard in the backwood country as any people in the whole creation."

My Tennessean grandparents were Presbyterians of Scotch-Irish descent. Legend has it they were somewhat shocked, initially at least, when one of their daughters, my mother Betty, came home from Vassar College over the holidays with my future father, Steve Zimmerman, who was raised in a Reform Jewish family on Long Island.

Betty married Steve the day after her college graduation in 1953 and, no doubt unlike many of her high school classmates, never returned to Greenfield to live. Instead, the three Zimmerman kids were raised in the New York suburb of Hastings-on-Hudson. My father commuted to Manhattan's "canyons of steel" where he earned a living as an ad man.

Even as a child, I sensed that there was a big difference between working on a Kool-Aid campaign and growing soybeans and milo. My mother's father liked to go bird hunting, but my brother and I were prohibited from using guns (or riding motorcycles). When I expressed an interest in learning how to farm, my parents assured me that I wouldn't like that way of life.

Yet Greenfield fascinated me. It was so different from the town in which I was being brought up. It even *smelled* different: green tomato vines, backyard fruit trees, the musty old house where my mother grew up (complete with antique toys and ghosts in the attic), the gas station where my Uncle Bob would hang out talking politics with his friends.

An early train engineer named the town in the 1870s after seeing its fields of wheat swaying back and forth in the wind. The area's first settlers literally had a tough row to hoe. They had to cut down forests of yellow poplar, oak, ash, and gum; burn the wood, check off the land, plant corn by hand, and cover it with a hoe. Once the stumps had been removed, grass was sown and cut by hand, and the wheat harvested with a cradle. Mowers and reapers could then be used, and the wheat cut and tied into bundles.

Later on, Greenfield became known as the "Okra Capital of the World." The town was once a shipping point for a variety of truck crops, including strawberries, beans, tomatoes, and a little cotton. Now its farmers concentrate their efforts on soybeans and feed grains.

During the last few years of Grandma Coats' life, I had the opportunity to spend several months with her, looking through an old trunk full of family photographs, letters, and clippings. At first Grandma, who was naturally reticent, couldn't understand why I would be interested in dredging through this material. For me, it was a way to catalog everything, because I knew once Grandma was gone, no one else would be able to identify who and what everything was.

The author's grandmother, Virginia Coats, and mother Betty, hold the fort in Greenfield, a small town in West Tennessee, 1932. Grandpa Coats, a farmer and entrepreneur, believed in the value of good land.

What made the experience special was learning more about this hidden side of my roots, for which I had always felt a certain empathy. Even some of Grandma's old expressions, like "Mr. Hootendasher," which was her version of "what's-his-name," made those hours pass very enjoyably.

Grandma often spoke of the Great Depression, when she and Grandpa "didn't have two thin dimes to rub together." This point was reinforced when she described the house where her half-sister, my Auntie, lived on the outskirts of town, which was basically a converted sweet potato storage shed. I can remember spending many hours there as a boy. The front yard was an enormous field of green beans, which Auntie, a home economics teacher at a high school in Dresden, harvested and put up for the winter. My uncle, Bob House, was once a minor league pitcher before injuring his arm, after which he tried his hand at local politics.

Growing up, I always associated the song "Jackson" with my grandparents, who had eloped to the nearby border town of South Fulton, Kentucky when my grandmother was 18. The tune starts with the line, "We got married in a fever/Hotter than a pepper sprout."

Later I found out that Jackson referred to the capital of Mississippi, not the Tennessee city between Memphis and Nashville. More recently, I came across the lyrics to "Tennessee Border," written by Jimmy Work in 1949, which, coincidentally, was the year my parents met. Aside from describing my grandparents' legendary elopement to a "T," the song features one of the most tenuous rhymes I've ever heard: "Her personality made me wonder/ On the Tennessee border."

Usually, after a hard day cataloguing, Grandma Coats and I would have our daily tonic — Jack Daniel's on the rocks with a splash — and watch *Love Connection* on TV. It was fascinating to hear her verdict on the various male contestants, vying for a date with the eligible bachelorette. I couldn't help thinking that these were the same standards used in selecting my mother's father some 60 years ago!

Then I would not-so-subtly mine her for more information about what it was like in Greenfield back in the 1910s and 1920s when she was growing up. The Coatses and Hillises on my grandfather's side were among the town's first settlers. When he was born, the different sides of the family all lived on the same block in facing or catercornered houses.

Back then, the local paper was a weekly, and because radio hadn't come of age and TV was still 40 years in the future, funeral announcements were printed and delivered door to door. The Coatses lived on Main Street, just a few houses from the Illinois Central railroad (built in 1873) and, just over the tracks, downtown.

Along the tracks near my great-grandmother Sheila "Granny" White's house, once stood the Greenfield Hotel, a two-story brick building. Salesmen would come to town on the train lugging trunks full of merchandise. They stayed upstairs and set up their trunks in a sitting room in the lobby, and local retailers would come by and select what they needed. How different from today's computerized cashless society!

Moving picture shows were the new rage, giving some healthy competition to tent revivals. In a diary my paternal great-grandmother, Lockie Hillis, kept, she mentions the first time my grandfather, Jean Coats, saw an airplane; it buzzed over town as part of a Liberty Drive parade in 1918.

Greenfield through Lockie's eyes seemed to exist in its own vacuum, somewhat affected by popular culture and yet also firmly entrenched in its own farming and small town-based mentality. In the same way, Grandma Coats wore flapper-style clothes without, perhaps, understanding their full connotation.

Grandma recalled driving to Nashville to see the *Grand Ole Opry* a few times, but she wasn't a particularly big country music fan. She preferred pop and big band music. I would go to the local library and check out records of music from that era and then ask Grandma about some of the songs. I loved the old song "Alice Blue Gown," and it turned out that "Alice" was Teddy Roosevelt's daughter who liked a certain shade of blue. Due to her notoriety as First Daughter, the color became known as Alice Blue. It was quite in vogue for a spell, and my Grandma remembered making her own dress in that tint — back then, she made all of her own clothes — and then singing the song in school. The picture is in the family scrapbook.

With Grandma's help, I began to see how American music and other aspects of its culture are interrelated. Music is not created in a vacuum; nonmusical factors play a role, among them geography, demographics, religion, transportation, and communications. This century, for example, regional styles largely have been absorbed into a musical melting pot, as inventions such as radio, records, and cars have erased physical boundaries.

———————

TENNESSEE HAS LONG BEEN CONSIDERED the buckle of the South's "Bible Belt," but its early settlers were decidedly irreligious, both before it became the 16th state in 1796 and for an ensuing generation or two. After visiting Tennessee, Methodist Bishop Francis Asbury wrote in 1800: "When I consider where they came from, where they are, and how they are, and how they are called to go farther, their being unsettled, with so many objects to take their attention, with the health and good air they enjoy; and when I reflect that not one in a hundred came here to get religion, but rather to get plenty of good land, I think it will be well if some or many do not eventually lose their souls."

That same year, the Great Revival spread like wildfire in southern Kentucky and north-central Tennessee, with Methodists, Baptists, and Presbyterians camping together and "singing hallelujah" in crowds reportedly as large as 10,000 people. While this cataclysmic movement only lasted a few years, it had a lasting effect: "Hence Tennessee was not devoid of religious background, beliefs, or inclination," writes John B. Boles. Here, too, were composed some of the state's first songs (excluding early Native American music, about which little is known). Participants brought their slaves, who worshipped in a separate area. From these activities came shape-note music and spirituals, the forerunners of gospel.

The effect of religion on the state's music has been nothing short of indelible. Regardless of the artist, while attending a concert in Tennessee you are likely to hear at least one sacred song, such as when I saw Tammy Wynette, recuperating from a life-threatening illness, singing "How Great Thou Art" at Opryland. It was truly an awe-inspiring moment.

Tennessee's first nonnative music, however, was Scotch-Irish fiddling, still in evidence at today's statewide old-time and bluegrass conventions. In the 1790s, James Gamble — apparently the state's first professional musician — wandered from town to town in Middle Tennessee, carrying his fiddle in "a sack of doeskin" and playing for dances. Many fiddlers gave up their instruments after the Great Revival — the fiddle was known as the "devil's box" — but Gamble kept playing. According to A.W. Putnam's 1859 *History of Middle Tennessee*, "he read his Bible, and fiddled; he prayed, and he fiddled; asked a silent blessing on his meals, gave thanks, and fiddled; went to meetings, sang the songs of Zion, joined in all the devotional services, went home, and fiddled. He sometimes fiddled in bed, but always fiddled when he got up."

AROUND 1760, THE FAMED EXPLORER DANIEL BOONE stumbled upon the Cumberland Gap, a passageway through the mountains where northern Tennessee meets Kentucky and Virginia. "The aspect of these cliffs is so wild and horrid, that it is impossible to behold them without terror," Boone wrote. "Over these [mountains] nature hath formed passes, that are less difficult than might be expected from a view of such huge piles."

Not all took the Gap. Some settlers came from North Carolina, following the Great Valley of the Tennessee and settling the Watauga and Holston valleys. Others traveled by river, such as the contingent of flatboats led by Col. John Donelson down the Tennessee and up the Cumberland to Nashville.

The large numbers of people who began migrating from points north and east sought fertile land and fewer governmental restrictions. My ancestors were among this exodus south and west. After Samuel Hillis, my great-grandfather five times removed, passed away in Rowan County, North Carolina, in 1784, his sons and daughters packed up and moved west. The wagonmaster's wife died in West Tennessee, and he refused to go any farther, so they put down roots there. This area's early settlers built log cabins with dirt floors, slept on straw beds, and mostly lived on cornbread and wild meat. They have been described as very friendly and unselfish, to the point of sharing their last half-dollar with a stranger.

By 1790, two million Scotch-Irish had migrated to the United States, representing roughly 10 percent of the country's white population. Many of Tennessee's Scotch-Irish pioneers came from neighboring Virginia, North Carolina (to which the state once belonged), and Pennsylvania. They shared certain basic needs, writes Malcolm Rohrbough in *The Trans-Appalachian Frontier*, "principally food, shelter, and physical security from the dangers of the wilderness," including bands of sometimes hostile Indians.

Instrument collector **Ellis Truett, Jr.** of Lizard Lick, southeast of Jackson, plucks "Amazing Grace" on a box dulcimer that was built locally some 150 years ago. "It's what the poor folks played," he says. Photograph by Perry Walker.

Over the next forty years, the population of Nashville alone grew nearly twentyfold, from 35,000 to 682,000. During the same period, the Federal government succeeded in "removing" most Native Americans west of the Mississippi River, culminating in the tragic Trail of Tears, which originated from southeastern Tennessee in the 1830s.

———————

SINCE THAT TIME, THE STATE HAS BEEN DIVIDED into three "grand divisions" of East, Middle, and West Tennessee, which turn up on the state flag in the form of three stars. The phrase is ubiquitous among Tennesseans, and although no one seems to know whence it came, the first mention appeared in public acts addended to the state's constitution in 1835-36, which established a supreme court comprising three judges, one from each division, "and the concurrence of two of said Judges shall be necessary to a decision in every case." The acts divided the state into Middle, Eastern, and Western divisions of 24, 22, and 17 counties, respectively.

Today, these original 63 counties have increased to 95, although the overall land mass (42,000 square miles) has remained roughly the same. The Tennessee Supreme Court now comprises five judges instead of three — at least one, and no more than two, from each division.

But the real differences are not judicial but sociological. As more than a few Tennesseans have observed, Bristol, Tennessee, is closer to Windsor, Ontario, than it is to Memphis. "There is probably not another state in the entire nation that is so clearly divided into three regions," or that has experienced the same degree of "intrastate sectionalism," according to Paul Bergeron. State historian Stanley Folmsbee adds, "Had the natural contours been followed, Tennessee would be three states or parts of three states, instead of one."

East and West Tennesseans feel that they are given short shrift as far as allocations, ever since Nashville became the permanent state capital in 1843. In addition, the people of West Tennessee's "cotton and river culture" (as novelist Peter Taylor describes it in *A Summons to Memphis*) and of East Tennessee's mountainous Appalachian region often feel looked down upon by their counterparts in Nashville, who tend to be better educated, more liberal, and wealthier.

East Tennesseans are apt to identify themselves as such, rather than as Tennesseans. They stress the state's first syllable (TEN-nessee, or as one East Tennessee fiddler jokingly told me, "TEN-nersee), while those hailing from Nashville and Memphis say "Tennes-SEE." East Tennessee's corn and tobacco farms are relatively small in comparison to the rolling pastures of Middle Tennessee and West Tennessee's vast cotton plantations. During the Civil War, East Tennessee's truck farmers, who had no vested interest in preserving slavery, sided with the Union, supplying some 30,000 volunteers to the cause (and only half as many rebels). West Tennessee, with its slave-based economy, was fervently pro-Confederate, while Middle Tennessee split.

Several years ago, Congressman Jimmy Quillen from East Tennessee proposed the creation of a 51st, "Cumberland" state, combining counties from northeastern Tennessee with those of adjacent Kentucky and Virginia. Quillen's idea echoes a 1939 state guide compiled by the Works Progress Administration (WPA), in which the East Tennessean views West Tennessee "as a swamp and resents the weight of the powerful Shelby County political machine in State-wide elections [this, written as Memphis politico "Boss" Crump's star was beginning to wane]. What West Tennessee is for, he is 'agin'."

TENNESSEE WAS ONCE PART OF A MUCH LARGER NORTH CAROLINA. The land was briefly called the Territory South of the River Ohio before becoming a state in 1796. Legislators named it after the former Cherokee capital of Tanasi, which was located south of Knoxville and now lies submerged beneath a Tennessee Valley Authority lake.

It is made up of a flattened anvil of land measuring 432 miles wide and 106 miles deep at its extremities. The land itself — notably the Appalachian Mountains and Mississippi River which bracket it, as well as the Tennessee and other interior rivers, valleys, and hills — has had a greater effect on Tennessee music than any mortal influence. Without the Mississippi, for instance, there would likely be no Delta blues; without the mountains, no hillbilly music. Other areas, such as the Sequatchie Valley and Cumberland Plateau, have spawned their own equally unique forms of music.

SLAVES ACCOMPANIED THE VERY FIRST SETTLERS, and if the fiddle has earned bragging rights as the frontier's basic musical instrument, then the five-string banjo — a three or four-string version of which blacks apparently imported from West Africa — must run a close second. Thomas Jefferson mentioned the "banjar" in his diary, and there is even evidence of biracial dueling fiddles and banjos in early Southern history (see Grady McWhinney's *Cracker Culture*).

East Tennessee's black population is small compared to other parts of the state. This separate cemetery for African-Americans, with large rocks for headstones, is located in the community of Hickory Tree, south of Bristol. Photograph by Perry Walker.

IN MEMORY OF DECEASED AFRO–AMERICANS

Mississippi's **James "Son" Thomas** (1926-1993), who picked cotton to raise money for his first guitar, is one of many musicians who migrated to Tennessee from its eight neighboring states. Many Delta bluesmen have earned their spurs in Memphis. Photograph by Frank Spencer.

This blending of black and white has defined the state's musical heritage, and musicians continue to spill over from Mississippi, with its majority black population, and from predominantly white Virginia and Kentucky, which border Tennessee to the north. Geography and the resulting demographics have had a stark influence on the state's regional musical forms; the arbitrarily drawn boundary lines pale in comparison. B.B. King hitchhiked to Memphis from Mississippi, for instance, while the Carter Family trudged down from Virginia to make its first recordings in Bristol.

Tennessee is where the Ku Klux Klan first organized (Pulaski, 1865) and the Rev. Martin Luther King Jr. was assassinated (Memphis, 1968). Good ole boy "roundups" still take place, such as a 1995 rally in the East Tennessee town of Ocoee at which a "Federal Nigger Hunting License" and racist T-shirts were confiscated. Paradoxically, the state is also where, in 1819, Jonesborough's Elihu Embree published *The Manumission Intelligencer*, one of the first anti-slavery newspapers; it folded a year later after his death. In 1905, blacks staged a streetcar boycott in Nashville. The Highlander Folk School in Monteagle conducted desegregation workshops as early as 1953, and Nashville's college students, led by James Lawson and Kelly Miller Smith, played a major, early role in the Civil Rights movement (see Juan Williams' *Eyes On the Prize*.) Today, Vanderbilt University's First Amendment Center serves as a watchdog of constitutional rights.

On a personal note, a black teenager named Mallie Wilson was once lynched in Greenfield on account of my great-grandmother Sheila Lewis, whom I used to visit in her house along the railroad tracks. According to an article clipped from the local paper and saved by my grandmother, Granny had been sleeping alone at home — my great-grandfather, J.P. White, was working late at the pharmacy — when she woke up and saw Wilson at the foot of the bed, with alcohol on his breath. She screamed, and he fled. Even though he had been guilty of nothing more than trespassing, they found Mallie Wilson and hanged him. The year was 1915.

People in my family avoided the subject, but the ghost of Mallie Wilson has haunted me ever since. The bottom part of the article was torn off, and I've often wondered which details had been excised from the collective family memory.

My ancestors also viewed Native Americans with similar distrust. According to my grandmother's high school primer, "They were brave and cunning, cruel and revengeful, very fond of gay colors and trinkets, very lazy and dirty, and were great liars and rogues. Indeed, they did not seem to think that there was much wrong in lying, stealing, and murder."

And it shall come to pass, that every thing that liveth, which moveth, whithersoever the rivers shall come, shall live.

~ Ezekiel 47:9

The insularity of Tennessee's remote mountainous regions contrast starkly with the navigability of its rivers. Even before the steamboat, merchants plied the smaller rivers in flatboats and keelboats. They transported their goods down the Mississippi to New Orleans and other ports-of-call, and returned to Tennessee on foot or horseback, following the Natchez Trace, an ancient route "graded" by buffalo and migratory Indians.

Twain once compared the steamboat in its waning years to "a crippled octogenarian who could once jump twenty-two feet on level ground." Indeed, trains connected Nashville and Chattanooga in 1854 and had soon rendered the steamboat all but obsolete. Now cars and planes have repaid the favor, rendering the train all but obsolete, and some fear a resulting decline in regional musical styles. However, dramatic differences still exist between the styles of music that you're likely to hear in Memphis and, say, Bristol to the east.

BEFORE RECORDING AND RADIO BURST ONTO THE SCENE in the late 19th and early 20th centuries, music in Tennessee was mostly relegated to amateur status and limited on a regional basis. Once records were distributed nationally and radio waves began to reach farther, people in Texas, Chicago, and California were given the opportunity to hear what was transpiring musically in other parts of the country, resulting in a fertile melting pot of influences.

The importance of the *Grand Ole Opry*'s broadcast from Nashville over the airwaves of WSM cannot be underestimated. The music had a dramatic effect on musicians who were glued to their sets thousands of miles away. Other stations played an equally pivotal role. For old-time, early country, and bluegrass music, some of the other pioneering programs included WCYB's *Farm and Fun Time* and the *WOPI Jamboree,* both out of Bristol, and WNOX-Knoxville's *Mid-Day-Merry-Go-Round;* a show on WDOD-Chattanooga was influential in southeastern Tennessee and bordering states. Later on, WDIA and WHBQ of Memphis, and Nashville's WLAC became the standard-bearers for rhythm and blues and soul music; down the Mississippi River in Helena, Arkansas, KFFA cornered the blues market.

Of course, these dramatic media also spread music *to* Tennessee. In *Singing Cowboys and Musical Mountaineers,* Bill Malone observes that Southern rural music "was built out of the cultural traditions of many interacting cultural groups, and in a context that, from the beginning of Southern history, was always changing in conscious or unconscious ways." Radio and records merely accelerated the process.

Nashville native **Kitty Wells** with *Grand Ole Opry* announcer George D. Hay, aka the "Solemn Old Judge," in 1954. A few years earlier she became the first woman to achieve a number-one country record with "It Wasn't God Who Made Honky-Tonk Angels." Kitty got her start on the *Mid-Day Merry-Go-Round* broadcast from Knoxville. Photo courtesy of the Country Music Foundation.

WHILE IN MEMPHIS, I MET WITH JOHN FRY, who opened a recording studio in his parents' garage 25 years ago along with his high school buddy Fred Smith, who now heads FedEx, the city's largest employer. Today, Ardent Studio is the biggest fish in town, recording and mixing everyone from Travis Tritt and R.E.M. to local wonder Alex Chilton.

Fry has witnessed many changes over that relatively brief span, such as the introduction of computers for everything from audio applications and accounting to graphic design. He remembers when there weren't even any record stores in town. "If you wanted to buy a record, you went to the department store or someplace that happened to have a music department," he said. "I mean, the record store is a fairly recent innovation. We don't think of it as being that today, but it is."

He added that many American record labels (including RCA, MCA, Columbia, Capitol, and Polygram) have been sold to large foreign investors and folded into big international conglomerates (BMG, Sony, Matsushita, EMI, and Phillips/Siemens). The only large American label yet to be swallowed up is Warner-Elektra-Atlantic-Asylum.

The business climate has changed, too. Fry used to go record-shopping at the Satellite shop at Stax where, he says, "I felt just as safe going down to McLemore and College as I did anywhere else in town. Today you go to a big city and you start thinking about, 'Am I going in the right neighborhood?' And there's a tendency for people to assume that it's always been that way. It hasn't."

I asked Fry whether he thinks mass transportation, particularly airplane travel, has changed the American musical landscape. He agreed that it has but feels optimistic about the prognosis for regionalism's survival, albeit in a different form.

"One of the reasons you had regional music to begin with was because it's hard for people to move around," he said. "People didn't have the mobility that they have today. And I think we're at a point where the verdict is out on what's going to happen to regional, cultural influences on music. To the extent that regional culture goes away, then its influence on music will go away, like its influence on everything else.

"If we wind up finally with a United States where you can't tell by talking to people or looking around whether you're in Tennessee or Oregon, then you won't have any more regional influences. And once whatever generation that is in, dies out, then that'll be the end of regional music in the United States.

"I hope we don't get to that point," he said, "because it'd be an awfully boring country if we do."

For the time being, however, regionalism is alive and well for those intent on seeking it out. State folklore director Robie Cogswell has been on the job for a dozen years and still feels like he is just at the tip of the iceberg.

He is probably right.

The Genres

I'm gwine back to Dixie,
No more I'm gwine to wander.
I'm gwine back to Dixie,
I can't stay here no longer.
I miss the old plantation,
My home, and my relations.
My heart's turned back to Dixie,
And I must go.
                         — C.A. WHITE, 1874

Old-Time

THE EAST TENNESSEE MOUNTAIN TOWN of Laurel Bloomery gets its name from an iron forge which was once located on Laurel Creek, now but a trickle of its former torrent. The bloomery — a "bloom" is a mass of wrought iron suitable for further working — was built in 1810 and shut down around 1870 after the local ore fields were exhausted. Before the forge was constructed, the small claim to fame of the locality was that explorer and frontiersman Daniel Boone had hid from Indians under a nearby waterfall.

Laurel Bloomery is just about as far east as Tennessee gets, an Appalachian town with more ties to the mountainous regions of Kentucky, North Carolina, and the Virginias than to the broad, cotton-heavy flatlands of west and middle Tennessee. Today it is a tiny, somewhat forlorn little hamlet of fewer than 1,000 souls. The green town-limits sign has been so riddled with buckshot that it is almost illegible. There is not a lot of commerce. In the words of the clerk at the local BP Groceries, "If you've seen a good cold Budweiser, you've seen it here."

All the towns in the area, Laurel Bloomery as well as nearby Mountain City, are threatened with being engulfed by the wild montane surroundings of Cherokee National Forest, where development is discouraged. The Federal government is eager to return this chunk of the Appalachia to near-pristine condition. There wouldn't be that much use for this land except for hunting, some pulp log harvesting, and, of late, second homes. The return is poor no matter how much development is put into it.

Probably the best hope is tourism, for this is undeniably pretty country, framed with rolling hillsides of blue-green, stippled with hickory, oak, and poplar, inhabited by a runaway population of whitetails. It is in the name of tourism, as much as love of music, that the little town of Laurel Bloomery wakes up every year to welcome the Bluegrass and Old-Time Fiddlers Convention, a one-night event held at the Old Mill Music Park.

I arrived at the festival early, when the grass field that served as the parking lot was virtually empty. There was a sign tacked up on a post, announcing that no alcohol would be allowed at the event, but virtually no other indication that the area was expecting an influx of fiddle-happy musicians.

I didn't think there'd be a quorum for the "convention," but by early evening, a long line of musicians waiting to perform wound around to the back of the semi-enclosed bandshell. The throng consisted of mostly middle-aged lovers of music, both male and female; some older tunesmiths and wayward teenagers, as well as a couple of the musicians' offspring, made up the balance. The conservatively dressed audience was predominantly older and sat upright in the folding chairs, listening and clapping politely. The whole scene had a Victorian air to it.

Backstage, and all along the grounds, small groups of pickers traded licks, accompanied by the occasional buckdancer, who responded deliriously to the sprightly rhythm. Many acts practiced in line while waiting to go on stage.

The low-level din was terrific, as ballads and breakdowns commingled. If there was a stringed instrument around, it was being strummed, bowed, picked, or plucked. I saw a "gutbucket" skiffle bass made out of #3 metal washtub, a broomhandle and a single piece of clothesline. The population of Laurel Bloomery had swelled by half that night, and a good number of the new arrivals played fiddle.

It was fitting that the pickers and pluckers had come to this area. It was here in the mid-1920s that the folk music of Appalachia first coalesced into a recognizable commodity that people would actually travel miles to hear. It was here that the music some people now call old-time, which used to be called mountain music or (derisively by some, with pride by others) hillbilly music, first came to be.

Briefly defined, old-time is traditional string music from the Appalachian Mountain region. It also has the distinction of being Tennessee's oldest form of music — excluding the songs of the Cherokee, which do not fall within the scope of this book. If old-time has a birthplace, it is this small, hilly triangle of northeastern Tennessee wedged between Virginia and North Carolina, known to natives as Upper East Tennessee.

Nearby Bristol probably has the biggest claim in this regard, but in 1925 in Mountain City, just 10 miles south of Laurel Bloomery, a milestone was passed in the history of music. What had been a loose and anarchic cacophony of folk tunes and traditional songs was transformed into the first wakening chords of something larger, grander, something which would lay an ever greater claim to the world's attention.

The first country records had been recorded a couple of years earlier. Back in the early '20s they were all amateurs — as many still are today— for there was no such thing as a professional fiddler or a professional player of mountain music. Almost everybody in these hills played, and your expertise was measured not in terms of musical skill but by how many fiddle

The **Crook Brothers**, shown here in 1930, was one of the *Grand Ole Opry's* earliest bands. It consisted of Herman and Lewis Crook (top), who weren't brothers, along with Blythe Poteet, Kirk McGee, and Bill Etters. Back in "the days that are no more," drums were not allowed on stage. Courtesy of Les Leverett.

tunes you knew. The best fiddlers, the ones their fellow townspeople would boast about, knew enough songs to keep people dancing all night. They played for food and drink or collected a nickel or 10 cents for every hour-long, three-song set — not enough to make a living but good for an evening's worth of beer.

By the mid-'20s change was afoot, and Mountain City was the first evidence of it. No one knew it was coming. No one had gauged the influence of two new developments: the growing popularity of radio, and the widespread distribution of phonograph records. Suddenly people who had merely been popular amateurs were transformed into regional celebrities.

It was somewhat out of the blue, then, that a fiddle convention, held in a small, isolated mountain town to raise funds for a local farmer who had fallen on hard times, suddenly attracted some of these hot new names in May of 1925. Performers like Fiddlin' John Carson, the Fiddlin' Powers Family, Uncle Am Stuart, Dedrick Harris and G.B. Grayson

showed up, as well as the original incarnation of a group that would eventually lend its name to the music itself, the Hill Billies Band, featuring fiddler Charlie Bowman from just over the mountains in Sullivan County.

Stranger yet, people from the surrounding region showed up, hundreds of them, an enormous crowd for these hills. They came from out of the hollows and from the small towns in all the three states that intersected here, over from Bristol and up from Elizabethton in Tennessee; from Boone and Jefferson in North Carolina, and from Damascus in Virginia. The crowd had listened to the music on records and heard about the convention on the radio. So many of them herded into the Mountain City high school auditorium that the floor collapsed and they had to be herded back outside again.

The musicians were surprised, wrote musicologist Joe Wilson, "that people who knew them only from their recordings and broadcasts were willing to lay down good money to see them in person."

So Mountain City was one beginning, where the people who played what had been folk music, and played it for free mostly, first got an inkling that they could make a living as professional musicians.

It was also another type of beginning, of the great tradition of gatherings and conventions and festivals devoted to this kind of music. It established early on what is still a characteristic of old-time music today: if you like this kind of music, you are most likely to play it, and enjoy spending your spare time around other people who play it, too.

———————

ROB NICAR IS THIRD OR FOURTH from the head of the line of musicians at the Laurel Bloomery festival, quietly observing and sizing up the competition. Nicar plays his fiddle every chance he gets, but he's never seriously entertained the idea of becoming a professional musician. The demand for his kind of music — old-time fiddling — simply isn't there.

So, like many other players here at the festival, Rob Nicar is literally an amateur, a word that originally described someone who did something purely for the love of doing it — which fits him perfectly. He and others like him may grouse about the lack of money, but they know that the sheer impossibility of making a living from playing old-time fiddle makes the joy of it that much purer.

In fact, it is Nicar's resolute amateur status that attracts me to him. "The pure joy of playin' music," is unquestionably the reason he does it, not the money. During the week, he manages his own construction company in Bristol, a small city in northeastern Tennessee on the Virginia border. In his free time, he plays old-time music.

Tall, dark, and handsome, Nicar looks a bit like Clark Gable and speaks in a slow but measured cadence which betrays his lilting East Tennessee accent. Within the ranks of old-time musicians, even top traditional groups like the Highwoods Stringband have barely managed to scrape by, he tells me.

It is as if old-time music rose up out of its amateur-only beginnings 70 years ago, attained a brief period of commercial viability, then collapsed back into its prelapsarian state of amateur

innocence. Occasionally Nicar's band — the latest incarnation of which is called The Hot Rods — performs for a pittance at the Down Home in Johnson City, but then it's back to pounding nails.

Fiddlin' **Rob Nicar** practices on his farm along the Holston River in East Tennessee. He does it for "the pure joy of playin' music." Tennessee's music has been influenced by its rural demographics. Three quarters of its people live in four of its 95 counties. Photo by Perry Walker.

Now in his early forties, Nicar took up his instrument 15 years ago. He developed an early interest in bluegrass, a form of music that evolved from old-time in the 1940s. His Sunday school teacher, a banjo-playing IRS agent named Mack Blevins, let him tag along to music conventions just like this one in Laurel Bloomery. In these parts, "conventions" or "competitions" denote get-togethers of amateurs, while the term "festival" suggests a more formal gathering of paid professionals.

It wasn't until Nicar heard the recordings of old-time fiddlers and string bands from the 1920s and '30s — people like Fiddlin' Arthur Smith, Dudley Vance, and Gid Tanner & His Skillet Lickers — that he was really hooked. He began trying to learn their music, which had evolved over several centuries in the same neck of the woods where he made his home. Like a wine connoisseur smitten with a particular vintage, Nicar is particular in his taste: old-time fiddling of the 1920s and '30s.

He considers himself fortunate to live in the musically fertile Bristol area, home to "hundreds of top-notch musicians," many of them amateurs like himself, who get together regularly for picking parties, or informal jam sessions. Among them are those who Nicar terms "the silent people." People like Blevins, Earl "Hump" Doyle, Leroy Canner, and Joe Bodum, who would "just open their doors to people like you and me," people with an interest in learning how to play traditional music.

"They've had a huge influence on musicians in this area without taking a lot of credit for themselves," Nicar says. "Some of them are masters on their instruments, but they

Picking party, circa 1972, at the general store in Hickory Tree, a community south of Bristol, featuring (from left) Howard Leonard, Raymond Jones, and Gerald Church. The store's first jam session took place in 1964, but rowdyism has ended the tradition. Photo by Perry Walker.

really didn't go out and get any kind of national acclaim for their music. They were good enough that if they had been under different circumstances, they probably could have played professionally, but there's not a huge market for bluegrass or old-time music, to where you can actually make a decent living."

I had become accustomed to hearing the litany of names, repeated with reverence, of musicians who reached their prime in the halcyon days of old-time music, when it enjoyed its brief currency on the national stage: Uncle Dave Macon, Sam and Kirk McGee, Vernon Dalhart, Obed "Dad" Pickard, and Uncle Bunt Stephens. To a person of my generation, exposed to groups like Led Zeppelin and the Isley Brothers, even the names of these artists smacked of the dictionary's definition of old-time: "of or like past times." As my Grandma Coats used to say, they sounded "old old."

To the outside world, these names would mean nothing, but to the people who play and enjoy their music, they live on. It was not nostalgia as much as a stubborn insistence on the values of the past that informed the passions of everyone at the Laurel Bloomery festival that July night.

Farther back in the line of musicians waiting for stage time are two of Rob Nicar's playing partners, Jeff Benedict and Charlie Hanley, performing here as a fiddle-and-guitar duo. They break into an up-tempo version of an old-time standard, "Fisher's Hornpipe," which Hanley has rechristened, "I Chased My Sweetheart Up a Tree and Kissed Her Gently Between the Limbs."

His modification follows a time-honored tradition, Hanley explains. Some old-time songs could be quite risqué; he cited "Cindy," which first surfaced in Thomas Jefferson's time, as a good example ("She's so sweet the honey-bees/Swarm all round her mouth"). But the old melodies were nothing if not flexible: the same "Fisher's Hornpipe" also served as a musical template for "The Old-Fashioned Bible" in a popular 19th-century hymnbook.

Like a lot of musicians at Laurel Bloomery, Benedict and Hanley belong to more than one band. In modern old-time — which is something of an oxymoron, like "jumbo shrimp" — the bands tend to be fluid, and groups and alliances permutate informally and often. Benedict and Hanley, for example, perform as a duo but also belong to a band that includes Rob Nicar and his wife, Amy, a guitarist whom Nicar met at an old-time festival while she was attending college in Greensboro, North Carolina.

Benedict and Hanley both see old-time as a distinct geographical phenomenon. "It's an Appalachian thing," Benedict tells me. "What's a North Carolina piedmont song and what's a Tennessee mountain song are actually the same thing." Thus, East Tennessee's music has more in common with mountainous southern Virginia and western North Carolina than it does with the flatlands of West Tennessee, which fall more under the sway of the Mississippi Delta.

Clandestinely sipping a little George Dickel whiskey and ice — Hanley claims the festival sign means no drinking *in public* — Charlie draws a parallel between old-time and jazz. To him, bebop saxophonist Charlie Parker "typified the urban environment." In the same way, "I like to think that what I play in old-time music comes out of what I do during the week," he said. "You know, I don't hoe 'bacco and do all that kind of stuff. But I think the energy that gets frustrated in me during the week at my office comes out in my music. It's a release."

Benedict said he wishes he had been around in the 1920s, when "all this music that's around right now first started to be recorded. Charlie Poole and Gid Tanner and all those people were coming out [and] it was commercialized. Gid Tanner had a million-selling record — a *million*-selling 78 [rpm record] — in 1932. Can you *imagine*? And they were playing all this hillbilly shit about possum hunts in north Georgia."

Nearby, a 17-year-old from Bluff City named Justin Cumbow, a great-grandson of the champion fiddler "Dud" Vance, is working through his repertoire. He's only been fiddling for two-and-a-half years and has had no formal training. Instead, he has learned everything he knows from listening to tapes; perhaps, too, it's in his blood. Despite these handicaps, a fellow fiddler from Boone, North Carolina, which is just over the mountains, is impressed.

"Some people have it, some people don't," said the anonymous Tarheel, nodding approvingly. "He's *got* it." After listening awhile to Cumbow's buttery tone and elegant phrasing, he adds wistfully, "Some people are just natural for it."

Another musician in the Laurel Bloomery lineup introduces himself as "Fiddlin' Alfred Michels." Until he speaks, Michels is virtually indistinguishable from the other contestants. Like some of them, he wears coveralls and a lumberjack shirt. Unlike them, he has a definite German accent. Over a decade ago, Michels left his native Germany and resettled in rural Ashe County, North Carolina.

Michels hopes to gain inspiration just by living near the old stamping grounds of his idol, Arthur Smith, a legendary old-time fiddler who belonged to the most popular stringband of the 1930s, the Dixieliners. According to Hanley, Michels has another skill highly valued in the old-time community. "Alfred is our local luthier, and he takes care of all our fiddles when they get screwed up in damp weather. He does an incredible job."

Michels came to these precincts to hone his waltzes, quadrilles and breakdowns — American country music that he had learned to know and love first in Germany, listening to cassette tapes. Like a prophet unhonored in his own land, old-time fiddling is much more popular in Europe than in its backyard.

That phenomenon isn't limited to Europe, either. Nicar reports he once took a trip to Asia and brought his fiddle along, intending only to practice in his hotel room. While in Hong Kong, he noticed that one nightclub was listed as a country music bar.

"I thought, 'I've got to check *this* out.' We went down there one night, and outside there were big signs: 'Manny the Fiddler.' I thought, 'That doesn't even sound like a Chinese name.' I go in there and, sure enough, there's a country band playing real rough, ragged country music. That place was *packed*.

"I ended up playing. The whole band was from the Philippines. I guess they were probably influenced by Americans who were in the Philippines. I played with Manny's band. A couple of them I don't guess had ever seen a real live American playing the fiddle."

The Dixieliners, consisting of the great Fiddlin' Arthur Smith and brothers Sam (l) and Kirk McGee — all Tennessee natives — may have been the greatest string band in country music history. This photo was taken in 1935, at the height of their popularity. Courtesy of Les Leverett.

Uncle Dave Macon, aka David Harrison Macon, master of the clawhammer banjo, came from the McMinnville area and didn't break into show business until he was in his fifties. Here "The Dixie Dewdrop" is shown with Alabama's Delmore Brothers, Rabon (left) and Alton, circa 1935. In old-time, the banjo is downpicked rhythmically, as opposed to the arpeggiated three-finger roll used in bluegrass. Courtesy of Les Leverett.

Not everyone at the Laurel Bloomery festival is a fiddler; there is a smattering of other instruments favored in old-time music. Bill Birchfield, front man for the Roan Mountain Hilltoppers, a band that he inherited from his father, crouches over a '20s-vintage autoharp in an attempt to hear himself play the quaint "Little Darlin' Pal of Mine," popular in these parts. The autoharp, a box zither of German origin, reached the height of its popularity during the Victorian era. In mountain music, its most famous practicioners were Ernest V. "Pop" Stoneman and Maybelle Carter of the famed Carter Family.

Wayne Taylor, a broker-auctioneer from Meridianville, Alabama, vigorously plucks his spalded maple Appalachian dulcimer. In a clear voice, Taylor sings "'Gwine Back to Dixie," written in 1874 and popularized by one of the legendary forefathers of country music, Uncle Dave Macon. Like the fiddle and several other stringed instruments (the banjo, for example), the dulcimer and the autoharp produce a droning sound, lending to the music a melancholy timbre of lament over which the melody is played.

The weather had been damp and cold, with intermittent showers, but the festival crowd seemed oblivious. Around one in the morning I decided to climb into the back of my Chevy Caprice wagon for some shut-eye. Drifting off to sleep, I could hear the emcee on stage intoning, "And now the fifteenth contestant in old-time mandolin. . . . "

Several hours later, with the first light, I woke up and looked out the car window. Someone's dog had made fast work of a potato I had left outside. With the exception of a handful of campers, everyone had cleared out of Laurel Bloomery, heading home or perhaps on to the next event on the old-time festival circuit. In the pale, damp dawn, and in my own morning befuddlement, it was as if the Bluegrass and Old-Time Fiddlers Convention at Old Mill Music Park in Laurel Bloomery had been a mirage.

IN THE LAST HALF OF THE 18TH CENTURY, the first European settlers traveled along Virginia's river valleys and trekked over the mountains and through the Gap, following Daniel Boone's famous Wilderness Road. A few of them settled and built communities in East Tennessee, peopling the western flank of the Appalachian Mountains with small mining and farming communities.

They weren't the first inhabitants of these mountains, of course, nor even the first who played music there. When they arrived, the pioneers found the woodlands inhabited by various tribes of Cherokee, Creek, Shawnee, and Chickasaw. These aboriginals created a traditional music with flutes, drums and rattles based on a diatonic scale. But through a sometimes brutal series of wars, relocations, and forced marches — the Trail of Tears originated at Red Clay, near Chattanooga — the Native American presence in Tennessee was virtually erased by 1835.

Many of the European early settlers were Scotch-Irish Protestants, originally from Scotland, who migrated first to Ireland and then to America, trying to escape poverty, political chicanery and religious intolerance. In 1790, this ethnic group constituted some 10 percent of the U.S. white population. They brought their easily portable fiddles and, in their heads, memories of their native songs. "The fiddle was the basic musical instrument of the frontier," according to Charles K. Wolfe, "light, easily portable, repairable, and capable of a wild variety of sounds and moods."

The Scotch-Irish influence still lingers in old-time fiddling. Rob Nicar told me that fiddlers sometimes tune the their instruments to AEAE (as opposed to the standard violin tuning of GDAE), thus producing a droning on the strings, which are tuned to the key of A. The resulting sound resembles that of the Scottish bagpipes. Traditionally, old-time fiddlers tuned "to whatever pitch sounded pleasing on their instruments," writes Joyce H. Cauthen. "Such tunings . . . made fingering easier. By raising or lowering the pitch of a string, the fiddler could bring into easy reach a note that otherwise would require a tricky stretch. Moreover, the cross tunings usually enriched the sound of the instrument."

Modern fiddlers (and banjo players) continue this practice. For show tunes like "Black Mountain Rag," for instance, the fiddle is often tuned to ADAC#, Nicar said. "It gives the fiddle a completely different sound [and] even changes the tone of the instrument." In addition, old-time fiddlers use a variety of techniques — such as slides, rolls, smears, and hammer-ons — that are vastly different than those employed by classical violinists. The banjo is played rhythmically by frailing or downpicking the instrument. Like blues and bluegrass, most old-time songs are built around three basic chords, such as G, C, and D, and the resulting melodies are easy to whistle. The lyrics range from syrupy and sentimental to broadside and whacky.

The tunes Nicar and his friends play today have been handed down and modified over many generations. In 1916, a pair of music teachers named Cecil Sharp and Maud Karpeles came to these same southern Appalachian Mountains. Working out of Rocky Fork, 45 miles southwest of Laurel Bloomery, they found people singing age-old ballads, including one published in Ireland in 1740.

There were other influences than that of the Scotch-Irish, of course. Old-time draws its inspiration from myriad sources, from the German waltz to 19th-century minstrelsy, the latter derived from African-American tradition.

Early settlers had brought black slaves with them; the slaves, in turn, brought rudimentary versions of the banjo. By 1800, there were 13,000 slaves and 300 free blacks in Tennessee. Slavery was always more predominant in the agricultural lands of the west and middle parts of the state; it did not take hold on the small subsistence farms and mining camps of the mountains. Statewide, the slave population climbed to 80,000 by 1820 and to 275,000 at the beginning of the Civil War, of which only 10 percent lived in East Tennessee.

The country blues, Piedmont-style. **Walter "Brownie" McGhee** (left) of Knoxville and **Lesley Riddle** of North Carolina worked together in Kingsport in the 1920s and '30s. Riddle collaborated with the Carters and taught "River of Jordan" to A.P. McGhee was associated with harmonica player Sonny Terry. Courtesy of Kip Lornell. Photo courtesy of the Blue Ridge Heritage Archive.

The stereotypical old-time fiddler was a white mountaineer, but blacks also made a distinct contribution to repertoire and style. Blacks gave Southern fiddling its "'hoedown' quality," according to Cauthen. "The African fiddler . . . played sedate tunes for his master's cotillions, then added bow shuffles and syncopations to the same tunes to power the rhythmic, emotional, leaping, hand-clapping dances of the slaves." Janette Carter of the Carter Family, perhaps the prototypical old-time music group, told me that Lesley Riddle, a black guitarist, taught A.P. Carter "tunes and guitar runs."

In music historian Bill Malone's view, scholars have often placed too much emphasis on country music's Anglo or Celtic roots and generally "have not hesitated to make bold and sweeping judgements about the South, its people, and their music." African-Americans and other ethnic groups also had a significant impact on old-time music. "Rural southerners made their own music or inherited it from their forebears," writes Malone. "But they also absorbed songs, dances, instrumental pieces, and performing styles from whatever source was available within the total southern context in which they lived."

Indeed, old-time songs are wonderfully varied. Wayne Erbsen has divided them into eight major categories: minstrel, fiddle dance tunes, lonesome fiddle tunes, ballads, "knockdown" banjo, gospel, parlor, and joke songs. The fiddle repertoire alone derives from numerous sources: quadrilles from France, waltzes from Germany, reels from Scotland, hornpipes from England, airs from Ireland. "The quality that unites the eclectic mix of tunes in the [old-time] fiddlers' repertoire is oldness," Cauthen writes. "The tunes may be ancient, but if they are not, they are played in a style that makes them sound that way."

Each district, however, has a number of airs, that are, to some degree, peculiar to it, being more generally known there than they are in other parts. They had probably been composed in that district: the scene of the poems that are sung to them is frequently laid in it: they relate to its particular manners and customs, to its history and inhabitants. These airs, therefore, may be properly enough considered, as the peculiar music of that district.

~ Patrick McDonald, *A Collection of Highland Vocal Airs,*
Country Dances or Reels, and Bagpipe Music, 1784

SONGWRITER AND OLD-TIME FIDDLING AFICIONADO John Hartford, a Missouri native, proposes a river-based model for the development of old-time in which the genre belongs to a musicial continuum spanning some 500 years. I met John Hartford — perhaps best known for his composition "Gentle on My Mind," as well as his guest appearances on *The Smothers Brothers Show* in the 1960s — at the Uncle Dave Macon Days festival in Murfreesboro, where he and Uncle Dave's great-grandson were playing fiddle and banjo in a back room. (On stage, John is a one-man show, playing banjo, fiddle, and guitar while dancing softshoe on a piece of amplified plywood.)

Taking a break, he scratched a crude map on a paper tablecloth and theorized that a "river of sound" originated in the Shetland Islands and Norway (where one in three schoolchildren plays the fiddle even today) and flowed south to the British Isles, eventually crossing the ocean, where it cut a swath from Newfoundland to Texas. Hartford, who has worked as a river boatman and still keeps a current license, said that in the old days, each region and each particular river valley had its own distinct style. As the music developed, the lines of communication and transportation — and the regional influences — followed the great rivers. A fiddler along the Big Sandy River in Kentucky, for instance, would sound different than one who lived on the Tennessee River or the Ohio.

The great flatpicker Doc Watson, now in his seventies, concurs with Hartford's regional approach to understanding old-time music. He told me: "Back in the days before the media came into play, even before the Victrola, each hollow had its own version of a ballad, just almost."

THE BOYS FROM NORTH CAROLINA

Some say it comes a-rollin' down the hollers of old Ireland
And up the mountains of East Tennessee from back in North Carolina
With Scottish tones and Indian moans and wails of railroad liners
They helped along that old-time song, the boys from North Carolina.

It rolled and growed all in the West way out in old Missouri
And then took off around the world like lightning in its fury
There ain't no way you sound the string in major or in minor
It disappears all in the years and brings a laugh throughout the tears
From the boys from North Carolina.

Kentucky is the Bluegrass State her sunny skies define her
The Western Slope of East Tennessee there nothing could be finer
The northern boys, who make more noise to pick could not be finer
To make that sound and get it down, it helps if you have been around
The boys from North Carolina.

They stood in line around the block right back here at the Ryman
To hear that lick, that old mule kick from the boys from North Carolina
Gastonia to Boiling Springs, from Flint Hill back to Charlotte
They tried to find the place of birth, still talking about who played it first
Of the boys from North Carolina.

~ John Hartford Music (BMI)

To stand in the bottom of any of the valleys is to have the feeling of being down in the center of a great round cup . . . Travelers from the level lands always complained that they felt hemmed in by our hills, cut off from the wide skies and the rest of the world. For us it was hard to believe there was any "rest of the world," and if there should be such a thing, why, we trusted in the mountains to protect us from it.

— Jean Ritchie, *Singing Family of The Cumberlands*

The music of the Carter Family represents the very soul of old-time, and their story furnishes lessons on the permeability of state borders in Upper East Tennessee. The Carters also demonstrate the enduring influence of mountain music on bluegrass and country, as well as later forms such as rockabilly and, yes, even rock and roll.

The original group consisted of two cousins, Maybelle Addington and Sara Dougherty, and Sara's husband A.P. Carter. In 1927, RCA talent scout Ralph Peer set up shop in Bristol, Tennessee — "about 20 feet from the Tennessee-Virginia line," according to one music historian. He brought along his wife, a couple of sound engineers, and two carloads of recording equipment, determined to record the music of Appalachia.

A story on Peer's recording project was featured in the local newspaper. On August 1, 1927, responding to the article, A.P., Sara, and Maybelle, along with A.P.'s nonmusical brother Ezra, loaded into their Hupmobile and drove down to Bristol from Maces Springs, Virginia. The songs that Peer recorded, including "Bury me Beneath the Weeping Willow" and "Little Log Cabin by the Sea," endure as classics not only of old-time but of American music in general. (Two days after he recorded the Carters, Peer also lured a Mississippi-born singer from nearby Asheville, North Carolina. Jimmie Rodgers became known as "the Father of Country Music.")

Peer recorded the Carters' first six songs; by the time of their last record date in 1941, the "First Family of Country Music" had cut a total of 250 songs. Toward the end, the group moved to Del Rio, Texas, where their music was broadcast on three 50,000-watt radio stations. Joining the original three members were A.P. and Sara's two children, Janette and Joe, and Maybelle's three daughters, Helen, June, and Anita.

Johnny Cash has said, "I don't think you can listen to eight bars of a country music song without hearing the influence of the Carter Family." Of course, Cash may be somewhat biased, since he's married to June Carter, one of Maybelle and Ezra's daughters. The group's close family connections — brothers married to cousins — are indicative of the region's tight-knit family groups.

"WELL, THEY'RE KIND OF A MIXED-UP FAMILY, you know, but . . . that's the way it is, see?" offers a mischievous Janette Carter. Now in her seventies, she runs the Carter Fold Music Barn in Maces Springs, a tiny hamlet a few miles from the nearest post office in Hiltons, a windy 20-mile drive north from Bristol.

Every Saturday night like clockwork, Janette Carter emerges from her hillside home and descends several dozen steps to the barn, where she sings and plays her autoharp. Guest artists appear as well. The annual Carter Family Memorial Festival takes place at the Music Barn each August.

Sitting on her porch on a summer weekday morning, birds twittering about, Carter explains, "I'm just a-tryin' to keep alive their music. Well, I wouldn't have nothing else here in the valley. It'd be a dishonor to have anything but their type music."

Carter acknowledges that carrying on the family tradition can be wearing. "You give 20 years of every Saturday night to some organization like I have down here, you are tired. You love your work, you enjoy it, but you are tired. You know, your weekends, every once in a while you'd like to be somewhere else besides here.

"Like I went out over to Kingsport over there, to the mall, with my daughter and them last night, and people recognize me because they come from everywhere down here, you know, and there's some woman [who said], 'Well, Miss Carter,' she said, 'I didn't believe you *ever* got out of Hiltons, Virginia,' says. I said, 'Yes, I do,' [laughs] 'I'm in Kingsport.' I said, 'I do get out of Hiltons, Virginia.' "

Then, after a pause, Carter exhales a long moment and adds, "But I guess I'm just a part of Hiltons, just like that ol' tree there. I'm *here*, you know."

Before talking with "Miss Carter," I had driven up from Bristol, following the valley which runs alongside the Clinch Mountains. Arriving in the early morning, I stopped in at Hiltons Restaurant for a plate of biscuits and cream gravy and at the counter met Gene Harper, third cousin to June, who escorted me to Mt. Vernon United Methodist Church, where A.P. and Sara Carter are buried.

"This is the little church I was saved in 27 years ago," Gene said as we stood in the churchyard.

People all over the Appalachian region still honor the Carters' music, and on the last Sunday of every July, the Mt. Vernon United Methodist Church holds an all-day singing and dinner on its well-groomed grounds.

For Janette Carter, the early years of the Carter Family were unforgettable. "They had radio, of course, way back, but they didn't have the TV and they didn't have all the stuff that they have now," she told me. "When I was a girl a-goin' with them to the schools and things, they didn't have microphones. A lot of the schools didn't even have electricity. I think the lights come through the valley in the '30s."

She pauses. "It was quite a bit different. They sold most of their records through Montgomery Ward and Sears Roebuck. They just didn't have the distribution like a lot of the musicians now that carry their albums everywhere they go and sell them, you know, at concerts. And the Carter Family done a lot of personal appearances. 'Entertainments,' is what they called 'em back then — programs.

Maybelle, Sara (with autoharp), and A.P. (Alvin Pleasant) Carter made up the original **Carter Family**, whose musical programs were advertised as "morally good." They came to Tennessee from Virginia's Clinch Mountains, north of Kingsport. Courtesy of Hatch Showprint.

"But people didn't have a lot of money, you know. They'd just charge about 25 cents for an adult to come in and see a concert. And they worked at the schools and the churches and the reunions and, back then, the theaters — you know, there used to be a lot of theaters. In between the movies, why, they would put on a little program and then they'd show the movie. Then, before the next one come on — maybe they'd put on two or three programs at this theater."

In its songs, the Carter Family stressed the dignity of mountain life by focusing on traditional values: "images of morality, stability, and home-centeredness," as one writer stated it. In 1970, the Carters became the first group to be inducted into the Country Music Hall of Fame in Nashville.

———————

LIKE ROB NICAR, FRED McCLELLAN IS NOT A PROFESSIONAL MUSICIAN, but he cares deeply about preserving traditional music.

By vocation, "chicken-sellin' Fred McClellan" (as he's known around town) is a Bristol businessman, the owner of a "chain" of Hillbilly Chicken convenience stores. By *avocation*, he is a tireless promoter of old-time music, specifically of the idea that old-time, and thus country, music began in Bristol, Tennessee. The Birthplace of Country Music Alliance, of which McClellan is president, hopes to promote the region's rich musical heritage.

Standing behind his store counter, McClellan serves customers and talks about his love for old-time music. He still remembers the two-story brick building where Ralph Peer first recorded the Carter Family and Jimmie Rodgers before it was demolished; the site is now occupied by a Rite Aid pharmacy. Bristol is also the birthplace of Tennessee Ernie Ford, the country and gospel singer, who started out in the '30s as a DJ on the town's WOPI radio station, pulling down $10 a week.

When McClellan was in high school, he focused not on music but on basketball, hoping to nail down a spot in the pros, as two of his classmates did (one of them earned a ring with the Celtics — as a bench-warmer). Because he was busy shooting hoops, McClellan never took up an instrument. He now regrets that lapse but takes a very personal interest in the old-time string music of Appalachia.

McClellan spent his early years in Kentucky. His father, Gene, worked in the coal mines but he played banjo so well that he was hired on in the company-sponsored band, the Tug River Ramblers. The Ramblers played on a famous radio show in West Virginia. From the *Wheeling Jamboree*, Gene McClellan vaulted to the big time: the *Grand Ole Opry*. He stayed for two years before deciding that he would rather toil in the mines than starve in Nashville. He moved back home, only to die in a mining accident.

McClellan showed me old photographs of his father's band. Some of them show the band members wearing farcical hillbilly outfits: patched clothes, goofy oversized brogans, hayseed hats, even big fake ears. Ashamed of the photos, Gene McClellan wouldn't allow them to be hung in his house. He was incensed that the Ramblers were asked to wear

Fred McClellan's father played banjo with the **Tug City Ramblers**. Gene McClellan (far right) decided against trying his luck as a musician in Nashville, opting for steadier work at home; he later died in the coal mines. Courtesy of Fred McClellan.

such silly outfits, that their music couldn't stand on its own. Sometimes, when an orchestra backed the group, Fred's father felt that the orchestra musicians snubbed him and his bandmates.

Today, Fred McClellan is trying to eradicate the negative stereotype of the hillbilly that his father detested. He feels that young people in East Tennessee should be proud, not ashamed, of their Appalachian heritage. Part of the problem is with the word "hillbilly," which summons up connotations of rude mountain folk. In his opinion, the word is synonymous with "mountaineer."

It originally referred to "a group of people from the Appalachian Mountains with a strong will and spirit to live against adverse conditions," he said, adding, "I don't run away from the term. I hold it dear, and wish that we be given the opportunity to build our own pride around who we are and tell others, 'I think you've been misinformed.'"

The next moment, chicken-sellin' Fred McClellan snaps open a brown bag with one hand and purrs to an older female customer, "Today is Friday, darlin' — all day long and half a night."

FRONTIERSMAN DAVY CROCKETT served West Tennessee for three terms in the U.S. Congress. Best known for his wilderness skills — he once killed 105 bears in a single winter — Congressman Crockett is also said to have played a mean fiddle, once jamming with a bagpiper at the Alamo (where he and Sam Houston met their end).

Tennessee has had a long tradition of politician-fiddlers. East Tennessee brothers Bob and Alf Taylor competed in the 1886 state gubernatorial election. The race included fiddle competitions as well as other unorthodox electoral strategems. For instance, they used the same poster, replete with illustrations of their parents and seven siblings, the Happy Valley house where both were born, and the lyrics to their uncle's "Ode to East Tennessee." Newspapers called it "the War of the Roses" — a jocular reference to the fight for the English throne by the royal houses, Lancaster and York, back in the 1400s. Centuries later, this family struggle was based on ideologies, not bloodlines: The Taylors belonged to different political parties.

In a governmental cost-cutting measure which may never again be repeated, the two traveled together on the campaign trail. Following is an exerpt from *Bob and Alf Taylor: Their Lives and Lectures* (1925):

> . . . Often, when the battle lines brought them to some lone hostelry far from the more modern towns, they slept in the same bed. Like the rain which falls equally on the just and the unjust, the same quilt would warm the slumbers of Republican Alf and Democratic Bob; and early the next morning, refreshed by their rest, they would set forth anew to rend each other's parties into bleeding fragments for the cheering electorate to see. So deadly earnest were they on the platform, so scathing in their denunciations of the opposing faiths, that folks expected to see the brothers turn on each other and settle the argument with fists.
>
> Far from it! Often, Alf told the biographer, he and Bob would discuss their speeches as they rode to their next appointment. Sitting astride their horses or side by side in a buggy, they would offer criticisms and suggestions while jogging down a country pike towards that crossroads junction where the welcoming processions, resplendent with bunting and bands and roses, would be waiting to escort the candidates into town. . .

The 1886 race for Tennessee governor featured fiddle-offs between **Robert Love Taylor** and his brother Alfred. Bob ended up serving three terms, and Alf one, at age 72 — after Bob's death. Illustration by Libby Davidson.

Once, the brothers held a fiddle-off instead of a scheduled debate, and judging by a tally of the votes in 1886, Bob was the superior fiddler. Robert Love Taylor ended up serving three terms as Tennessee's governor, but time has dimmed memories of his legislative agenda; it is his fiddling that has earned him a place in the history books. Alf later followed in his brother's footsteps, winning the race for governor in 1920, eight years after Bob had passed through the pearly gates.

Well-a, old Uncle Doody in the shade of the tree
Played on the fiddle in the key of C.
Sheep's in the meader and the cow's in the co'n,
But old Uncle Doody don't give a doggone.

I WAS THINKING ABOUT CROCKETT and the Taylors as I drove around Carthage, the Middle Tennessee hometown of Albert Gore, father to the U.S. vice president and himself a former U.S. senator. Like a lot of Tennesseans, Senator Gore, now in his late eighties, has a distinctly warm and informal approach to interpersonal relations — he doesn't stand on ceremony.

I caught up with him at the door to Gore's Antique Barn. He was just leaving but he offered to speak with me provided that I accompany him on a few errands. We took his slightly worse-for-wear 1975 Buick to the post office and visited one of his properties, and talked about fiddling and politics.

"[Country music star Roy] Acuff ran for governor when I ran for senator," Gore said. "But there was a difference. When Acuff fiddles, he's making his principal appeal. I play a tune or two to get attention." This difference may have been crucial: Gore won his 1948 race and Acuff lost.

Senator **Albert Gore** stands outside his home outside Carthage, east of Nashville. Other public servants from Tennessee include Admiral David G. Farragut ("Damn the torpedoes! Full speed ahead!") and Cordell Hull, mastermind of the United Nations (and the Income Tax Law of 1913). Perry Walker.

A decade earlier, during his first campaign, Gore's friends predicted that if he fiddled, "on the very next day I would be called Nero," after the infamous Roman emperor.

"I went to Jamestown for a speaking engagement on a very hot day," he recalled. "People were sitting in the windows. I saw some fellows doing square dances, holding up a guitar, banjo and fiddle. Someone thrust a fiddle at me and said, 'Here, Albert, play us a tune.' The people applauded. I told the crowd that I had been warned not to play the fiddle, but [said] 'I'll play this fiddle if you vote for me.'"

That afternoon, Gore worked through crowd pleasers like "Soldier's Joy" and "Turkey in the Straw," telling a story between each tune. Sure enough, Gore recalls, in the next day's paper, "each of my four opponents were quoted calling me Nero."

Inside his spacious but unassuming home overlooking the Caney Fork River, Senator Gore showed me a copy of Val J. Halmandaris' *Heroes of the U.S. Congress*. "I'm one of the 100 — Al isn't," he chuckles, referring to his son, the vice president. "That's a touchy thing in the family." On the wall were photographs of a lifetime in politics, including Roosevelt's dedication of Great Smoky Mountain National Park, which Gore attended.

Gore has long since hung up his fiddle. He enjoys classical music, particularly opera. As for rock, he believes that songs with X-rated lyrics are "not worthy of our people or our culture" and he supports his daughter-in-law Tipper's call for parental discretion labels.

A PRIMORDIAL FOG ENSHROUDS ROB NICAR'S PRACTICE BARN on an early morning in October. When the owner rattles up in his red pickup truck, the raucous strains of Gid Tanner & His Skillet Lickers disturb the autumnal peace.

"The only time I really listen to old-time," he said, "is when I'm trying to learn a song, unless I'm just drivin' down the road. But at home, as far as just background music, I love to listen to Alison Krauss and to the Front Porch String Band, which is a band out of Alabama with a girl singer named Claire Lynch [see page 101]. Claire's got a voice equal or maybe even better than Alison Krauss. Why she hasn't gone to Nashville . . . she could make it easy in Nashville with her voice." He also likes the New Dixie Entertainers, an old-time band from Harriman, particularly the fiddling of Mike Bryant (whose wife Marcia plays bass).

I try out John Hartford's "river of sound" theory on Nicar, who lives near the Holston River. Along with the French Broad, Nolichucky, and Clinch rivers, the Holston runs southwest, ultimately feeding into the Tennessee River near Knoxville. Nicar doesn't profess to know the difference between regional river styles, but speaks instead of his personal experience: "I'm more in tune with southwest Virginia, western North Carolina, and East Tennessee."

Nicar plays fiddle in the staccato, "round peak" style that is heard throughout Appalachia and often identified with Galax, Virginia and Mt. Airy, North Carolina. "We do a lot of sawing, or whatever you want to call it," he says with a smile, alluding to the cartoon image of a frantically bowing fiddler. By contrast, a smoother "long bow" style, in which fiddlers play more notes per individual stroke, is the norm in West Tennessee and Texas.

The most famous long-bow fiddler was the aforementioned Arthur Smith (1898-1973), a native of Bold Springs, Humphreys County, who at various times collaborated with Tennessee natives Uncle Dave Macon, and Sam and Kirk McGee, as well as Alabama's Delmore Brothers. Smith's use of double-stops and his bluesy phrasing influenced many Southeastern fiddlers in the 1930s and continues to impress people like Rob Nicar today.

Nicar removes his fiddle from its case and plucks the strings to see whether the instrument is tuned to his liking. He starts out with what appears to be a rather challenging tune "that comes from just down the river" in Bluff City, Dudley Vance's "Tennessee Mountain Fox Chase."

It consisted of several distinct passages, one of which was plaintive and eerily discordant, the other relentlessly rhythmic. Asked if the song is technically difficult to play, Nicar laughed heartily and said, "Oh, no, no, not really. It's just a little unusual; it's got a little rhythm pattern to it."

Is it supposed to sound like a real fox chase? "Yeah, it is. It's a bad [one] to start out [with] for your first tune. You need to be a little more warmed up playing it, to get the full effect of the hounds chasing the fox, but yeah, that high part, I guess, is . . ."

He plays a passage.

"I guess that may be the dogs howling," he says. "And I always took that middle, the second part, as being the chase."

Rob and Amy Nicar get together with Jeff Benedict and bassist Rick Moore for summer jam sessions in a downtown Bristol parking lot on State Street. A mural in the background celebrates the town's boast as "the birthplace of country music." Jimmie Rodgers and the Carters, among others, cut their first records down the road. Photo by Perry Walker.

He runs through four or five more tunes, including a couple of Arthur Smith originals, before pronouncing the barn too cold and damp for fiddling.

Nicar hopes the Birthplace of Country Music Alliance will succeed in attracting attention to the musical heritage of northeastern Tennessee. He believes that Bristol, rather than Owensboro, Kentucky, could have been the bluegrass capital of the world if local politicians and "people with the money" hadn't looked down on the genre.

"And now I think people are realizing that Bristol missed a wonderful opportunity," he said. "Or they *will* miss it if they don't get something going.

"Tourism is gonna have to play an important part, long-term. We've got a beautiful area here, and we've got great talent. We're not ever gonna be a Nashville or a Branson, Missouri, here in Bristol, Tennessee. But I think we've got something to offer the people who are more interested in string music than the country-pop that you hear out of Nashville and Branson."

As we head out to the truck and a ride back to the present day, the sun finally breaks.

"Yeah, it's gonna be a beautiful day," Nicar says, "it really is."

Three Old-Time Fiddlers

by Robert J. Fulcher

Bob Douglas, Charlie Acuff, and Frazier Moss — who range in age from their late seventies to nearly 100 — literally represent the old school of old-time fiddling. All dabbled with a dangerous profession that left many men poor, bitter, and alcoholic. None made it onto a major record label or the *Opry*, instead plying their art at medicine shows, local radio and stage programs, and at fiddle contests. But even through decades of musical change, they never abandoned their passion for old-time fiddling.

Fiddlers don't agree on many musical issues, but the great ones rarely claim any benefit from instruction or severe practice. Rather, they feel "gifted" by God to play the instrument, although the gift comes with a share of suffering, especially for fiddlers so deeply bewitched that they try to make a living at it.

BORN IN 1900 NORTH OF CHATTANOOGA, Bob Douglas continues to perform in his nonagenarian years at festivals, fiddle contests, and small-town country music shows. His father Tom was a tenant farmer, fur trapper, and ginseng digger, in addition to being Sequatchie Valley's first-rank fiddler. In 1917, Bob joined his father and Uncle Ab Ferguson "on the road" along a 150-mile wilderness circuit from Bon Air to Jasper, playing in coal towns and, between the camps, holding square dances in private homes.

"We travelled mostly by trail," he said. "Dad knowed every pig trail on that mountain. He'd been all out in there turkey hunting."

For 10 years, Tom and Ab carried their instruments (the ubiquitous fiddle and banjo) in meal sacks while Bob carried a guitar on his shoulder. He said they always managed to find shelter when it rained. Tom was reluctant to lose his guitarist, but finally handed over his fiddle to Bob in 1928. That September, he entered the All Southern Fiddlers Convention in Chattanooga — his first fiddling contest — and handily defeated Clayton McMichen, Tom "Sawmill" Smith, and other champs.

A month later in Atlanta, he made a "hillbilly" recording with Lee and Austin Allen, his first and only commercial disk. There followed jobs with an Indiana medicine show, as house fiddler for WSB-Atlanta's Tennessee Firecrackers, playing in Bill Gatins' jug band, and touring the Midwest with the Georgia Wildcats. Frustrated by the the impossible hours and modest income, Douglas moved to Chattanooga in 1938, fitting music gigs between factory jobs.

On a trip to Nashville with Curly Fox, Bob decided to turn around for Chattanooga and steady work at a textile mill, while Curly stayed put and soon found himself on the *Grand Ole Opry*. For the next 30 years, Chattanooga had Bob Douglas all to itself, on the radio and at contests, amateur hours, jam sessions, bank openings, and dance hall gigs. His fiddle turned out whatever people wanted: square-dance tunes, Western swing, pop, blues, or country. His own band had a 10-year run during which he hired the teenaged Louvin Brothers for their professional job.

Douglas was rediscovered during the 1960s folk revival, and he went on to press a dozen LPs at custom recording studios, selling the records at contests and gigs to admirers (and competitors). In 1975, the Smithsonian Institution invited him to Washington to participate in its National Fiddle Contest, and nearly 70 years after winning his first trophy, Douglas won again.

Five years ago, he took his first flight, a transcontinental jaunt to Port Townsend, Washington, to perform at the Festival of American Fiddle Tunes. It took nearly a century, but he has now finally played his music from coast to coast.

"I was just one of them fellers that didn't care about trying to get rich," he said. "I'm still a poor man, but I've got enough to live on, and I'm gonna play as long as I'm able."

PITCHING ACE DIZZY DEAN crowned Roy Claxton Acuff "King of Country Music" because his voice rang true, with compelling authenticity. He always carried his fiddle on stage, although beginning early in his career he hired gifted fiddlers to handle the job. Those fans who have wondered about the musical background that tempered his ringing voice, and wondered why he always had a fiddle in hand (though they may have never heard him play it), can best find their answers from Roy's first cousin once-removed, Charlie Acuff. *(continues)*

Like many Tennessee musicians, Charlie believes that bloodline, as much as practice, makes perfect. "There's so much of it borned into you," he said. "See my daddy played, and my grandpa played, and all of my daddy's sisters played some kind of instrument, except one." Born in 1919 in Maynardville, northeast of Knoxville, Charlie was named after his fiddling grandfather, Charlie Boyd Acuff, who put a fiddle in his 12-year-old grandson's lap. Charlie, who had to overcome the obstacle of being left-handed, said, "If my grandfather was living today, I doubt you could tell much difference in our old-time tunes."

Grandfather Charlie had already taught some fiddle tunes to his nephew, Roy, who went on to become a household name. During World War II, Japanese soldiers hollered across the battle lines: "To hell with Roosevelt! To hell with Babe Ruth! To hell with Roy Acuff!" But while Roy was making money and thrilling *Opry* audiences and USO tours, Charlie was living a fiddler's life in East Tennessee.

In high school, he and his guitar-playing brother Gale would perform tunes like "Dance All Night With a Bottle In Your Hand" at square dances. They played an early-morning shift on WROL in Knoxville, advertising Hub Department Store (and their own gigs). They supplied music during intermissions at movie theaters in Maynardville and toured mining camps in Kentucky, eventually landing a half-hour slot back in Knoxville on WNOX.

The war brought good jobs to East Tennessee, and like Bob Douglas, Acuff opted for the sure money of factory work. He and his new wife moved to Alcoa, Tennessee, where he worked for the next 40 years, in addition to doing some part-time fiddling and raising a family. He joined employee jam sessions after hours at the company credit union and musical gatherings at the union hall.

Since retiring in 1982, his love for fiddling has been rekindled. He performs with an old-time string band, the Lantana Drifters, at contests and festivals, and works as a staff musician two days a week at the Museum of Appalachia in Norris.

Acuff's style is touched with a light vibrato that brings a sweet flavor to his sustained notes. "My grandaddy called those 'tremble notes,' but he told me, 'Charles, you take a tune that's got them rolling notes in it — that's what's pretty.'" Charlie's five fiddles were made by his father, Evart, with tools crafted by a fiddling great-great uncle.

FRAZIER MOSS "WAS FOND OF A FIDDLE" the first time he heard it at a schoolteacher's wedding. His dad bought him his first fiddle when he was eight, and four years later, Moss won his first fiddle contest in Gainsborough, Tennessee, for which he earned a five-dollar gold piece. The year was 1922.

Moss learned from the old men who played their fiddles and banjos at square dances that could last for a week in the Jackson County countryside. After showing his stuff at a vaudeville tent set up outside the courthouse, he was recruited to tour small towns, coal camps, and schools throughout central Tennessee and Kentucky.

Now almost eighty, **Charlie Acuff** lives near Knoxville, where he continues to entertain locals with his unorthodox lefthanded style. Not as famous as his late cousin Roy, Charlie worked in a factory for 40 years to support his fiddling habit. He believes that music is "borned into you." Photo by Bob Fulcher.

With one partner, he perfected 13 acts, performing comedy routines and buck-and-wing dancing while fiddling crowds into an uproar.

He still couldn't make enough money in those lean times and supported his fiddling habit by working as a carpenter for 35 years. He held a regular radio slot in Cookeville, the largest town between Knoxville and Nashville, and worked at local dances. People took to calling him "Fiddler" Moss instead of "Frazier."

In 1977, he struck out for Weiser, Idaho, and the National Old-Time Fiddlers Championship. After three days of competition against the more popular Texas and Canadian styles, Moss took the grand prize and a title won by no other Tennessean, before or since.

Anyone who has met Moss remembers his high, keen voice and laugh, and it has always seemed that his fiddle mimicked that somewhat nasal tone. His melodies are meatier than Texas style and more elaborate than hillbilly music. Capable of playing whatever he desired, he never strayed far from the music he mastered first.

"Course, I've went through this world of modern music that we have," he said. "A lot of it I don't even play, but I still play the old authentic music yet myself, and I think it's the best music that we've ever had, and I don't think they'll ever make music that will be equal to it."

Bob Fulcher works for Tennessee State Parks as a regional interpretive specialist and formerly served as its director of folklife projects.

Although **Joshua "Peg Leg" Howell** and **Memphis Minnie (Lizzie Douglas)** were contemporaries — both made their first recordings in the 1920s — there is no evidence that they made music together. Minnie was born in Louisiana, moved to Mississippi at age 7, and later ran away to Memphis, singing the blues and accompanying herself on guitar. She recorded with the Memphis Jug Band, led by the city's own Will Shade. Howell worked out of Atlanta and, like Minnie, played country blues guitar. He lost one leg in 1916 after getting shot by his brother-in-law, and the other to diabetes in 1952. Peg Leg Howell should not be confused with South Carolina's Peg Leg Sam, who played harmonica. Mixed media by Florence Zinman.

Blues is a feeling that's when something get on you and you get to
thinkin' about it, it's a real feeling when, you know, like your woman
left you or your wife left you or girlfriend or something, or something
get to worryin' you — that's the way I express the blues. Blues is just
words and music to me, but you can express the blues as, like I say,
when you fell in love with somebody and well, they done you so wrong,
you set down and think and say, 'Oh Lord,' you know, 'she got me
walkin' the back roads.' Or climbing the walls backwards, you know?

— Earl Banks

Blues and Roots

The first time I saw Earl "the Pearl" Banks, at a rainy outdoor concert in
Memphis, he was playing a shiny red electric guitar as a guest artist with the legendary Hi
Rhythm Section, which backed that record label's great soul singers of the late 1960s and
early '70s, notably Al Green and O.V. Wright. (The group's front man, guitarist "Teenie"
Hodges, is profiled in the soul chapter.) After the band had warmed up on a few instru-
mentals, Banks strode onto the stage exuding confidence like a prizefighter.

From head to toe, he was nattily dressed in white, bright against his dark brown skin.
He wore a loose-fitting suit reminiscent of Cab Calloway and a sharp hat somewhere between countrified and ghetto. It is unlikely that this seasoned blues guitarist was experi-
encing any stage fright — he had been doing this sort of thing for 40-plus years. Playing
to the hometown crowd didn't hurt, either. When the audience cheered for the Pearl, one
sensed that more than a few had gotten to know him personally over the years; judging by
his gentle ribbing, the emcee certainly had.

Smiling, Banks looked relaxed and in his element, guitar slung low across his midriff.
He played in the characteristic sparse style favored by most Memphis-area guitarists,
searching for notes and riffs and, finding ones he liked, bending and sustaining them.
This was a man cut from B.B. King cloth, with perhaps a dash of Texas' T-Bone Walker. Although his solos excited and even incited the crowd, they were Delta-derived, an electric
extension of earlier acoustic "country bluesmen" like Bukka White. They bore little re-
semblance to the dazzling pyrotechnics of such guitarists as Seattle's Jimi Hendrix and
Louisiana's Buddy Guy (whose partner Junior Wells came from West Memphis, Arkansas).
This was "strictly blues," as Banks later described his music to me.

It was as if he were thinking, "I don't *need* to play so many notes, as long as I can get
the same emotional mileage out of a few choice ones."

And he pulled it off. The audience cheered his solo on "Every Day I Have the Blues,"
written in 1948 by pianist Peter Chatman, aka Memphis Slim (who also wrote "The
Comeback"). Banks delivered this hometown favorite with a seemingly incongruous mix
of emotional intensity and almost effortless nonchalance.

Before this show, I had never heard of Earl Banks, but I liked his playing. Afterwards, I introduced myself and asked him for his number, which he cordially provided.

When I phoned him at home, Banks suggested that I stop by his daytime job at the now-closed White Way Pharmacy on North Cleveland, not far from downtown Memphis, where he delivered prescriptions in his workmanlike compact car.

We met before work one day at 8 a.m. and sat at one of the little tables in the pharmacy, talking about his days in Memphis. Banks is one of perhaps dozens — perhaps hundreds — of talented blues and R&B artists kicking around Memphis and environs. They play gigs as they crop up, almost as a hobby, while holding "regular" jobs, such as Banks' at the pharmacy, to make a living. It is not easy making a living in Memphis as a musician, partly because there are so many good ones and partly because the locals have grown to take this glut of talent for granted.

Musicians' success depends on how they prioritize music in their lives, and how well they get along with people and handle adverse situations. In Banks' opinion, fate also has a hand.

IN CONTRAST TO HIS LARGER-THAN-LIFE STAGE PRESENCE, Earl the Pearl was rather slight of build in person. His disposition was self-possessed, but I also detected something deferential in his demeanor. Perhaps it was because we were strangers and his guard was up a little. I also felt that Earl Banks is a man who prefers to tread lightly. He is a gentleman, a sensitive person who does not like to step on others, who tends to walk away from, rather than face, any potential confrontation that comes his way.

Talking with him, it was also my impression — and perhaps I'm mistaken — that there was a tension in the fact that we are members of different races: black and white. Not that he didn't like me because of my ethnic background; rather, he appeared to treat me with inordinate respect because of my whiteness. Sometimes he made me feel that, in his eyes, I was "The Man." I attributed this mostly to our generational difference: Banks is in his sixties, roughly twice my age. It was interesting to encounter this deference compared with younger black musicians, such as the aforementioned Teenie Hodges, who learned guitar from Banks. They seemed bolder and more strident in expressing themselves when I asked them virtually the same questions.

Banks' eyes occasionally met my own as he pondered what might have been, why his musical career had faltered, why he had "never gotten anywhere" while people like B.B. King, whom he used to jam with at Roosevelt Lake,

For Information Call
Phone 744-8453
Earl The Pearl
HI RHYTHM BAND
RECORDING ARTISTS
Memphis, Tenn.
I PLAY THE BLUES

had catapulted to worldwide fame. Riley King has become the "King of the Blues"; Earl Banks delivers drugs for White Way and plays an occasional gig.

In the 1950s, back in his salad days, Banks was hot. He recalls gigging with such legends as the one-man band Joe Hill Louis, aka "the Bebop Boy," in Moscow, Tennessee. Memphis emissary Rufus Thomas, of "Walking the Dog" fame, featured Banks' band on his WDIA radio slot. Banks also played with Roscoe Gordon and most everyone who was hanging out on Beale Street and around town.

Nowadays, the club engagements are few and far between. Banks attributes this to a certain lack of fire in his belly. As he traced his development as an indigenous Memphis blues artist, he sounded almost apologetic at times, leaning forward and perching on the edge of his seat so he could hear over the pharmacy's early morning hubbub.

Banks believes that he never really developed a knack for making the right contacts — networking, in the '90s vernacular (others have a more derogatory term for it).

"I didn't have the knowledge to try to get with somebody that would send me out there, you know, because it's gonna take a person like you" — meaning, I surmised, someone

Earl "the Pearl" Banks strikes a pose outside the White Way Pharmacy, his former employer, now defunct. By his own confession, Banks lacked the drive to make a big name for himself in music, but he remains a local favorite at clubs and festivals. Banks grew up in Germantown, east of Memphis. Back then it was farmland; now it's Tennessee's 11th-largest city. Photograph by Perry Walker.

white with contacts — "to get me out there and get a name. It's like when [guitarist] Albert King come along back in them days. I was coming along, you know, but evidently they got with somebody that pushed him, and B.B. and them. I coulda been the same place. If I'd just had somebody back in them days to kind of push me or pick me up and say, 'Well, hey'. . . ."

When he was young, Banks had a white friend named Rusty Pate who would come out to his house. He'd try to get Banks to go and hear Furry Lewis play (the legendary Memphis guitarist is covered later in this chapter) but Banks would decline.

"I said, 'I ain't going, I'm gonna stay at home.' He would come by to get me, to bring me down there. See, if I'd have went on down in those days, somebody might have discovered me and might, you know, but . . . I guess I was a lagger. I'm just stay-behind."

At the time, although Banks wanted to become a musician, he ended up quitting music for two years on account of a relationship. "Two years, that will take a lot out of your music," he said. "[But] I was in love. When you fall in love, man, that's . . . ." He shook his head and sighed. (We didn't discuss why he couldn't play his music *and* have a relationship; on the other hand, I could see his point.)

As with amateur old-time fiddler Rob Nicar, music means more to Banks than money alone. Rather, it is an integral part of his character. People like him are the backbone of the music industry, the unsung (and, mostly, uncompensated) heroes of their own songs. These men and women continue to make music in counterpoint to the more mundane demands of everyday survival.

Earl Banks' career has been further hampered by his fear of flying. It's simply not practical to make a gig in Europe, for example, when you're traveling by boat. He is equally high-strung about other modes of transport.

A couple of years ago, he was scheduled to fly to Toronto in order to back singer Carla Thomas. When he got home that afternoon, Banks related: "An old lady said, 'Earl, have you seen the news?' I said, 'No, what happened?' She said, 'Another plane done fell.' I said, 'Hell, uh-oh,' I said, 'No, no, I'm not flyin' up there.'

"We had to be there that Friday. So I left on Thursday and got to Detroit, Michigan, about 2:30 that night, and spent the night at [a friend's] house. I went to the bus station the next morning and caught the bus out, Detroit into Toronto.

"I sat behind that bus driver — because I got a bus myself — I sat behind him all the way. I was the first person got on that bus, and I got that seat right behind him. I said, if anything go wrong with him, I can go up and get that steering wheel.

"And every time he would go around a car, I would look at that mirror. And when he throw his light on, and come back over after he pass the car, I'd be lookin' in that mirror. And when I got to Toronto, Canada, I told him, I said, 'You're a good driver.' He said, 'Well, thank you.' He said, 'Why do you say that?' I said, 'Well, I got a bus, too, and I was watchin' you, and that's the reason I sat behind you — just in case somethin' went wrong.'"

EARL GREW UP IN GERMANTOWN, A MEMPHIS SUBURB some 15 miles east of downtown. He remembers being a kid in the '40s, back when it was a rural area. Banks' interest in music began to develop at age six after his grandfather bought a piano for his aunt. Every Sunday, a man by the name of Buddy Grim came by and played it, and Banks would stand by the corner of the piano and watch Grim's fingers dance over the keys. No doubt he scrutinized Buddy Grim as closely as he did the bus driver some 50 years later.

When he started school, he and a couple of other students started experimenting on the piano there, but since there was only one piano, the pecking order was first come, first served. "So that was Charlie Mathis, who was Teenie Hodges' first cousin, and there was Roy Evans, and myself," said Banks. "We was about the only three played the piano, so we would try to beat each other there, to play every morning in the chapel before school take in."

In 1958, Banks took up the guitar. He has always played "just plain blues," and like many blues musicians, he is entirely self-taught and cannot read music.

"I know some chords and notes, you know, the B-flat major, the B-flat minor, the C major, all the diminished, you know," he said. "But if you put a chart of music in front of me, I be lost just like you throwed me out in the ocean and said, 'Which way is the shore? What is the closer way to shore? Closer this way and this way?' You know? I be lost.

"But now, you can take a record and put it on, a tape player, and I set there, and play a part of it, a part of it, until I get it all down. That's the way I learn."

In his playing and songwriting, Banks draws heavily from his musical predecessors, and then adds his own slant. "You go back and try to get up some chords, you know, some *way* back there, ol' Rascal Williams, Elmore James. I'm right behind those guys. Muddy Waters, you know. Get some of these chords and just set down and put it together and play it. That's the way I would put my music together."

Several years ago, Banks' boss at the now-defunct White Way Pharmacy (whom he referred to as Mr. Lubin), arranged for Banks to record a 45. For whatever reason, the record never got pressed, so Banks scraped up the money and produced it himself. Both sides of that record are Banks' original compositions. "Too Much Cool in Your Blood" refers to a drug user (cool being slang for junk), while "Your Mind Is Snappin' on You" addresses those with hot tempers.

Banks said he tries to avoid the latter. "I'm a very easy guy to get along with, but you can make me mad. [If] I start talkin' to somebody in here and they just actin' crazy, I say, 'Hey, I'm through,' I'll back off, you know, I go on back. [Otherwise,] before you know it I'd be in a ditch, something."

Never one to give up, Banks is currently writing a new song and has another one in the studio. The latter has been recorded but not mixed. "It's an old record, and if I ever get the money to do it, I'm gonna do it, because this is a white lady that done this record here, and she's still living, and it's nobody ever done no record. I believe it might do something."

Banks has fond memories of Beale Street in the 1950s, but times have changed, and the renovations on Beale have created an entirely different environment, one which some musicians, including Banks, feel is harsher for people of their kind.

Back then, he would play piano with Joe Hill Louis, a Raines, Tennessee, native and Beale fixture who played the guitar, harmonica, and drums simultaneously. To Banks, Louis represented the street's heyday of great music and showmanship. "It was something!" he said. "You never seen a one-man band blow the harmonica, pick the guitar and singing, all that? That's the way it was back in those days."

Banks enjoyed his 15 minutes of fame in the late '50s when his band's music was broadcast over Memphis' influential WDIA radio station. He recalled that Rufus "Bearcat" Thomas, who later became a star on the Stax label, was the deejay who "broke" him.

A few years later, Banks and the Blue Dots would pack the Flamingo Room on Wednesday nights. The group included Banks' friends from Germantown: the Hodges brothers, their father Leroy Sr., and Willie Moody.

Banks also remembers jamming at the old Stax studio (see the Soul chapter for more on this important record label). Once, after spending hours recording some tracks, the engineer informed Banks that the band wasn't hot enough. Then, several weeks later, bassist Leroy Hodges reported that he had been listening to the radio and heard the music they recorded that day. Since he had neglected to copyright it, the music was released under another artist's name, and there was little Banks could do about it. The experience left a bitter taste in his mouth; however, in keeping with his turn-the-other-cheek nature, Banks prefers not to name names — on the record.

He feels equally disgruntled by the local musicians' union, to which he no longer belongs. "They ain't gonna do nothing," he maintained. "They want me to pay so much, and so much, and they'll try to start doing something for you. Well, look — when you paying your money and they ain't gonna do nothing. . . . If you pay out seven, eight hundred dollars, I want some action in!"

Instead, Banks relies on a plain business card to advertise his services. On it, he goes simply by his nickname, Earl the Pearl, and an equally abbreviated address ("Memphis, Tenn."), along with his slogan: I PLAY THE BLUES.

Regrettably, he said, Beale Street musicians "don't stick together like you and your organizations," ostensibly referring to white musicians.

"Beale Street is a nice place, and the way things going on Beale Street now, they just ain't right. I'm talking about far as us playing gigs down there. [The club owners] don't want to pay us nothing. They making all the money themselves. What they pay me on Beale Street, I been making that stuff back in 1975.

"But Beale Street is a nice place to play, and I played there at Blues City [Café], and I played at B.B.'s one night, well, two nights. It was during a thing there for Hi Recording. And we really got some good musicians here in Memphis. But the musicians here, while you may ask for $500, he'll come in and do it for $200 or $250."

It's hard for local musicians to get a leg up on visiting musicians. "When the musicians come [from] out of town, they paid those guys way more money than they do us," he said, even though the out-of-towners are no better than the local talent. Although the situation aggravates him, he doesn't fault the "scab" musicians. Clearly, it is a management problem, he said.

The unwritten laws of blues music, according to Earl Banks, are maintaining one's composure and, above all, having a good attitude. He believes that these traits are behind the worldwide success of B.B. King, who started out in Memphis and is Banks' elder by several years. "You can't — I don't care how good you be — you just can't go out there in this world and be playing in a club with five or six hundred people and then somebody come up and talk with you, [and] you say, 'I ain't got time to talk to you,' you know, 'I got something to do, I'll talk to you later.' You know?

"You talk to that person for a few minutes, I don't care who they are. 'Well, hey, I gotta move on, it's been nice talking to you, nice meeting you.' You just can't talk to people that way. See, that's the reason I think my brother Albert [King] didn't get no further. He had an attitude. But he's a good man. Now to me, he played better than B.B. But you gotta have a good attitude."

Glancing over at Mr. Lubin, I asked Banks if perhaps we should end our conversation. I didn't want him to get in trouble with his boss. He said not to worry, that Mr. Lubin knew he was being interviewed. As we left the pharmacy, Banks invited me to his upcoming engagement.

"Why don't you jot it down on the card? I'm gonna be at Lester's, on Park Avenue and Pennington," he said. "Just come out. Bring some payin' customers with you, and I'll talk to the manager. If things go right, I got to talk to a little lounge here at Magnolia and Front. I might be there Friday night."

IT IS NOT QUITE THE MIDNIGHT HOUR when B.B. King finally and triumphantly ambles onto an enormous makeshift stage which has been set up in a Memphis park along the Mississippi River. The crowd roars, and King himself is clearly happy to be back home. His band has already worked through an instrumental, and B.B. — or just plain "B" as he is known to friends — teases the audience with a few choice notes. This sparse style, similar to Banks', is the preferred one around Memphis.

King has been described as "the world's greatest guitar soloist" and "King of the Blues." This is a big step up from when he first arrived in Memphis in the late 1940s after hitchhiking from Itta Bena, Mississippi. He got his start in show business as a deejay on WDIA. Fifty years later, he has become a household name, an international superstar.

Ironically, the park where he's playing is named after a certain Tom Lee, who, according to an obelisk erected not far from the stage, was "a very worthy Negro." In 1925, Lee saved dozens of lives in his boat *Zev* after a steamer capsized 20 miles downstream. Perhaps in another time, B.B. King might have been described in much the same way — as "a very worthy Negro" — which just goes to show, rather poignantly, how much the times

Riley "B.B." King with his Gibson guitar, which he calls Lucille. His simple, sparse approach epitomizes the blues, Memphis-style. Photograph by Erica Lansner.

have changed over the past 70 years.

While neither the most polished singer nor the most technically skilled guitarist, King is the consummate showman and knows how to work the crowd. When he's singing, he claps the back of one of his hands into the palm of the other; and while playing his cherry-red electric guitar, which he has christened Lucille, he looks possessed, at times rolling his eyes up into his head, smiling with his mouth ajar, grimacing and contorting his face. King is a hard worker: one year (1956), he endured a staggering 342 one-night stands.

Watching B.B. expose his emotions in such a heartfelt manner is a moving experience, as anyone who has seen his live show can attest. On this particular evening, King is clearly *feeling* it, and enjoying the effect his music is having on the hometown crowd. He walks to the front, stoops down, and shakes hands with his kid brother. "I can call him 'Son,'" he deadpans. "I'm the oldest."

If it is true, as the Bible says, that "by sadness of countenance the heart is made glad," then B.B. King is living proof: singing the blues makes him feel better about having them. His songs run the gamut from deprecating self-pity ("Nobody loves me but my mother/And she could be jivin' me, too") to unabashed joy ("I've got a sweet little angel/I love the way she spread her wings").

The audience in Tom Lee Park has been thoroughly warmed up by three disparate but geographically related bands. Dr. John folded funk and salsa into his New Orleans-style piano, and Georgia's Little Feat churned out its blues-and-soul-tinged Southern rock, including a rousing version of "Fool in Love" (made famous by Tennessee native Tina Turner). Just before King's appearance, a group of musicians including bassist Calvin "Fuzz" Jones and drummer Willie "Big Eyes" Smith, representing the Chicago school, and who collectively logged some 60 years with the Mississippi-born Muddy Waters, laid down a powerful hypnotic groove on Muddy's powerful "I'm a Man."

Although the four groups were touring the country, no place could have been more appropriate for them to meet on stage than Memphis, the self-ordained "capital" of the Delta, whose culture has spawned such a panoply of musical forms.

ONCE, WHILE APPROACHING Memphis from the north, I drove past the industrial section and through the sprawling housing projects. The road passed over the Wolf River, a tributary of the Mississippi, where a few people were fishing from a crumbly old bridge.

The fishermen were black and, since I had recently arrived from Middle Tennessee, where the African-American population is much smaller, they seemed to be of an especially dark hue. The air was heavier here, the foliage lush, and people of all races seemed to move about at a drowsier pace.

Much has been written about slave life on the large, labor-intensive cotton plantations of the Mississippi Delta in the first half of the 19th century. Tennessee was split almost sym-

Memphis native **George Coleman** started out playing tenor sax in B.B. King's band. In the '60s, he moved to New York and recorded some classic albums with Miles Davis (*Seven Steps To Heaven*) and Herbie Hancock (*Maiden Voyage*). Today he leads his own acoustic jazz quartet and octet. Photo by PZ.

metrically during the Civil War: the eastern third, with its smaller farms and fewer slaves, supported the Union, while the western plantocracies were solidly pro-Confederate. Middle Tennessee was divided on the slavery question and its people fought on both sides.

The state continues to be defined along racial lines. After emancipation, some blacks left the South in search of jobs, but many elected to stay put. Today, African-Americans make up more than half the population of Memphis — the state's largest city — and each of the surrounding six counties is more than 25 percent black. By contrast, the African-American population in 31 of East Tennessee's 33 counties is less than five percent.

"The cultural difference between upper East Tennessee — which is really the heartland of the old Anglo strain — and Memphis, is not just mountains and Delta — it's also Anglo and Afro," says John Seigenthaler, former publisher of *The Tennessean*, the state's largest daily paper. "That Delta area around Memphis is an extension of the Mississippi in terms of character, color, and culture."

———————

NO ONE KNOWS EXACTLY WHERE OR WHEN the musical form known as the blues originated, although its development as a popular art form is often traced to the Mississippi Delta region. Tennessee has also produced its fair share of blues greats, a fact which has often been obscured by the state's association with country music. A young Bessie Smith sang for pennies on the streets of her native Chattanooga. Jackson's John Lee "Sonny Boy"

Walter "Brownie" McGhee

by Happy Traum

In 1957, while a college student at NYU, I made a phone call that would have a profound impact on my life. I called up the legendary blues guitarist Brownie McGhee and asked him to give me guitar lessons. I had just about worn out my 10" Folkways LP called *Brownie McGhee Blues,* with such wonderful songs as "Sportin' Life Blues," "Betty and Dupree," "Pawn Shop Blues," and "Blood Red River," and was captivated both by Brownie's warm, honey-tinged voice and his rock-solid, clear-toned fingerpicking guitar technique. When I found his name in the New York City telephone directory I nervously decided to take a chance, dialed the number, and was rewarded by an invitation to come to his apartment in East Harlem.

For the next three years I made many trips to East 125th Street for a series of freewheeling, informal sessions that often consisted of dinner with the family, informal jams with Brownie's partner (the harmonica virtuoso Sonny Terry), and visits with his brother, guitarist "Sticks" McGhee (who wrote "Drinkin' Wine, Spo-Dee-O-Dee"). Mostly though, Brownie's teaching method consisted of playing songs and guitar solos over and over while I picked along behind him, trying to keep up, making mistakes and playing hour after hour. I finally developed a solidity and understanding of the blues that I never would have achieved through a more conventional system. Brownie was always patient and accommodating to this young white college student from the Bronx, and our friendship at that time resulted in a book we co-authored, *Brownie McGhee Blues Guitar.* His example has remained with me for nearly 40 years.

Walter Brown McGhee was born on November 30, 1915 in Knoxville, but his family soon moved to Kingsport where his father "helped to build a city." His first instrument was the piano, but he started playing guitar at the age of six — actually a Prince Albert tobacco can with rubber bands on it. "I would strike those strings and beat it with the back of my hand while my father would play his guitar. My father was a very

Williamson revolutionized blues harmonica playing, and slide guitarist Mississippi Fred McDowell actually grew up in Rossville, Tennessee.

The Nashville-born pianist LeRoy Carr wrote such classics as "Hurry Down Sunshine" and "In the Evening (When the Sun Goes Down)," as well as the music to "How Long, How Long Blues." When he was only 30, Carr succumbed to nephritis aggravated by acute alcoholism, although it has also been conjectured that someone put a spider in his whiskey at the brothel/dancehall where he was living. Other Tennessee-bred blues greats include Sleepy John Estes and Walter "Furry" Lewis, both covered later in this chapter.

The Georgia-born singer Gertrude "Ma" Rainey, under whom Bessie Smith apprenticed (and not to be confused with the younger, Memphis-based "Baby Ma" Rainey), claimed that

good guitarist — not professionally known but after a hard day's work he relaxed his mind. From that I got my musical education.

"Later, we left Kingsport and moved further down south in Tennessee, out in the country about eight miles from any store. There was nothing out there but guitars and banjos, a few French harps (harmonicas), and so on, so I started strumming guitar."

When Brownie was a young boy he was stricken with polio, leaving him with a short leg. He was on crutches until his last year of high school when an operation, partly funded by The March of Dimes, allowed him to walk again. "Today, instead of having my foot five inches from the ground it's an inch and a quarter. No crutch and no cane, pretty good. But anyway, I never quit, and that's when I really fell in love with the guitar, when I felt I could carry it with me. I picked up the guitar and haven't quit walking yet."

Brownie, who died in 1996, fingerpicked the blues in a way often referred to as "Piedmont" style, a technique popular with guitarists from Virginia, East Tennessee, the Carolinas and Florida, in which the thumb keeps a steady rhythm on the bass strings while the fingers pick out syncopated notes in the treble. His particular style was heavily influenced by the North Carolina bluesman Blind Boy Fuller. In fact, Brownie was billed on his earliest recordings as "Blind Boy Fuller #2."

The other dominant traditional blues guitar style, known as Mississippi Delta blues, was made famous by artists such as Robert Johnson and Charley Patton. Somewhat less refined but often technically very complex, this style typically uses bottlenecks or knife blades on the strings to achieve a whining, emotionally raw effect. Even when not using slide techniques, Delta blues is generally less structured rhythmically and harmonically than the ragtime piano-influenced East Coast styles.

Brownie's guitar playing actually falls somewhere between these two instrumental traditions but with a definite North Carolina/Tennessee emphasis.

Happy Traum owns Homespun Tapes, a Woodstock, New York, company which makes instructional music videos.

she was the first person to call the music "blues." This was in 1902 at a tent show in Missouri, where she heard a local woman sing a "strange and poignant" song about being jilted. Noticing the audience's enthusiastic response, Rainey learned the song and incorporated it into her act as an encore. Others say Jelly Roll Morton and Son House were first to hear and play the blues.

A decade later, while standing behind a cigar stand in a Beale Street saloon, cornetist and bandleader William Christopher Handy (1873-1958) became the first person to transcribe a blues song onto sheet music, for which he's often called the "Father of the Blues." The Florence, Alabama, native came to Memphis after a stint in Clarksdale, Mississippi, where he had conducted the black Knights of Pythias band. It was during this time that he first heard the blues, late one night at the Tutwiler, Mississippi, train depot. He described the experience in his autobiography:

> A lean, loose-jointed Negro had commenced plunking a guitar beside me while I slept. His clothes were rags; his feet peeped out of his shoes. His face had on it some of the sadness of the ages. As he played, he pressed a knife on the strings of the guitar in a manner popularized by Hawaiian guitarists who used steel bars. The effect was unforgettable. His song, too, struck me instantly.
>
> *Goin' where the Southern cross' the Dog.*
>
> The singer repeated the line three times, accompanying himself on the guitar with the weirdest music I had ever heard. The tune stayed in my mind. When the singer paused, I leaned over and asked him what the words meant. He rolled his eyes, showing a trace of mild amusement. Perhaps I should have known, but he didn't mind explaining. At Moorhead the eastbound and the westbound met and crossed the north and southbound trains four times a day. This fellow was going where the Southern cross' the Dog, and he didn't care who knew it. He was simply singing about Moorhead as he waited.

Handy, who had formally studied music, was not immediately won over. He soon became a convert, however, at a concert in Cleveland, Mississippi. The audience's reception to his orchestra's arrangements was lukewarm compared to that garnered by an informal, three-piece Mississippi string band. Handy, who was black, described the leader as "a long-legged chocolate boy," and this chance encounter represented a turning point in his career:

> . . . A rain of silver dollars began to fall around the outlandish, stomping feet. The dancers went wild. Dollars, quarters, halves — the shower grew heavier and grew so long I strained my neck to get a better look. There before the boys lay more money than my nine musicians were

being paid for the entire engagement. Then I saw the beauty of primitive music. They had the stuff the people wanted. It touched the spot. Their music wanted polishing, but it contained the essence. Folks would pay money for it. The old conventional music was well and good and had its place, no denying that, but there was no virtue in being blind when you had good eyes.

Handy's most famous composition, "St. Louis Blues," was actually conceived in Memphis. His lyrics have become part of the blues vernacular, such as "Joe Turner Blues" ("If you don't b'lieve I'm leavin' / count the days I'm gone"); and "Shoeboot's Serenade" ("I'll have to leave this town / just to wear you off my mind"). Since his blues were orchestrated and incorporated elements of jazz and popular forms, they are considered less spontaneous than the pure, guitar-driven Delta variety. Still, Handy's sheet-music success early this century undeniably contributed to the genre's widespread popularity, hence his honorific. His music came on the cusp of radio and records, before these media could spread the sound to millions.

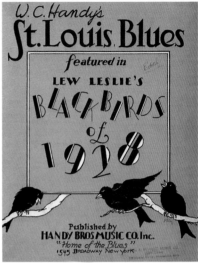

"Nobody ever wrote a greater tune than the 'St. Louis Blues.'"

~Jazz pianist Willie "the Lion" Smith

One Memphis musician informed me that Handy referred to members of his race as "they" in his autobiography (I was unable to find this passage). Yet in a 1948 interview at his New York office, he claimed credit for "pioneering the roughs and cementing the highways against musical disasters and administrative chicanery for all Negro artists." If nothing else, W.C. Handy was certainly opinionated. He believed that the blues originated on the large plantations and small cities of predominantly black Mississippi, further maintaining "that all real work in typical Negro music can come only from one to the manner born. It's his mother tongue. The art of writing blues or spirituals can be assumed but cannot be delegated outside of the blood."

Handy's theory linking race and music has been argued over and, I believe, found wanting, both in terms of whites playing "black" music (such as soul songwriter Dan Penn) and vice versa (DeFord Bailey, a black harmonica player on the early Opry). Smokin' Joe Kubek may not sound like Mississippi Fred McDowell, but they are both playing the blues.

THE SONG THAT HANDY WROTE DOWN AT PEE WEE'S SALOON — that first transcribed blues, described earlier — was titled "Mister Crump," which the composer subsequently renamed "The Memphis Blues." Composed for Edwin Hull Crump, who was running for Memphis mayor in 1909 on a reform platform, the song was also performed by Handy at the opposition's rallies, perhaps to show his impartiality (or make a few extra silver dollars).

Handy first came up with the melody and then added the lyrics, basing them on the spontaneous and often rowdy comments offered up by his band and audience members, to whom Crump's reforms, he later wrote, were "about as palatable as castor oil." The resulting lyrics were not exactly pro-Crump:

> *Mister Crump don't 'low it, ain't goin' have it here,*
> *Mister Crump don't 'low it, ain't goin' have it here.*
> *We don't care what Mister Crump don't 'low,*
> *We gonna bar'l-house anyhow,*
> *Mister Crump can go and catch hisself some air.*

While leafing through an old songbook, I came across a popular tune from the 1890s called "Mama Don't 'Low" (later a boogie hit for Charles "Cow Cow" Davenport), whose lyrics and melody seem to have directly inspired "Mister Crump."

> *Mama don't 'low no drums a-drummin' here,*
> *No banjos, guitars a-strummin' round here.*
> *Well she's not here to rave and shout*
> *And the Joneses living next door went out,*
> *Mama don't 'low no drums a-drummin' 'round here.*

I had once heard Bill Monroe, the Father of Bluegrass, sing "Mama Don't 'Low" while picking it on his mandolin at the Long Hollow Jamboree in Goodlettsville, north of Nashville. A member of the *Grand Ole Opry* from 1939 until his death in the fall of 1996, he and his Blue Grass Boys dressed conservatively, with matching cowboy hats and suits. A Kentuckian who lived in northern Tennessee for many years, Monroe readily acknowledged his musical debt to black blues and old-time fiddling, both of which he had heard while growing up.

Yet Monroe's version of "Mama Don't 'Low" sounded downright starchy compared to the irreverent, in-your-face "Crump" I later heard performed by a Memphis "roots" band called Mudboy and the Neutrons, a quartet of local musicians that disbanded following the death of lead guitarist Lee Baker in the fall of 1996.

The concert was part of the town's Mid-South Music and Heritage Festival held in July spotlighting sub-genres of Delta music, from fife-and-drum and calliope to rockabilly. Playing guitars, piano, and washboard, Mudboy basically mimicked the late-1920s rendition of "Crump" recorded by the Beale Street Sheiks, a duo comprised of the legendary singer Frank Stokes (a Whitehaven native) and his partner, Dan Saine. Mudboy's pianist and spiritual leader Jim Dickinson ad-libbed a verse of his own for good measure: "Told my baby like the Arab told the Jew/ You gonna get mad at me, I'm gonna piss off at you."

The definition of roots music varies by region, Dickinson told me, adding that Mudboy's version borrows from Delta blues, early Memphis jug-band music, and "hillbilly harmonies." Many of the band's covers are frequently overlooked gems from the first half of the 20th century; the band also expropriates early rock and soul, from Bo Diddley to Buffy Sainte-Marie. It is as if its members, who first met in the '60s, are declaring war on the banality of slickly produced modern music. They are determined "to bar'l-house anyhow."

No one member of the band is Mudboy. Rather, Mudboy is some sort of primeval spirit that the band hopes to conjure up through its music. The washboard player, Jim Crosthwait, offers that, astrologically, he and Baker were the band's earth elements, and Dickinson and rhythm guitarist Sid Selvidge its water signs. Thus, mud.

One local musician called Mudboy "the Grateful Dead of Memphis," referring to the group's small cultlike following (which includes Bob Dylan). Selvidge described their music as "gonzo rock," as in "filled with bizarre or subjective ideas, commentary, or the like," and the late Baker called it "the world's most dysfunctional band." As for Dickinson, he would probably rather be compared to his childhood yard man, Timothy Teal, whom he recruited to sing and chop wood on his Delta *Experimental Projects Compilation* double-CD, on which Dickinson plays everything from Moog to Zulu dung drum.

"Louder! Faster! More!" shouted one fervent fan, as Mudboy launched into Leadbelly's "Bourgeois Blues" after completing a rather lively version of "The Ship Titanic," which was introduced as "America's number-one camp song." The fan's enthusiasm is understandable, for it was hard to see a Mudboy concert and not come away feeling impressed that these four musicians cared deeply about preserving the region's early musical traditions. As the long-

Mudboy and the Neutrons succeeded in turning Memphis on its ear for years before the "roots" group finally disbanded in 1996. From the left, Sid Selvidge, Jim Dickinson, Jim Crosthwait, and Lee Baker. Courtesy of Jim Dickinson.

bearded Crosthwait observed with one of his trademark guffaws, "We're certainly not doing it for the *money!*"

So why are they doing it? Dickinson provided an answer of sorts in his uninhibited belting-out of "I'd Love To Be a Hippy" ("but mama, my hair don't grow that long"). Lest it pollute their souls, the band members appear to deliberately thumb their noses at money — while at the same time scrounging to make some. A few years ago, before *Known Felons In Drag* and *Negro Streets At Dawn* were finally reissued as *They Walk Among Us*, finding Mudboy recordings — even in the band's hometown of Memphis — had been catch-as-catch-can.

Memphis Music Women

by Sid Selvidge

In the 1920s there were only a few men, and even fewer black women who, through their music, could escape the fields of the Delta and the kitchens of Memphis to lead the relatively easy sporting life of the itinerant musician. If to become an "easeman," playing rent parties, juke joints, and medicine shows, meant that men like Robert Johnson had to wrestle with the devil and leave their souls at the crossroads, then the *women* who embarked on this life must have had to clasp him in a lover's embrace. That the sporting life was not respectable is patently demonstrated by the fact that musical documents from this period mention only a few African-American women, and no white women at all.

I have quit many a job to go and make fifteen cents a night.

~ Lillie Mae Glover aka Ma Rainey II

Medicine show singer Ma Rainey II hit Beale Street in 1928 like a freight train jumping its tracks. She turned down respectability and low wages for music and even lower wages, rubbing shoulders with Memphis Slim (who quit Memphis for the accolades of Paris), carrying on with Bessie Smith, and encouraging a young and discouraged B.B. King to follow his dream to stardom. She sang for decades and lived to see the faint glimmers of a city on the verge of embracing a culture the rest of the world had celebrated for generations.

And there was Hattie Hart, who did the "Beedle Um Bum" with Cannon's Jug Stompers, and Van Zula Hunt, who sang "Selling Jelly" in Noah Lewis' band. Guitarist and singer Memphis Minnie cut over 200 sides, including "Me and My Chauffeur" and "Black Rat Swing," in a career spanning six decades. Alberta Hunter ("Downhearted Blues") left town at 13 and, hand on hip, became the first blues singer to perform on the European continent. Memphis native Koko Taylor participated in the "Wang Dang Doodle," Chicago-style, while the classically trained pianist Lillian Hardin played in jazz bands led by King Oliver and her husband, Louis Armstrong.

This scarcity is a source of mild amusement to Crosthwait, whom I interviewed over a plate lunch at the Midway Cafe in midtown Memphis, where he knew the waitress on a first-name basis. "We're a big hit in Belgium," he said without apparent irony.

Crosthwait has traced his surname to ancient England. It means someone who plays a stone xylophone. He started out as a puppeteer and still puts on shows for schoolchildren at the Pink Palace, built by Clarence Saunders, the Memphis businessman who founded Piggly Wiggly, America's first self-service grocery chain. Music is Crosthwait's sideline. He considers himself primarily a visual artist, working in metal, glass, ceramic, and wood; he sold me one of his "Zen wind chimes" which, in typical Crosthwait humor, makes no sound.

These women sustained careers against terrific odds. In the 1970s and '80s they were joined by such luminaries as "The She Wolf," Jesse Mae Hemphill, who helped herself to a Handy blues award for her recording *Feeling Good*. Ruby Wilson, majestic as a royal ship of the Nile, continues the tradition night after night, as the Queen Bee of Beale Street; Mobile transplant and former Waylo artist Lynn White plays her saucy set of blues out on the road and garners a cover article in *Living Blues* magazine.

But not every Memphis woman has sung the blues. In the post-war 1940s, two women came out of the Bluff City to entertain the country in the cardigan sweater, pop style of the period. Anita Kerr formed the Anita Kerr Singers. And Kay Starr belted out hit after hit; the most notable, "Wheel of Fortune," still rolls in our consciousness as a game-show title. While these girls were soothing a war-weary nation, a strange brew was cooking back in Memphis. Cordell Jackson had her superb ear to the ground and became a "rocking mama" and record executive for her own Moon label.

Of course, it was Sam Phillips who really got everything rocking and rolling when he took the rich black mud and staunch white clay of the Mississippi River and squeezed it together into the world's most outrageous music. Along with the likes of Elvis, Jerry Lee, Charlie Rich, Johnny Cash, Rufus Thomas and Howlin' Wolf, his stable of artists included Barbara Pittman, Maggie Sue Wemberly, Anita Wood, Shirley Sask, and Bobbie Jean Barton.

In the early 1960s, Estelle Axton, with her brother Jim Stewart, formed Stax Records and brought together young black and white musicians who toured behind artists like Carla Thomas ("Gee Whiz") and Shirley Brown ("Woman To Woman"). At the competing Hi label, Ann Peebles scored a hit with "I Can't Stand the Rain," while West Memphian Sandra Posey was gathering gold at American studios. Dr. King's assassination in Memphis and Stax's subsequent engulfment by corporate giants becomes in retrospect all too ironic.

Memphis-born Aretha Franklin teamed up with Jerry Wexler and recorded some of her most of memorable sides with Memphis musicians in nearby Muscle Shoals, Alabama, and in Miami. From Nutbush, Tennessee, Tina Turner, meanwhile, began her climb out of ex-husband Ike's abusive shadow with the classic "Proud Mary" in 1973, and continued through the 1980s with the Grammy-winning *What's Love Got To Do With It*. (One of the songs, "Private Dancer," is a strip-club staple.) *(continues)*

In 1967, Crosthwait moved to New York and helped open the Electric Circus, which is where Sly Stone found fame. He hasn't forgotten, he said, how quickly success turned Sly into an ogre. "And that, I think, is what we are all smart enough to want to avoid. In answer to your question, 'Why just sit here and hardly do nothin?' You know, but why do *that*, you know? We all have great lives here.

"I've done a few things in my life that I'm really proud of and glad I did and received really almost no recognition for what it was, but I enjoyed doing it. It's like, art is a process as much as a product."

Gospel is the mother of the blues, and nowhere is the duality between the sacred and the profane celebrated more than in the stunning body of work of Mavis Staples. She is the heir to such Memphis gospel greats as Cassietta George and Queen C. Anderson, sang first with the Staple Singers before becoming a solo R&B performer in the 1970s.

Memphian Brenda Patterson's credits include her Epic debut album *Keep On Keeping On,* a stint with Frank Zappa's label, a duo with Coon Elder on Polygram, touring with Furry Lewis, and singing on soundtracks.

The city is also amply represented in the field of country (Debra Allen, Roseanne Cash, Charly McClain, and Linda Gail Lewis, Jerry Lee's little sister), alternative (Lorette Velvette, the Marilyns, the Alluring Strange, and Nancy Apple), classical (Marguerite Piazza, Mignon Dunn, and Kalen Esperian), and rock (guitar wizard Lilly Afshar).

Then there are the Memphis Glamour Girls — Dixie Carter and Cybill Shepherd — who have integrated singing into their acting careers. Cybill, in particular, continues to sing and perform using musicians from Memphis; her recordings include "Vanilla" and "Somewhere Down the Road."

The multifaceted Joyce Cobb has run her own club on Beale, sung with the symphony, and hosted a show on WEVL radio. Becky Russell and Sandy Carroll also entertain around town. Local songwriters include Donna Weiss ("Bette Davis Eyes") and Margaret Ann Rich, while Jackie Reddick and Jeanie McQuinn work with gospel superstar O'landa Draper.

Dawn Hopkins handles sound engineering duties at B.B. King's and produces at Soul Unreel studio, and last but not least, Bettye Berger — a pioneer deejay on all-girl radio WHER — continues as a publisher whose catalog includes many of the songs penned by the late Ivory Joe Hunter.

Guitarist Sid Selvidge works for the Blues Foundation in Memphis. An expanded version of this article appeared in *Memphis Magazine.*

It's hard for Crosthwait to talk about music without mentioning Jim Dickinson in the same breath. Way back in '62, it was Dickinson who picked up Crosthwait's current washboard while passing through Waco, Texas. Together they cut their first record, "jug band stuff" produced by Bill Justis and recorded in Nashville (of all places). Crosthwait, who played drums, was just 16.

"'Nobody Wants You When You're Down and Out' was one side," he said. "Can't remember the other side. 'She'll Do It All the Time' I think was the name of it. We pulled what was called a smoker, where you go and they redo the session again, but you just sit around smoking cigarettes because the thing's already been taped — but you weren't in the union when it was taped. So you get in the union, then you go back into the studio where it's 'recorded' at that time.

"The leader of a band would get double the amount of the other members of the group, and the drummer would get two dollars more [than the others], because there was more equipment to haul, or whatever. But the contracts would read, like, 'four musicians and a drummer.' Separate and distinct breed of cat there on the stage." He laughs.

Memphian **Alex Chilton** belted out "The Letter" with the Box Tops in 1967, when he was just 16. Later he formed Big Star, a "pop rock" band named after a local grocery chain. The group recorded three albums, disbanded in '74, and then reunited several years ago (without Chris Bell, who died in a car accident). On his solo CD titled *Clichés,* the never-predictable Chilton tackles standards such as "There Will Never Be Another You." Poster courtesy of Lynn Porterfield/Artstar.

Most of his memories are distilled — literally — from those early years. After the early 1970s, they become foggier, due in part to his admittedly heavy use of alcohol. He has now regained control but admits that for a time he was a piece of work for his bandmates to put up with.

Born in 1945, Crosthwait grew up in Memphis on a street once written up in the *Press-Scimitar* as having the most kids, about 70 of the first Baby Boomers. He now lives out in the country northeast of town with his girlfriend and father, and a Bouvier named Attila the Hound but still occasionally waxes nostalgic for the experimentation of the early '60s, particularly the Market Theater hootenannies organized by Dickinson.

At one of these, he recalls, "for some reason I took a bunch of garbage cans and turned 'em upside down and was beating on them with mallets, and kinda chanting and whatever, and getting people to chant along with me. It was really surprising to say the least, that people would do that. At first I made the mallets out of sticks — like, branches from a tree — and tied rags around them with rubber bands, to kind of soften them up, and give it a little more timpani sound."

Then came gigs with the New Beale Street Sheiks, a takeoff on the old Memphis jug bands featuring a jug blower in lieu of a bassist. He recorded with songwriter Alex Chilton, another native Memphian, beating on a cardboard box with maracas. He also experimented with primitive Haitian drums and Indian tablas and lent his services to the Tangiers Rock and Rhythm Blues Band. He got a special charge out of accompanying guitar legend Bukka White at the first Memphis Country Blues Festival, held in 1965.

Crosthwait's Waco washboard is constructed from a series of metal rods attached to a wooden core, enabling him to get a different sound from that than from the more common corrugated-metal variety. Alluding to Dorothy's magic slippers in *The Wizard of Oz,* he said of his technique, "It's almost like the red shoes — if you had 'em, you could dance, you know?"

I asked Crosthwait about the difference between playing the washboard and the drums. "Drums should be the pulse and heartbeat of a band — they should be the driving force," he said. "Whereas with the washboard, I'm more like a tap dancer." As Crosthwait talked, he drummed his fingers on the table. "I'm almost, like, doing it *with* it, as opposed to behind it, *kicking* it, you know what I mean?"

Crosthwait believes that the Mississippi River, which drains some 330,000 square miles of the North American continent, is what defines Memphis. "I mean, goddamn it, if you could harness that sucker right," he said, "you could light the globe from pole to pole, in terms of force and energy. And it's a thing that's actually happening all the time right here, you know? You forget about it or you don't think about it or whatever, but there's an awful lot of power coming down that river. Maybe I'm being a little too . . . [makes a spooky noise] . . . but there is a momentum, a moving body the likes of which doesn't exist in nature but in a few places on the planet."

IN ADDITION TO BEING MUDBOY'S PIANIST AND LEAD SINGER, Jim Dickinson has accompanied, engineered, and produced a wide range of musicians, from Grandma Dixie Davis to John Hiatt. His last "normal" job was sacking groceries at 16, and he is proud to list "musician" on his driver's license and passport. To Jim, Memphis is the ideal place to record, due to the city's air, water, elevation, and geography.

"Even before there were studios here," he said, "the Delta blues people came here and recorded, you know, remotely, in hotel rooms and that kind of thing. I mean, there were other places to go, why didn't they go *there*? Where I started thinking about this is from my own work. I've noticed that I play differently here than I did in Los Angeles or Miami or New York or Nashville. And I've noticed it about other people as well. Something happens to my left hand when I'm in Los Angeles and I lose the depth of the groove that you have here.

"But see, if you take it in terms of elevation and humidity, and geography, as you drive down Highway 61 down the river towards New Orleans, you can almost *feel* it get deeper and heavier. When you get to New Orleans, where you are actually below sea level, it's very difficult to record. And this is not a provable fact, but it's true. I've recorded in three places below sea level, and it's very difficult to do. For what reason, who knows?"

Strategically sandwiched between three states, Memphis both draws from and exerts an influence over the entire area, Dickinson said. "Memphis is more a part of Mississippi and Arkansas than it is Tennessee. There's no major city in Mississippi or Arkansas. Memphis is 'town' to all those people."

Jim Dickinson thinks he plays piano better in Memphis than anywhere else, although he's not exactly sure why. Photo by Ebet Roberts.

Perhaps most significantly, Memphis is "where the races collided," he says, adding that he doesn't actually play the blues, but plays at them. "I used to think white people could play the blues. They can't. But that's what rock and roll is: rock and roll is white people trying to play the blues and not being able to." (This from the man who backed Aretha Franklin with the Dixie Flyers and Albert Collins on his *Trash Talkin'*.)

Dickinson was born in Little Rock but *conceived* in Memphis. He now lives in Hernando, Mississippi, close to Memphis yet a comfortable distance from its ever-encroaching suburbs. (Hernando also happens to be the hometown of jugbander Jim Jackson and bluesman Rev. Robert Wilkins.) The Delta, with its biracial culture, is where he feels comfortable living and raising his kids. Sons Luther and Cody have formed their own band, DDT, and Dad produced their first CD, which includes the original compositions "Stomp on Me," "Violence at the Ballfield," and "Bottle O' Hell."

By contrast, from a purely racial standpoint, Dickinson feels uncomfortable in Middle Tennessee. He likes interacting with blacks and living where there are more of them. "There's nothing whiter than Nashville," he said. "Go to Opryland — you've never seen so many ugly white people in all your life. (Jackson, Mississippi, he adds, runs a close second.) When I go to Nashville and I cross the Davidson County line, I realize how black people must feel all the time. I don't even feel *safe* anymore, you know?"

Dickinson appenticed under Sleepy John Estes in the Brownsville, Tennessee, bluesman's later years. Sleepy John was on another wavelength, Dickinson said. "Apparently I played like this guy 'Knocky' Parker, whoever the hell he was, that Sleepy used to play with. He'd call you up at 3 or 4 o'clock in the morning, you know, and talk about crazy stuff." Dickinson himself admits to having "no concept of linear time."

While in West Tennessee, I visited one of Sleepy's sons, Albert, who drives a van for a local human resources agency. Even though I stressed that I am a writer and not a lawyer, Albert Estes insisted on pleading his case with me: he hoped that I could somehow help him collect royalties for his late father's songs, which include "Diving Duck Blues." (Some say he also wrote "Milk Cow Blues," although his contemporary, Kokomo Arnold, often gets the credit.) Despite the best efforts of Tennessee's Chief Justice Lyle Reid, a fellow Brownsvillian who helped manage Sleepy's affairs, Albert said that the family has not received one thin dime for the use of Estes' songs, even though they continue to turn up on recordings by other musicians.

———

ONE THEORY GOES THAT SLAVES CREATED THE BLUES to ease their suffering and pass time while working in the fields. This might explain their overall tone and rhythm, but what about the lyrics?

Doc Watson, who draws from blues and hillbilly music, believes that the blues always tell a story. I met Doc backstage at a concert in Bristol, not far from his home in Deep Gap, North Carolina. We talked about one of Jimmie Rodgers' "blue yodels," which, coincidentally, the early country star had recorded in Bristol in the late 1920s. In it, Rodgers proclaims

that he would "rather drink muddy
water, sleep in a hollow log," than be
in Atlanta treated like a dog. "That
comes from black blues, I think," Watson said. "He'd borrow lines just like
[blacks] borrowed lines from some of
the white blues. I've heard that line in
many songs. Skip James' 'Cypress
Grove' has a line close to that in it.

"To get any sense out of a line from a
blues song, you have to listen to the
whole lyrics. You can't take one line and
say, 'Well, what does this mean?' Usually a blues song tells a story of sorts —
Skip James and 'Cypress Grove,' for instance. He's married to a girl who wants
to do as she pleases, not as his wife, but
she wants, probably, all the guys, all the
rest of the privileges to go with it. Instead of lovin' the guy and tryin' to help
him along, as well as herself, she wants
to do as she darn pleases."

Watson paused a moment, and then
asked me whether I had grown up in
the city, and I replied that I had come
from a suburb of New York. Since I had-
n't grown up in the country, he said, I

Brownsville's **Sleepy John Estes** (1899-1977)
specialized in "crying the blues." Courtesy of the
Schomburg Center for Research in Black Culture.

wouldn't know what Skip James means. He translated: "The expression 'treated like a dog'
means where people are really mean to you. Poor, cur dog comes around, people'll kick it
and won't feed it; they're as mean as they can be to it. And he'd rather sleep in a hollow
log in the woods and be able to fend for himself than be treated mean tryin' to do so.
That's simple."

Watson befriended James and other black bluesmen at music festivals in the 1960s.
"They're real people, just as down-to-earth and real as they can be," he said. "Some of
them had literally been treated like a dog, in their hometown."

These same festivals also made a lasting impression on Dickinson. "Seeing the old men
at the country blues festivals showed me that there was a future," he said. "Because it appears to be youth music, especially when you're a kid. And at the first [Memphis] country
blues festival, there was a guy named Nathan Beauregard who was 107 years old — he
looked like a mummy — he was playing electric guitar and feeding back, and singing
about *screwing 12-year-old girls*. And I saw him and thought, 'Alright, there is a future for
what I'm doing.'" (For the record, Beauregard was only 102 at the time.)

Since Dickinson had been friends with Sleepy, I asked for his views on the meaning of blues lyrics. For example, if Sleepy John's 1931 milk cow is a metaphor for his woman, then why does he want her driven home after he has apparently written her off? The bit about the cow doesn't seem to be part of the "story." In a later version, Estes focuses on a down-and-out philanderer whose body has been ravaged by consumption, and he doesn't even mention a cow. The lyrics seemed almost deliberately unclear, I said.

"That's the point!" Dickinson said. "White folks not *supposed* to understand it!"

How about "Shake, Rattle and Roll"? Is the 'one-eyed cat peeping in a seafood store' a veiled sexual reference?

"It *is*. It is. Obviously," he said. "'Over the hill, way down underneath.' What does that mean? 'Bout feeling up a woman, is what. I mean, go back to Robert Johnson and dig up what his songs are about. He's singin' about being impotent. I mean, that's the point: the blues is about more than 'my baby left me.'"

I believe I'll buy me a graveyard of my own,
I believe I'll buy me a graveyard of my own,
I'm gonna kill everybody that have done me wrong.

~ "Furry's Blues"

ACCORDING TO MUDBOY'S SID SELVIDGE, the blues have more to do with emotional content than anything else. "It's on the outside looking in at your emotions, to be able to deal with them," he says, "and so one verse is as good as the other."

Selvidge, who works at the Blues Foundation and performs solo around town, studied under Walter "Furry" Lewis, considered *the* prototypical early Memphis blues musician. Born to Mississippi sharecroppers, Furry started making music on a homemade guitar at age six, played in Memphis jug and blues bands, lost a leg in a train accident, and spent 30 years as a city trash collector before making a comeback during the '60s folk revival. Later in life, Furry became a Memphis institution, admired for his offbeat outlook and ribald humor. He appeared in a Burt Reynolds movie and toured with Leon Russell. Joni Mitchell wrote a song about Furry, and the State of Tennessee even named him an Honorary Colonel.

Even though Selvidge probably knows as much about Furry's songs as anyone, he often has a hard time deciphering certain archaic expressions, such as "donie," which he thinks is synonymous with "whore," as in "see your donie/make me think of mine." With a laugh, he adds that these days, "we're kind of beyond" the early blues culture, and therefore, "psychological archaeology" — figuring out what the lyrics really mean — "is a difficult task."

Blues lyrics are not neccessarily logical, and Doc Watson's narrative view has been colored by his having been brought up in the storytelling tradition of Appalachia. Sometimes you have to read between the lines, Selvidge said, citing "Pearlee," a Lewis tune dating to the 1920s in which three thematically unrelated songs are incorporated into one.

For several decades, **Walter "Furry" Lewis** (1893-1981) shelved his career as a country blues-man and worked as a Memphis garbageman instead. Although he had never left town, Furry was "discovered" during the '60s folk revival. "Furry could say more in a couple notes than Stevie Ray Vaughan could say in twenty-four bars," said Mudboy's Lee Baker. This shot dates from 1966. Courtesy of the Mississippi Valley Collection.

"If you'll listen to it," Selvidge said, "a lot of it doesn't make that much sense. 'My home's on the water, I don't like dry land, my home's on the water, I don't like...' And it repeats itself. Well, that's a whole song [called] 'My Home's On the Water' that Furry did. And 'Take Me Back, Baby' is another song. And 'Pearlee' is yet a third song.

"By the time I got to Furry, he was combining all those songs. And again, he would use and/or make up words to songs. He would be singing 'Casey Jones' in a bar, for example. So you're goin' along with the story of Casey Jones, and then all of a sudden you've got 'Come on boys, if you want to flirt, yonder comes a lady in a miniskirt' — this is from the '60s — 'Got a half a yard of ribbon wrapped around her leg, steppin' like she's steppin' on scrambled eggs, on the road again' — which is [Memphis jug-bander] Gus Cannon's line, you know.

"So what does that mean, in the context of Casey Jones? I mean, there were no miniskirts in Casey Jones' time. Another situation in the same song is 'Come on boys, let me tell you the news, Memphis women don't wear no shoes, got it written on the back of my shirt, I'm a natural born easeman, don't have to work.' That doesn't have *anything* to do with Casey Jones."

Musically, the blues developed from what African-Americans did with European instruments such as the piano and, especially, the guitar, Selvidge said. A good example of this adaptation is the slide guitar on which continuous tones are played instead of half-tones.

When he first arrived in town from his native Mississippi, Selvidge only knew how to play the twelve-bar blues popularized by Handy; in fact, he didn't realize that there was any alternative. He soon learned otherwise, however, after a "very succinct lecture" from Lewis, whom he was trying to accompany. "He told me to do it his way because that was the way he wanted, and as far as he was concerned, *that* was the right way. And fuck twelve bars, you know? Play it like you feel it."

"That's one of the things that makes blues unique," Selvidge added. "One reason you're playing a little bit behind the beat is so that you can wait and make the change at the last minute. It's just like holding back your swing in baseball. And you've *got* to, because you don't know where it's goin'."

WHILE NASHVILLE BILLS ITSELF "MUSIC CITY U.S.A.," Memphis has chosen to be known as "America's Distribution Center," a rather drab nod to its proximity to a large percentage of the American population. Indeed, Memphians tend to take their music for granted. "There's being some attention paid now in terms of the tourist value of music," Selvidge said, "but still, people don't really support it here. I mean, [pianist] Mose Allison comes to town occasionally, and people just talk right through him. Don't listen to a thing he's doing. They feel it, but they don't listen to it."

(continues on page 81)

Tav Falco and Larry Lee

by Peter Zimmerman

Search the world over, and you're unlikely to find two people as different as Tav Falco, who happens to be white, and Larry Lee, who is black. Both are "non-commercial" musicians with strong Memphis ties, after which any apparent similarities soon fade.

Roots rocker Falco, an Arkansas native-turned-Austria transplant whose influences range from Handy and R.L. Burnside to Rico Discépolo, Stockhausen, and George Raft, makes films and writes poetry; in the mid- to late 1980s, he produced a series of Counterfests in answer to the Memphis in May festivals, which had become too "stilted" for his liking.

Blues and soul guitarist Lee, a one-time Hendrix sideman, prefers the quiet life tending his tomato plants on McLemore Avenue (near where the Stax soul studio once stood) and keeping a vigilant eye on his grandchildren. Although Lee, now in his fifties, is only a decade older than Falco, his generation is a markedly different one. Born and raised in Memphis, he grew up without television and made his first guitar from a John Ruskin cigar box, some roofing nails, and wires from an old transistor radio. He was first "impressed" with the guitar after seeing Gene Autry and Roy Rogers. "At the time I came up, white people's music was our music," he said. "There wasn't no black stations, so whatever the music was, it was just music."

When I first met Tav Falco, he was back in town to perform at the bare-bones Barrister's and plug his new CD called *Shadow Dancer*. I ambushed him at an early-evening sound check and dropped rockabilly guitarist Roland Janes' name, whereupon Falco invited me to dinner with his band, the Panther Burns (named after the Percy plantation in Mississippi). We never made it to dinner. Instead, the Burns and I piled into their rental van and drove to their friend's house, where the band showered and shaved and dressed for the show.

The interview was conducted in a room strewn with empty bottles and cans and decorated with an antique sewing table, a poster of early Dolly, and a bong fashioned from a Mrs. Butterworth's syrup bottle; the bathroom was decorated with 13 Elvises and one Buddha. Tav, who talked as he dressed, started out in a pair of ink-stained skivvies. Less than an hour later, he had donned a rather theatrical costume that included a shirt with ruffled sleeves. It was 11:30 — time to hit the stage — and he posed for a picture with one of his trademark disarming smiles.

After fronting his band in Memphis for 17 years, Falco moved to Vienna four years ago. He said the city is a source of fascination for him, representing "the old Europe that I like," similar to what Paris must have been like in the 1920s and '30s. Like Memphis, it stands on a river, the Danube, at a crossroads between East and West.

(continues)

He spends a lot of time watching movies at the Albertina Museum of Visual Art or eavesdropping on conversations uttered in the city's many exotic tongues. While Falco loves Memphis, he views it as little more than a "Middle American *dorf* that's become very urban," a place defined by narrow attitudes, a place that "kills" artists.

Soon after moving to Vienna, Warner Chappell signed him to a three-year song-writing contract, paying a $7,000 advance. "That would never happen to me in Memphis," he said. "It would never fuckin' happen over here. I'm still trying to figure it out. They have a different attitude towards music and artists. You're considered an artist over there, not just a musician."

"Memphis is rather blind to its musical heritage, and blindness breeds fear and disillusionment," he adds. "The fear of the unknown, you know?"

Tav Falco says artists are treated better in Vienna. Courtesy of Josefish/LEX.

Falco's music is as diverse as it sounds, infusing tango and surf with a rock beat and attracting a cult crowd bordering on groupiedom. Originally the self-described "product of the '60s" came to Memphis with the intention of becoming a filmmaker, but he was unable to make any money at it. "So out of frustration, I started a rock and roll band," he said. Comparing his present state to the early days earning "chump change" in Memphis, he jokes that "we're now riding in a van on our tours rather than running along beside one."

He remains unflappable, however, in his commitment to preserve roots music. "In Panther music we draw on different genres of music, new and old. We're a modern band playing music that is connected to earlier forms, and we feel we have a sense of history, a sense of past, and this is the real frontier for us. If we can come to terms with that, then we can know ourselves in the present and be able to meet the future with some sort of modern outlook and attitude. Because if you just try to live totally in this instant, it can be gratifying, but it can also be very misleading. You have to have a sense of perspective."

Falco is not planning to sell out any time soon. "I mean, everybody likes to make money, but it's not the ultimate criteria," he said. "You can't base your life on that totally, can you? Call yourself an artist and do that?"

"YOU'RE GOING TO ALWAYS THINK ABOUT WHAT YOU'VE LEARNED in the past," said blues guitar ace Larry Lee. "That's what common sense is. Or add what you've learned with what you've had to go up against."

We are sitting in his living room, with an entire wall crammed with miscellaneous amps and guitar cases. Lee is turning over an early Percy Mayfield cassette in his large hands. Someone sent it to him, wondering if he played guitar on the session. Lee thinks he might have, but the Memphis native has never been one for self-promotion.

Once I saw him sitting in on Beale Street at a place called the Daiquiri, which was a glorified hot dog and ice-cream stand with a back patio featuring live music. The gig wasn't listed in the paper, nor was it advertised out front — strictly a walk-in-crowd. Some musicians would turn up their noses at such a low-profile venue, but it's the kind that Larry Lee prefers. He doesn't want to be a recording artist — he has never put out a record under his own name — and turns down most interview requests. He just wants to play.

That night, with his feet planted firmly and eyes closed, he took a long, exquisitely phrased solo on "Red House." Unlike the flashy Falco, his performance was short on theatrics. His soulful guitar said it all, encompassing the entire blues, rock, and soul lexicon in one delirious, 20-minute swoop.

It's tough making a living in Memphis as a fulltime musician, but the financial rewards are of secondary importance to Lee. "How I get my money [has] got to make sense for how I expect my life to grow," he said.

Memphis guitar legend **Larry Lee** believes in keeping things in perspective. Photograph by Perry Walker.

At Woodstock, Lee played second guitar to Jimi Hendrix, whom he called "my idol and my friend." He's also toured with Al Green and jammed with Carlos Santana, among others. And although he does not belong to any particular denomination, their spirituality has affected him. "If there is a God," he said, "it's up to each man to be worthy of the God. And you should pray to him and show him that you might deserve some of these blessings. Because look around, man, this world's in pretty bad shape."

Occasionally Lee returns to his old stomping grounds in New York. On a recent visit he was disppointed to see the gentrifying changes being made on 42nd Street. He preferred the old, down-and-dirty version.

"We'd stay there for two and three weeks at a time at the Apollo, man, never under two weeks," he said. "So, I've had my little paths up and down New York, and I always like to walk and check out things and see if it's different, you know, since the last time."

New York has become more dangerous these days, I told him.

"You know what," he said, "I don't do nothing but walk and stay in the crowd. Yeah, I've been careful, man. I was careful my first time coming up here. I've always been careful. My first time was when Jimi called me."

Nowhere is this lack of empathy more apparent than at International Elvis Tribute Week in August, honoring the city's ultimate "roots" musician, who drew heavily from blues, country, and gospel (he won his only three Grammys in the latter category). Fittingly, Presley's first single, released in 1954, covered Bill Monroe's "Blue Moon of Kentucky" and Arthur "Big Boy" Crudup's "That's All Right (Mama)" on the flip side. As Francis Davis wrote in *The Atlantic Monthly*, "The key to his originality may have been his enthusiasm for so many different kinds of music and his refusal to distinguish among them."

Some, on the other hand, view Elvis as a marginally talented copycat who just happened to come along at the right time. "Here was a white kid that could rock 'n' roll, or rhythm 'n' blues, or whatever you want to call it, and the girls would swoon over him," Ray Charles told *Bone* magazine. "Black people been goin' out shakin' their behind for centuries." Indeed, Jim Jackson sang about rocking chairs and rolling balls a good quarter-century before Elvis' appearance at Overton Park, and Memphis Slim was "Rockin' the House" in '48.

Either way, Elvis has come to represent both the apotheosis of rock music and the inscrutability of Memphis, his adopted hometown (he was born in Mississippi). Even those who like his music appear more interested in his status as an American icon. Some 20 years after his death in 1977 at age 42, Graceland still receives hundreds of thousands of visitors a year. On the anniversary of his death, airlines offer special rates to Memphis for those who wear appropriate garb or sing all the words to "Jailhouse Rock." The city's Leader Federal Bank for Savings has come out with an Elvis credit card.

His saga has been recounted in hundreds of books, including one by his hairdresser and spiritual adviser, and Ole Miss now sponsors an annual Elvis symposium. There are even competing (and countersuing) troupes of skydiving Elvis lookalikes, the Flying Elvises and the Flying Elvi. A woman from Dayton, Ohio, even had her dentist print the King's first name on her gold cap.

The little British island of St. Vincent issued an Elvis stamp; a later version by the U.S. Postal Service earned $50 million. In Israel, Elvis impersonator Uri Yoeli has erected a 13-foot fiberglass statue of Presley outside his truckstop restaurant, which is decorated with 728 photos, busts, framed concert tickets, and felt rugs. "Elvis is not only for the Americans," Yoeli says. "Elvis is for all of the world."

Most people have their own thoroughly subjective associations — positive or negative. Mine are hearing "Suspicious Minds" on the radio while driving around St. Thomas, and in high school, watching one of his kitschy movies, the one in which Ann-Margret lures him — fully clothed and serenading, guitar in hand — into a swimming pool.

"Elvis gave his life for tourism," according to Tommy Foster, founder of the First Church of the Elvis Impersonator and Viva Memphis! Wedding Chapel in the city's bohemian Cooper-Young district. In his opinion, Graceland — which administers Presley's estate — is

(following pages) **Elvis Presley** fraternizes with Brook Benton, who sang "Rainy Night In Georgia." Born in Mississippi, Elvis moved to Memphis as a teenager and cut his first record at Sun. According to the critic Lester Bangs, "He was the man who brought overt blatant vulgar sexual frenzy to the popular arts in America." Leonard Bernstein called him "the greatest cultural force in the twentieth century." Photograph by Ernest Withers/Panopticon.

just a big moneymaking machine. Foster, who likes Elvis' music, believes that Presley was unable to adapt to fame and its restrictions. "You kind of feel sorry for him, what he got himself into," he said. "Can't go anywhere, can't see anybody, can't go out."

Mudboy's Jim Dickinson would rather focus on the early years. He recalls seeing Elvis at the downtown Ellis Auditorium, one of his first shows after appearing on national TV. The north and south halls had never before been opened simultaneously.

"Elvis opened them both and played to both sides, and everybody in the place was seeing him," Dickinson said. "He couldn't possibly have been facing both sides at once, and yet he appeared to be. I thought I was in the presence of a god. It was something that was superhuman. I saw the Beatles on their first national tour, and I've played [piano] with the Stones in front of thousands of people. There's no comparison. What Elvis did *by himself* walking on the stage without an instrument is beyond the Beatles, and beyond the Stones."

Like many fans, Dickinson believes that Elvis flowered as "the walking embodiment of an idea" while at Sun Records, only to later fall from grace in Nashville, Hollywood, and Vegas. Yet even in the '50s, Memphis was "ashamed" of Elvis, he said. When I suggested that while some people worship Elvis, others just kind of laugh at him, this raised Dickinson's hackles.

"Depends what you think rock and roll was, and whether or not it was important to you," he said. "Elvis represented the antithesis of the socially acceptable high school hero. When Elvis came along there was no place to put a teenage musician, there was no such thing. That all came about after the Beatles.

"Believe me, it was not socially acceptable to play black music and be a white man in the city of Memphis in 1956, it was not alright. Now it is. Now there's a place to put it. It's safe. Elvis is dead. That's why they talk about him."

The Lord will save me,
and we will sing to stringed
instruments,
all the days of our lives,
at the house of the Lord.
~ Song of King Hezekiah, from Isaiah 38:20

Gospel

BLACK AND WHITE, TRADITIONAL AND CONTEMPORARY divide the sacred music known as gospel. I spoke with mandolinist, singer, and bandleader Doyle Lawson over breakfast at the Bonfire, a 24-hour restaurant in Bristol, where he lives. When the waitress asked if he wanted regular or decaf, he thought for a second and then requested half of each. This small gesture symbolized the East Tennessean's notoriously meticulous attention to details: he's picky.

Next to his religious conversion, the seminal experience in Doyle Lawson's life occurred as he sat with his mother one evening, listening to the *Grand Ole Opry*. The music that night was different from anything Lawson had heard up to that point in his short life. He was only four or five at the time, but he remembers that moment well. "I said, 'Mama, who is that?' And she said, 'Why, that's Bill Monroe' — as if I should know. And I said, 'What does he play?' She said, 'He plays mandolin.' And I decided right then that I wanted to play that kind of music, and play mandolin." And play it he does, with absolute devotion and remarkable virtuosity.

Lawson was around 10 years old when he took up the mandolin. His family was living in Sneedville, Tennessee, just south of the Virginia border. In the beginning, it was frustrating trying to learn an instrument that no one else in the area played, but all that changed when he met Jimmy Martin. The legendary bluegrass guitarist, himself a Sneedville native, began teaching Lawson when he would return home from touring or playing sessions in Nashville.

"He sat me down and showed me how to use my wrist properly, because I couldn't play fast," Lawson said. "He told me to go home and practice that over and over and over and over, and not to do anything but use my wrist, and do tremolo. And that's what I did for hours and hours every day, and finally it was just natural."

In the early days of bluegrass, Lawson says, there were not nearly as many bands playing music as there are today, thus reducing a musician's chance of being hired. Concerned that there would not be enough of a demand for a mandolin player, Lawson decided to expand his repertoire. He taught himself the banjo in order to "boost his odds." Always one to set his sights high, Lawson's goal was to work for his mentor, Jimmy Martin, or even Bill Monroe.

His hard work and strategy paid off. In December 1962, Martin called Lawson and asked him to join the band in Nashville. He arrived in Nashville at 3 o'clock in the morning, called Martin's house, and spoke with his wife.

"He wasn't in," Lawson recalls, "but she said, 'Well, he's expecting you. Soon as he comes in I'll have him come pick you up.' And, you know, it was 3:30 by then, and I probably had never been that far away from home, by myself, ever, and scared to death, you know? And I said, 'Here I am in the middle of the night, I wonder if he's gonna show up.'"

Martin did show up, along with the band's banjo player.

"We lost out to Sheriff Taylor," joked Doyle Lawson's office manager Mary Jane McClellan, referring to the 1996 gospel Grammy won by Andy Griffith.

"Soon as I got in the car, [Martin] said, 'Get your banjo out.'" Lawson did as he was told and Martin asked him to play "Cripple Creek." He played it, and Martin said, "You're hired."

"And that," says Doyle Lawson, "is how I got the job."

Lawson's music is a hybrid of a hybrid: bluegrass-gospel. His group, Quicksilver, which he formed in the late 1970s, pioneered the form, which weds string-band instrumentation with various forms of sacred music. It's the bluegrass ode to the Christian faith. The music is virtually always played by white musicians who sometimes draw on black spirituals and gospel.

Though his music is virtually ignored by commercial radio, Doyle Lawson, always his own man, insists on following his own path. That path is the straight and narrow, the way of a man who who has managed to integrate two of the most important elements of his life: music and religion.

Raised in northeastern Tennessee (he was born in Kingsport), Lawson had a strong religious upbringing, growing up within "sixty paces" of a church. Both his grandfather and uncle were missionary Baptist preachers, and he recalls being saved at the age of eight. Over the years, however, he "strayed from living the way I should." In 1985, he rededicated his life to Jesus Christ. He calls this renewed commitment "the best thing I've ever done, for me and my career. I have an inner peace now that I never had all those years before. It's hard to explain to somebody what it is. But once they get it, they'll recognize what it is."

This particular incarnation of **Quicksilver**, at a bluegrass festival in Connecticut, features (foreground) Owen Saunders, Doyle Lawson, Donnie Catron, and (background) Barry Abernathy and Dale Perry. Catron has since left the band.

Quicksilver's songs, including Lawson's own compositions, often touch on spiritual themes. The band consists of typical bluegrass instrumentation: banjo, fiddle, guitar, standup bass, and Lawson's mandolin. Occasionally the group sings *a capella,* as on its 1988 *Heaven's Joy Awaits.* Lawson uses a system of musical notation based on "shape notes" which dates back to the early 1700s.

Shape notes originally consisted of four distinctive note heads used to delineate tones of the musical scale: a triangle for fa, an oval for sol, a square for la, and and a diamond for mi. Invented around 1800 by two New York schoolteachers, the shape-note or "fasola" method quickly spread to the South's many singing schools. In fact, the introduction of shape notes facilitated the growth of these schools, enabling choral students to quickly learn how to sight-read music.

"The most obvious advantage of a shape-note notation," writes Dorothy D. Horn in *Sing To Me of Heaven,* is that it "dispenses with the whole wearisome business of learning key signatures." Although the first shape-note songbooks were published in New England, the system soon spread to the South and declined in popularity elsewhere. In his introduction to *The Sacred Harp,* George Pullen Jackson wrote that this hymnbook, originally published in 1844, was at one time — after the Bible — "found oftenest in the homes of rural Southerners."

Eventually the four-note system was expanded to seven notes. According to Lawson, "Once you recognize the shape of a note, and you know the pitch where that note is,

[then] you know your notes, *do* through *do*." A pitch pipe (or tuning fork) is used to find the most workable key for all four singers and enable the group to deviate from singing the song in its original key.

The shape-note style succeeded in transcending genres. For example, Memphis' Blackwood Brothers and Statesmen quartets are known to have influenced Elvis, who particularly admired the unorthodox leg-shaking antics of Jim "Big Chief" Wetherington, the Blackwoods' bass singer. Such moves, however, would have been frowned upon by Ananias Davisson, author of the 1816 *Kentucky Harmony*.

"All distortion of the limbs or features while singing has a tendency to excite ridicule, and should be carefully avoided," he wrote. "Nothing is more disgusting in singers, than affected quirks and ostentatious parade, endeavoring to overpower other voices by the strength of their own, or officiously assisting other parts while theirs is silent. On the other hand, nothing is more praiseworthy in a choir of singers, than a becoming deportment, and a solemnity which should accompany an exercise so near a kin to that, which will through all eternity engage the attention of those who walk in 'climes of bliss'."

Doyle Lawson can recall when his father, who taught him how to read shape-note music, attended a singing school convention in the 1950s. "A guy named Cecil Dewitt would come through every so often, usually in the summer, and he'd hold these singing

This example of **shape-note music** is taken from *The Eclectic Harmony,* compiled by Andrew W. Johnson and published in Shelbyville in 1847. Courtesy of the Center for Popular Music, Middle Tennessee State University.

schools," he said. "And I think he had to have at least 25 students a week, at $5 a week, or something like that, in order just to pay for the school and his keep, and I guess he made his money on the sheet music and the songbooks that he carried with him and sold."

When Lawson was three years old, the family temporarily moved to eastern Kentucky, where his father worked in the Leatherwood coal mines. In his spare time, Lawson's father began singing in gospel quartets. This exposure to gospel music undoubtedly affected Lawson's musical career, although Lawson's father never sang professionally. "He never would have dreamed of anything like that," Lawson says. People like his father sang for singing's sake and because "they believed in what they were singing about." For Lawson, there's a special feel to testimonial music that he feels is absent in other kinds of music.

There lies the unique appeal of gospel music. To the believer, the word of God feeds the soul and the musician, reveling in the pleasure of the moment, lets loose with the sound of his joy. Lawson admires the "heartfelt expression" exhibited by amateur church singers such as his father. "They don't claim to be professional singers or musicians — it's just their way of worship," he says.

Church music was not always so exuberant. In the beginning, it consisted mostly of solemn Methodist and Baptist hymns written by Englishmen like John Wesley who, along with his brother, Charles, founded the Methodist Church, and Isaac Watts, the father of modern English hymnody; the latter is sometimes wrongly credited with composing "Amazing Grace," by John Newton.

Around 1800, the Great Revival swept through the Cumberland region of northern Tennessee and southern Kentucky. Its multidenominational participants were swept away in their enthusiasm. "Sabbath evening exhibited the most awfully solemn scene I ever beheld," wrote Reverend William Hodge. "About the centre of the camp, they were lying in heaps, and scattered all around; the sighs, groans, and prayers seemed to pierce the heavens, while the Power of God fell upon almost all present."

These outdoor gatherings, known as camp meetings, had an enormous impact on the traditional notion of hymn singing. The first one in Tennessee took place at Desha's Creek in Sumner County, northeast of Nashville, led by John McGee, a Methodist minister from Smith County. Often traveling long distances and bringing their own provisions, the participants camped out for several days while attending continuous religious services that included praying, shouting, and group singing.

For several reasons, camp meetings can be viewed as the precursor of modern gospel. Illiteracy, for one — not everyone could read the hymnal. Also, camp meetings were often held in the evening, which meant that no one could see to read the words, even if they had been able to read. In order to allow everyone to participate, simple refrains or choruses were set to the music.

> *Were you there when they crucified my Lord?*
> *Were you there when they crucified my Lord?*
> *Oh! . . . Sometimes it causes me to tremble, tremble, tremble,*
> *Were you there when they crucified my Lord?*

INITIALLY, BOTH BLACK SPIRITUALS SUCH AS "Were You There?" and white hymns like "The Wayfaring Stranger" (copyrighted in 1939 by R. E. Winsett of Dayton, Tennessee) were handed down orally, but they were also written down, published, and distributed, thus accounting for the spread of modern Southern gospel. Songbooks became readily available, selling in the general store for five cents a copy. Singing was so important to the lives of parishioners — Methodist, Baptist, and other Protestant sects alike — that all-day Sunday singings became a regular part and parcel of the Sabbath.

Doyle Lawson remembers when his father's quartet would get together for "visits" on Wednesday nights, alternating between the four singers' homes. "Since I was living on a farm, there was not much going on," he said. "I would go to hear them sing and watch them practice the shape-note parts. First they sang the individual notes through the song without the words. This embedded the melody in my mind."

He was also swayed by the black gospel quartets of the 1930s, '40s, and '50s, "which I love dearly," he says, quickly rattling off the names of some of his favorite groups: the Swan Silvertones of Knoxville, the Soul Stirrers, the Bells of Joy, Five Blind Boys and the Chosen Gospel Singers. "I still *am* impressed," he says, "not as influenced, as impressed." He said he borrows a little from black gospel, adding that while he likes to "dig into the material," he never tries to imitate it.

Black gospel and white gospel developed at the same time. Out of concern for the souls of their black slaves (and to keep an eye on them), white slave-owners would bring their slaves to church and to camp meetings. The slaves were often segregated from whites, sometimes conducting their own singings. Music historians have theorized that the result of this exposure of blacks to the white man's music (as musically prudish as it was at the time with its emphasis on Scripture) was a new hybrid combining the black's more advanced sense of harmony and rhythm with the dirge-like hymns.

The critic H.L. Mencken, writing in the 1920s, noted that blacks, as composers of spirituals, contributed an essential

Bristol's **Tennessee Ernie Ford** was the first country music entertainer to tour the Soviet Union (1974), and the first to receive the Presidential Medal of Honor (1980, from Ronald Reagan). His biggest hit was "Sixteen Tons," but he is remembered most for his sacred music.

Along with her Cumberland Mountain Folks, singer **Molly O'Day** (1923-1987) joined Knoxville's *Mid-Day Merry-Go-Round* in 1945 and a few years later she briefly hosted the Opry. Then she found religion and concentrated her efforts on gospel music. Dubbed the "female Hank Williams," O'Day hailed from rural Kentucky where "you had to break daylight with a sledgehammer and the groundhogs carried the mail." Courtesy of the Country Music Foundation.

missing ingredient to church music. "The Negro is a harmonist far more than he is a melodist," he wrote. "He doesn't care much for tunes; the things that interest him are harmonies and rhythms. Let a crowd of colored fellows begin to sing any current song, however banal, and they will presently give it a new interest and dignity by introducing strange and often entrancing harmonies into it. A gang of white boys, attempting song together, will stick to a few safe harmonies of the barber shop variety, but [blacks] almost always plunge out into deeper waters, and not infrequently in the midst of harsh discords, they produce effects of extraordinary beauty."

However one separates the strands, white and black religious music have always affected each other. Historically, they have also kept at arm's length and continue to do so today. One notable exception was a recent collaboration between the Nashville Bluegrass Band, whose members are white, and the Fairfield Four, a Nashville-based spirituals group which formed in the 1920s and still tours. Certainly the two forms continue to be categorized separately. In fact, it's said that there are four gospels: traditional white (shape-note), contemporary white (Southern gospel), traditional black (spirituals), and contemporary black (gospel).

As for bluegrass, it initially fell under the broader aegis of "country" before becoming its own genre, spearheaded by Monroe, in the mid-1940s. From then until the early 1970s, bluegrass was "a real force," Lawson told me. Now, although bluegrass has declined in popularity, he believes that "what goes around comes around." He sees signs of its resurgence, often with a focus on gospel. A good case in point is the pairing of bluegrass fiddler Alison Krauss with the Cox Family, a Louisiana gospel group.

IN TODAY'S WORLD, OF COURSE, RECORD COMPANIES and radio stations decide what brand of music is served up. As a boy, Lawson recalls hearing Flatt & Scruggs announce their upcoming dates on a noontime radio show called *Farm and Fun Time*. When he toured with Jimmy Martin, the group often paid impromptu visits to the local radio stations. Deejays "stopped whatever they were doing" and interviewed them, he said. "It was good for business to have a celebrity come through."

With the advent of Top 40 and format shows, however, deejays were forced to make their choices based purely on the charts. The music is now "all in a rack," and the DJs are less accessible to the recording artist, Lawson said. "It would be impossible to simply walk in with a record and say 'Give that a spin while we're talking.'" Indeed, most radio stations now subscribe to a satellite service or download their songs. They no longer have records, or even CDs, so deejays have no control over what gets played or in what order.

To compound the problem, record companies have decided that bluegrass gospel music is not commercial. At one time, there was at least a smattering of bluegrass artists signed to major labels, a list that Lawson has preserved to memory: Martin, Monroe, and the Osborne Brothers were on Decca, Jim and Jesse McReynolds on Epic, Mac Wiseman (Capitol), Carl Story and the Stanley Brothers (Mercury), and Reno and Smiley on King. (In addition, Flatt & Scruggs recorded on Columbia for most of their career.) At the time of our interview, he knew of only one bluegrass artist, Bill Monroe, recording for a major label, and he died in 1996.

To Doyle Lawson, the underlying faith is what is important. "I believe, and the Bible tells us, that by grace, through faith, we are saved." Lawson reiterates his own personal belief that gospel's commercial aspect is secondary; whether the music sells big numbers is irrelevant.

Nearly 20 years since its formation, Quicksilver is "still plowin' away," he says proudly. "I've undergone several changes over the past several years, but the sound has pretty much stayed intact. People have asked me how I do it, and it's real simple. I don't change through people that come into the band — they have to change for me. If you change sounds every time you change musicians, you'll have no identity."

Monroe adopted a similar approach, he said, adding that "Jimmy [Martin] says it about as good as anybody: 'If I let each musician that I hire play whatever they want to play, pretty soon I'm just a guitar player up here with a bunch of musicians and nothing happenin'." (As a rule, bluegrass-gospel solos tend to be conservatively based on the song's melody.)

Lawson is equally fastidious in his choice of secular songs, steering away from subjects which he deems "too suggestive." He wants to play music that is appropriate for his listening audience, which ranges from the thousands of Quicksilver fans in Europe and Japan to his three children, who are young adults.

He feels that as a public figure and possible role model he should "try to uphold a sense of values and moral standards, and not be afraid to express that I'm a Christian."

"On the other hand," he added, "I don't want to go and beat people over the head with religion." While he concedes that the musicians in his band are "pretty much" as religious as he is, this is not a prerequisite. "I can't answer for you at that final roll call, when it's time to tally up."

AFTER APPRENTICING WITH MARTIN FOR SEVERAL YEARS, Lawson grew restless. He had always been fascinated by the work of banjo player J.D. Crowe, and one day — Lawson figures it was the summer of 1966 — he decided to look him up. Lawson was living in Louisville, Kentucky, at the time and made the trip to Lexington to see Crowe play. Lawson had been learning the guitar and played it when he got "picked out" on his other two instruments, banjo and mandolin. "I sat in with him that night at the club they were playing," Lawson said. It was the first time he had played guitar in a "band situation." He soon became fast friends with Crowe and began visiting Lexington on a regular basis. "[I] played guitar most of the time, or *all* the time at that point."

One night, Lawson noticed that Crowe's mandolinist was struggling and offered to show him a thing or two. He said the student looked over at Crowe and grinned, and Crowe looked back and "kinda smirked." Lawson then took the mandolin and easily played what he thought would fit the song.

"Boy," he said, "you coulda probably driven a taxi in their mouths." Crowe said, 'Why didn't you *tell* me you could play mandolin?' And I said, 'Well . . . you didn't ask.'"

For the next five years, he split his time between Tennessee and Kentucky, Martin and Crowe, mandolin and guitar. In 1971, he moved to Washington D.C. to join a group called the Country Gentlemen, a gig which lasted seven years. "Musically, for us, those were good years," he said. In the 1970s, bluegrass music was at the height of its popularity, and the band's thrice-weekly show at the Shamrock in the Georgetown district was often packed.

An influx of Southerners into the Washington area helped increase the awareness for traditional music, yet the band was considered "progressive" by bluegrass standards, Lawson said, adding that he and bassist Bill Yates, from Big Rock, Virginia, were the only "real, true, down-South boys." (Not to split hairs, but I have since been informed that the lead singer, Charlie Waller, came from Louisiana — the deep South — while Ricky Skaggs, who was fiddling for the band, grew up in northeastern Kentucky.)

In order to fit in with the band, Lawson had to conform to the existing style. He changed the way he phrased and toned down his East Tennessee accent. That does not mean, however, that he lost his accent. "Wherever I am," he said, "I've never tried to lose it. I believe that you oughta be yourself."

Towards the end of our conversation, I asked Doyle why spirituals and gospel often focus on the somewhat gory subject of Christ's crucifixion. The music is meant to be up-lifting, not macabre. "It was written, I believe, in reverence rather than to frighten people. A lot of it depicts the fact that Jesus came to earth, he took on the likeness of a man, he walked as we walked, he lived as we lived. And he could have willed himself not to suffer the agony of crucifixion, because as I read and I understand it, that was a horrible, horri-ble way to go. But he did that for our redemption. And the way that I read it, as Gentiles we had no hope for eternal life until that price was paid."

For the past dozen years, Doyle Lawson has sponsored his own festival in Denton, North Carolina. He has spent a good part of the past 30 years on the road, which has en-abled him to visit every state as well as dozens of foreign countries. He has noticed, and he finds it remarkable, that even foreign audiences — those without a strong grasp of English — can sense and appreciate when the band switches over from bluegrass to gospel. "It does have a different feel," he added. "Many times people say that when we sing bluegrass, and then go into our gospel part, that *we* change."

Spirituals and Black Gospel In Tennessee

by Kip Lornell

> "They are the music of an unhappy people, of the children of dis-appointment; they tell of death and suffering and unvoiced longing towards a truer world . . . Through all the sorrows of the Sorrow Songs there breathes a hope, a faith in the ultimate justice of things."

The "Sorrow Songs" so poetically described above by W.E.B. DuBois have their roots in the slave spirituals created and sung prior to the Civil War. Rising from the musical culture of the early 19th-century camp meetings, spirituals helped to guide the way for the men, women, and children who worked hard and longed for a better life, both in the United States and in the hereafter. Singing provided a major re-lease and relief for the slave population; and their songs, often containing veiled allu-sions to movement and freedom, provided blacks with hope. Spirituals helped to voice both despair and the hope to "steal away" from slavery to greater freedom in the North.

A familiar refrain like "free at last, free at last, great God Almighty, I'm free at last," reverberated strongly enough in black culture to resound from the era of spirituals all the way through to the Civil Rights movement more than a century later. Even today,

Formed in 1928, **The Spirit of Memphis** was known for singing just above a whisper, for harmony, not hollering. (front row left to right) James Morris, Clarence Smith, Bobby Mack; (back row l to r) Earl Malone, Jet Bledsoe, Pee Wee Jefferson. This photo was taken in 1957. Courtesy of Kip Lornell.

early spirituals such as "Michael Row the Boat Ashore," "Trampin', Trying to find My Way Home," or "Roll, Jordan, Roll," can still be heard in popular and sacred culture.

The jubilee song movement, which was spearheaded by the Fisk University Jubilee Singers, built upon the heritage created by the recently freed slaves. Founded in 1866, Nashville's Fisk University soon launched a traveling group of fundraising singers. Called the Fisk Jubilee Singers, this small troupe of men and women built their musical reputation upon their heritage of spirituals. (Another Nashville school, Central Tennessee College, sent out its own jubilee group, the Original Tennesseans, in 1873.) The Fisk singers initially toured the mid-South and lower Midwest to promote and raise money for their struggling university. After a few months of travel with mixed results, their touring gained momentum and ended as a financial and critical success.

Through its written and aural arrangements of spirituals and early gospel songs, the Fisk Jubilees succeeded in moving the spiritual into a new and popular realm, breaking ground for other "jubilee" groups from such traditionally black education institutions as Hampton and Tuskegee. Jubilee groups proved so popular that professional troupes soon emerged to compete with the students. Frederick J. Loudin's Fisk

(continues)

Jubilee Singers used the name of the famous Nashville school (Loudin was an alumnus but the group had no other legitimate connection).

MOST BLACK SACRED MUSIC STILL OWES A GREAT DEBT to the aural tradition exemplified by spirituals. This century, however, gospel composers have played an increasingly prominent role. Building on the work of composers such as the Reverend C.A. Tindley, who was based in Philadelphia, a small but increasing number of black Christians began to write and publish sacred songs. By the 1930s Thomas A. Dorsey and the National Baptist Conventions were nurturing a group of songwriters whose compositions were being disseminated and performed by way of small paperback books such as *Gospel Pearls.*

In the 1920s and '30s, as the gospel movement was spreading across the United States, three noteworthy gospel composers emerged in Tennessee. The first of these songwriters was Memphis' Lucie Campbell, the first black woman to publish a gospel song. Campbell's exceptional career composing sacred songs began in 1919 with the publication of "Something Within," and continued through her final contribution, "Come, Lord Jesus, Abide with Me." For 32 consecutive years beginning in 1930, Campbell presented a new song to the National Baptist Convention! Campbell was a buoyant figure who typically wrote songs with a message of hope on Earth and salvation in Heaven. "Heavenly Sunshine," composed early in her career, was typical: "Yes, there is sunshine in the shadows, sunshine in the rain/sunshine when we're burdened, sunshine when we pray."

The Reverend W. Herbert Brewster, another Memphian, eventually became as well known as Lucie Campbell. During the 1940s and '50s, Brewster published several dozen notable compositions, including "Move on Up a Little Higher" (popularized by Mahalia Jackson) and "Surely God Is Able." Brewster created black religious musicals using individual songs to underpin nearly every element of these productions. His songwriting output slowed in the late 1950s, while his stature as a leader in the local black community, especially in the Civil Rights movement, grew. At the time of his death in the late 1980s he had gained worldwide recognition and the Smithsonian Institution had hosted a conference studying his work.

A contemporary of Campbell and Brewster, the third major Tennessee gospel composer was East Tennessean Cleavant Derricks, best known for writing "Have a Little Talk with Jesus" and "We'll All Be Done with Trouble and Trials." Both of these 1930s songs became almost instantly popular and have since become classics. Rev. Derricks became the first black composer and compiler to publish a shape-note songbook, *Pearls of Paradise.* He lived in Chicago and Washington for a spell before moving back to Chattanooga, where he performed with the Derricks Family, who recorded several albums for Canaan Records.

A COMBINATION OF SPIRITUALS AND COMPOSED GOSPEL SONGS formed the core repertoire of gospel quartets. For more than a century, black Americans have been singing sacred music in quartets, which usually consist of a bass, two tenors, and an alto. This style of harmony singing can be traced to traditional and popular music from the Reconstruction era. Minstrel shows, college jubilee singing groups, and the shape-note tradition are three of the most important early inspirations for the gospel quartets.

Around the same time, community-based quartets began to spring up across the South. While reminiscing about his Florida childhood during the 1890s, the noted black scholar James Weldon Johnson recalled:

> Pick up four colored boys or young men anywhere and the chances are ninety out of a hundred that you have a quartet. Let one of them sing the melody and others will naturally find the parts. Indeed, it may be said that all male Negro youth of the United States is divided into quartets. When I was fifteen and my brother was thirteen, we were singing in a quartet which competed with other quartets. In the days when such a thing as a white barber was unknown in the South, every barbershop had its quartet and the young men spent their leisure time "harmonizing."

These early quartets almost universally performed *a capella:* without the accompaniment of musical instruments. This gave the groups musical freedom to improvise and work out arrangements unencumbered by the inherent harmonic and rhythmic limitations of pianos, guitars, or other instruments. A capella quartets became an integral part of black America's musical landscape in both the South and the urban North, where migration had carried African Americans to greater perceived freedom and wealth.

Several centers for quartet singing had emerged by the 1920s. Nearly every urban center in the South had some quartet activity; Memphis became the regional center for quartet singing in the mid-South. Groups from Memphis such as the Middle Baptist Quartet and the Hollywood Specials traveled to nearby towns in Arkansas, Tennessee, Mississippi, and Missouri in order to sing in weekend programs. Scores of these harmony groups were active in Memphis, although most went undocumented. However, the I.C. Glee Club Quartet made several fine commercial phonograph records for the OKeh company in the late 1920s.

The commercial popularity of gospel quartets increased throughout the 1930s. By the late 1930s, a few groups, most notably the Famous Blue Jay Singers of Birmingham and the Texas-based Soul Stirrers, had taken to the road full time. Following World War II, the interest in quartet singing virtually exploded. Every sizable black

(continues)

community supported several quartets and every city spawned at least one professional or semiprofessional group. Tennessee quartets such as the Spirit of Memphis, the Swan Silvertones (who were based in Knoxville for a time in the 1940s), and the Fairfield Four of Nashville (who sang spirituals and jubilee material) toured the country and recorded frequently. Most of the early recordings were done for independent regional labels, including Dot and Bullet, both of which were based in Nashville.

Radio contributed to disseminating the music made by Tennessee's black quartets. As gospel quartet historian Doug Seroff observed of the Fairfield Four: "They began broadcasting over 50,000-watt WLAC in 1942, after winning a local contest sponsored

The Fairfield Four, formed in Nashville in 1921, broadcast over WLAC in the '40s, disbanded in the '50s, and reunited in the '80s. They became National Heritage fellows in 1989; Warner Brothers released the group's *Standin' In the Safety Zone.*

by Sunway Vitamins. Their WLAC program was transcribed and broadcast over power-ful sister stations from Philadelphia to Salt Lake City . . . Their broadcasts were so popular that the group was in constant demand for personal appearances and soon be-came the South's greatest box office attraction." Taking their name from the Swan Bak-ing Company, which sponsored their WNOX broadcasts, the Swan Silvertone Singers began their rapid rise to prominence by way of weekly radio appearances that quickly became a daily fifteen-minute program.

Some of the biggest names in popular music emerged from gospel quartet singing. Many of these singers spent time singing in church choirs, but the quartets served as their more formal apprenticeship. Sam Cooke and Lou Rawls, for example, sang for groups like the Soul Stirrers and the Pilgrim Travelers before switching to popular music in the late '50s. Both O.V. Wright of Tennessee and Joe Hinton emerged as first-rate soul singers in the early '60s after being lured away from the Spirit of Mem-phis by Don Robey of Peacock Records.

No survey of black sacred music in Tennessee is complete without a brief mention of Pentecostalism. The black Pentecostal movement, also known as Holiness Churches, can be said to call Memphis its home — the city is headquarters for the Church of God in Christ. Founded in Lexington, Mississippi, by Memphis-based minister Charles C.H. Mason in 1895, the Church of God in Christ moved its base of operation to Memphis early in the century. It remains the largest and most powerful Pentecostal church, and nearly five percent of all black churchgoers belong to one of its sects.

Black Pentecostal church music has influenced many other forms of black and white music, both popular and sacred. Pentecostalists believe in baptism by the Holy Spirit, the so-called second baptism that people receive because of special calling. This spiritual rebirth is reflected in fiery, highly emotional music which has influ-enced nearly all types of 20th-century black music, such as sacred, soul, and many styles of popular music.

Emotion is especially evident in Pentecostal singing, which often takes a highly ornamented, dramatic turn. Aretha Franklin's singing is a good example of this style. Franklin grew up in Memphis, and as a child often sang at the church of her father, the Reverend C.L. Franklin. Although Reverend Franklin was a Baptist preacher, Aretha's singing contains some of the hallmarks of the holiness churches that dot the Memphis landscape.

Kip Lornell has written six books, including *Happy In the Service of the Lord*, considered the definitive work on Memphis black quartets in the 1950s.

Bluegrass guitarist **Lester Flatt**, mandolinist **Curly Sechler**, and banjo master **Earl Scruggs**, looking in the chips in 1949. Courtesy of the Country Music Foundation.

Someday we'll meet again sweetheart
We'll meet and never more to part
Someday we'll meet again sweetheart
Don't cry so, please don't break my heart.
~ Lester Flatt and Earl Scruggs

Bluegrass

BORN IN POUGHKEEPSIE, NEW YORK, Claire Lynch now lives in Hazel Green, Alabama, five miles south of the Tennessee border. Although she doesn't consider herself a "blue-blooded Southerner," Hazel Green is home, and these days she is definitely in an "Alabama State of Mind," the title of one of her songs.

The 40-something singer has had to straddle the fence of career and family, gospel and bluegrass, traditional and contemporary. She is the mother of two, and in her spare time she tours with the Front Porch String Band, for whom her husband Larry plays mandolin. Her album *Moonlighter,* which features some of Nashville's finest pickers, earned Lynch a long-deserved Grammy nomination, and she won the International Bluegrass Music Association female vocalist of the year award in 1997, but things haven't always been so easy.

She and Larry met at the University of Alabama in Huntsville and together they built the Front Porch. Its eponymous first album, released in 1981, was critically acclaimed but commercially marginal; it has been rereleased by Rebel Records. In her words, "It was a landmark bluegrass album and we didn't even know it." Soon thereafter, she gave birth to her first child, Kegan and also began finding work as a studio artist, backing Patty Loveless and others.

"Then I got pregnant with Christi and pretty much lost those opportunities," she said, "and the people who were interested in communicating with me and working with me pretty much lost interest. There are realities of raising children that some of us won't face, and others do, but record people know the realities, and know whether or not to ignore them. I'm always torn between the two, and the only choice I have is to balance the two and work at whatever level I can because of the fact that I'm a mother, too — which is better than nothing," she added with a laugh.

Not that Claire Lynch has any sour grapes. Major record labels, she said, "have every right to ask you to do those things [because] they're pumping money into your career. I would think they want all of you, whether you're a man or a woman." On the other hand, she believes it's easier for a man to have a career in music. "In my case, I can't leave my kids with my husband because he's in the band . . . so we've got double trouble," she said, laughing again. "We found a way to work it out, though."

Claire Lynch of Hazel Green, Alabama — just south of the Tennessee border — has had to juggle the responsibilities of being a musician and a mother. She hopes her music "will open people's minds when they hear the 'B' word."

Lynch grew up on church music, first in the Christian Missionary Alliance and later as a member of the nondenominational charismatic movement, which her parents had joined. She sang in trios with her older sisters. In the 1960s, they started listening to folk groups such as Peter, Paul and Mary and learning songs like "Fair and Tender Maiden" and "The Long Black Veil."

This background helped smooth the transition to bluegrass, to which she was exposed as a University of Alabama freshman. Her early influences included the Nitty Gritty Dirt Band's *Will the Circle Be Unbroken* and, more importantly, a band called Hickory Wind which she saw in Tuscaloosa. Larry, whom she had noticed in high school, was playing mandolin, and she was soon smitten by the music, and by the mandolinist. At age 19, she quit her job as an insurance underwriter, joined the band, and embarked upon "the paying dues thing."

The band's first real gig, as house band in a Birmingham banjo parlor, lasted three years. "It was really neat," she said, "it had peanuts on the floor, long tables with beer. And then they started bringing in national bluegrass acts, so all of a sudden these little amateurs were being exposed to the cream of the crop coming through town and doing dates."

Initially the band benefited by these headliners, but then they were forced to find work at other nightclubs. They hit the road for eight years, traveling on the Southeastern festival circuit and cutting four albums in the late 1970s and early '80s, including their masterpiece on Rebel. They ended up playing six-nighters "in club chains out in Texas, [the type] with a little bench on the podium and nachos — those kinds of things."

"We didn't feel like we were getting anywhere," she said. "We weren't getting the gigs we always had our eyes on, and then the baby came, and so we disbanded for awhile and Larry went back to school and got his degree, got a job." A few years later, they started hearing about the Front Porch's "cutting-edge" approach to bluegrass.

"It just came natural to us," she said. "We grew up on pop radio, and all of the boys in the band had been exposed to country music, so that was part of their heritage, but it was just our approach was different. And I was the [lead] singer, which was different because there weren't that many women in bluegrass at the time. Ginger Boatwright, Rose Maddox, Delia Bell — to name them all!" Bluegrass was, she added, "good ole boys' music."

For whatever reason, the 1981 album "just clicked." It's still selling, getting radio play, and influencing other bands, who cover their songs. With *Friends For a Lifetime* (1993), Lynch made a foray into gospel music, but she opted not to "cash in on it" by becoming a commercial Christian artist.

Come summertime, Claire is back on the road with the Front Porch. Over the past five years, she has become a much sought-after backup vocalist, working with the likes of Dolly Parton, Emmylou Harris, and Kathy Mattea. She views her devotion to bluegrass, and its relatively limited commercial appeal, with a mixture of realism and hopefulness.

"Well, I've got to say, and Larry and I have kept it between us for years, that all is fair in love and war and the music business. What else can I say? It's just unfair. You know what I mean? There is no justice sometimes, in the music business. Anything is fair. There is no justice in it. I don't think there ever will be. The thing that we cling to is the fact that we love it and it's an expression of art, and if we can make some money off of it, well that's great. It's like actors saying, 'I do what I love and I can't believe I get paid for it.' I mean, that's the attitude you have to take — either that, or quit. It's fun for us, too. If it wasn't fun we probably would find some other way to make moonlighting money."

The time is ripe, she adds, for a revival of bluegrass and other forms of roots music. Claire hopes her efforts "will open people's minds when they hear the 'B' word. It doesn't have the image that it used to have, which is good, because I've never been into that image anyway."

DEL MCCOURY FIRST SANG IN PUBLIC AS A BOY at his Missionary Baptist church in western North Carolina. In fact, he remembers singing as early as he began talking. His mother Hazel, whose lonesome "mountain blues" singing he compares to Virginia's Ralph Stanley, taught him his first song. She also taught his older brother, Grover Cleveland McCoury Jr., his first guitar chords, and G.C. promptly taught them to Del. Hazel also played piano and harmonica, and Del's father's side was musical as well.

Nearly half a century later, the Del McCoury Band, which includes his sons Rob and Ronnie, on banjo and mandolin, is one of the hottest tickets in bluegrass. During one recent stretch, the IBMA voted Del top male vocalist for three consecutive years, and in 1997 the band won entertainer and instrumental group of the year awards (it was nominated in 12 categories.)

For McCoury, making music has been neither an overnight success story nor a financial windfall. On the other hand, "it don't take much to please me," the guitarist said while resting in a Winston-Salem motel, his first night off in a week. "Boy, I tell you, I've been hittin' the road," he said, his voice sounding hoarse and lower than usual.

His love for the music is what has kept McCoury going. He started out singing such songs as "Farther Along" and "The Lord Keeps a Record" from the old Baptist hymnbooks, and then covered "hillbilly numbers" by Ernest Tubb, Hank Williams, and Bill Monroe. As with Doyle Lawson and Jerry Douglas (see the chapter on new acoustic music), hearing Flatt & Scruggs was the defining moment in McCoury's musical career, and remains so today.

"I think a kid gets a certain age and he hears something that really turns on a light in his head, and for me, it was Earl Scruggs," he said, pronouncing the name with reverence. "The best I can understand, it was 1950 — I would have been 11 — and G.C. bought a record of Flatt & Scruggs, and that banjo was something that I really *took to*. That stuff had some *spark*, you know? I mean, it had the *zip* to it. And actually, in my teenage years, that's what I did — I played banjo, the three-finger style of banjo-picking.

"Their timing was just so perfect," McCoury said of Flatt & Scruggs. "And it wasn't that they were trying. They were just natural at what they did. It was like breathing, you know? Those two guys."

Like many bluegrassers, McCoury is self-taught. His mother gave him lessons in her spare time, and his father borrowed his first banjo. He spent the next decade learning how to play it. "I got pretty good at it," he said, "good enough to play with Bill Monroe."

McCoury was living in York County, Pennsylvania, which is his home state, and playing in a band with his friend Jack Cooke (now with Ralph Stanley) in a little bar in Baltimore near the Martin airplane factory. Monroe passed through town in the winter of 1962 and hired McCoury to play banjo for an upcoming gig at the Chapel Café in New York.

Monroe urged McCoury to look him up in Nashville if he ever wanted a full-time job, and the following spring McCoury became the band's rhythm guitarist. Monroe also encouraged him to sing. "He heard something in my voice," said McCoury, who lasted a year, during which time he was joined by Kenny Baker and Bill Keith, considered masters of the fiddle and banjo, respectively. He quit after they had left the band.

In McCoury's opinion, what characterizes bluegrass — notably Monroe's mid-1940's bands — is the musicians' collective timing and rhythm, "playing on top of the beat, whether real fast or real slow," he said. "It's gotta sound like one man playing when five are."

After leaving Monroe, McCoury lived in California for a spell and then moved back to Pennsylvania. In recent years, he observed how much bluegrass had grown since he was a teenager and decided to relocate to Nashville, a move which has renewed his career. He likes being within a few hours' drive of the International Bluegrass Music Association headquarters in Owensboro, Kentucky.

Now in his sixties, McCoury is encouraged by his perception that while rock and country stars fade, older bluegrassers continue to tour and gain acceptance, regardless of their age.

"I can remember how this music excited me when I was young, and you know, these days it's kind of like a job," he said. "I enjoy doing it, but I'm sure I'm not as excited about it as I was then, you know? Course, kids are that way by nature. I still love to record and do new songs — that's what keeps me excited now — but bluegrass has never really been exposed or promoted like other [kinds of music] have been. And I make a comfortable living doing this. I mean, it's a lot better than farming. The work is a lot easier, and I'm satisfied as long as I can play music and do what I enjoy and make a living. And I know a lot of the country stars and rock stars, and they make *beaucoups* of money, but I'm not sure they're happy."

—————————

GUITARIST TIM STAFFORD RECENTLY BOUGHT A HOUSE out in the country near his hometown of Kingsport and he intends to stay put, except during the summer, when he will continue to travel the bluegrass festival circuit. He has started a family and wants to be around home to enjoy it.

Now in his thirties, Tim kicked around with a couple of bands — Mountain Memories, The Boys in the Band, and Dusty Miller — before getting his master's in history at East Tennessee State University, where he played in the ETSU Bluegrass Band. He then toured with the fiddler and singer Alison Krauss for a few years, which is the closest thing to super-stardom that you'll find in this form of music. Eventually he quit to spend more time with his son. He thought about giving up on music, finishing his doctorate, and getting a job in academia. But he couldn't tear himself away from it. Instead, in late 1994, he formed Blue Highway. A year later, it ranked as one of the top bluegrass bands in the country.

In addition to being a great picker, Tim is an avid scholar of the music, which has earned him a coveted spot on the IBMA board. Unlike many old-school bluegrassers, he didn't have any music to speak of "in the family," excepting a grandfather whom he never got a chance to hear. While a high-school freshman, he walked past

Kingsport native **Tim Stafford** is considered one of the best bluegrass pickers around. Here he shows a run or two to a Belgian tourist *avec magnétophone.* Photo by Peter Zimmerman.

the choir room where a band was rehearsing and had to ask what a mandolin was. Much to his own surprise, he soon took up the banjo and started playing bluegrass. "I tried desperately *not* to like it," he said. He grew up listening to his sisters' Beatles records, and all his friends were into rock and roll. He associated bluegrass with the *Beverly Hillbillies.* It was definitely not cool.

His band found a better banjo player and the guitarist quit, so Tim switched to guitar. "Three of the strings are the same so I did the best I could," said the self-effacing Stafford, who has been called one of the form's "most original and versatile guitarists."

For Stafford, what makes bluegrass special is the raw "emotional" sound of its nonamplified instruments, a quality shared by early blues and jazz, which he also loves. Rhythm is equally important. "I tell you, if you overlook the rhythmic aspect of blue-

For a few years, Stafford went on the road with **Alison Krauss**. He left Union Station in order to spend more time with his family.

grass, you're really overlooking a lot," he said. "A lot of people just focus on the lead, but the rhythm is just as important to me." Stafford constantly digs into his record collection for playing and songwriting guidance.

As a guitarist, he draws inspiration from Lester Flatt's solidity and timing, his unique and "intuitive" rhythmic style, and those killer thumbpicked downstrokes on the D and G strings. "Flatt was able to hold it together and center everything," he said, citing Tony Rice as another guitarist with a great sense of rhythm.

I interviewed Stafford at a bluegrass festival in upstate New York. We talked between Blue Highway's sets, sitting on their van's running boards. He would rather play at festivals and concerts than in recording studios. "If I could make a living playing sessions I probably would," he said, "but you've got to move to Nashville if you're gonna do the session thing. I love where we live."

Studio work is "more controlled, and more conscious," he continued. "This is, hopefully, less self-conscious out here and you're trying to have fun rather than worrying about the sound. I don't know . . . it's unfortunate. Years ago, people didn't know any better. They didn't have multitrack technology in the '40s and '50s, and they just had to go in there and cut it live. They stood around one microphone and did their regular show and just tried to get it as good as they could. We've totally lost that now."

Tim Stafford said he isn't expecting Blue Highway's success to spoil him. Although he is saddened that his old friend Alison Krauss now requires special security, he understands the need following the murder of the Tejano singer Selena.

"Bluegrass people are so used to the artists being accessible," he said, snapping his guitar case shut, "and the artists themselves are used to it. We won't ever run for the bus and hide. In this case, the van. I'm talking about if we ever *get* a bus."

WHILE I WAS WAITING TO INTERVIEW MARTY STUART before his concert at the state fairgrounds in Knoxville, the self-described hillbilly rocker came striding by on his way to the dressing room — on his tour bus. A middle-aged female fan, referring to his diminutive height, exclaimed to her friend, "Why, he ain't no more'n a fart!"

Since Marty is such a nice, friendly guy, I hestitate to repeat this story, but I feel certain that he would laugh out loud rather than feel insulted. For one thing, Stuart's stage clothes — rhinestone-studded jackets and jeans — transform him into a dazzling cross between, say, Ernest Tubb and Patti LaBelle. More importantly, his firecracker persona more than makes up for his shortness.

Stuart, who hosts his own show on TNN, bridges the gap between country's early stars and its slick, modern-day counterparts. He covers old songs in a new way and writes new ones that are firmly rooted in the past; he travels with an electric guitar but cut his teeth on bluegrass mandolin and guitar. His style and smile are as flashy as his wardrobe; once offstage, however, he immediately slips into a T-shirt. "I was born a country child," Stuart proclaims in one of his songs. Fishing is his favorite pastime.

Marty Stuart plays "hillbilly rock" and hosts a show on the Nashville Network. Originally from Philadelphia, Mississippi (also the hometown of Otis Rush), he started out working with Lester Flatt and Johnny Cash. To ignore their teachings "would be walkin' away from the bottom of my soul." Courtesy of MCA Records.

A longtime Nashville resident, Stuart was a child prodigy who quit school in his early teens to hit the road with Lester Flatt and then Johnny Cash (his former father-in-law). Now in his early forties, Stuart has forged his own unique style, which he calls "hillbilly rock." His repertoire taps into many different kinds of music. While growing up in Mississippi, he listened round-the-clock to WHOC ("1490 on your radio dial," he intones), which played an eclectic mix of country, gospel quartets, rock, R&B, and classical.

In the 1960s, Stuart was influenced by soul music. Specifically, he remembers the day Otis Redding died. A black woman was ironing clothes in his house, he said, "and I remember just seein' two big puddles of water on the ironing board. I said, 'Jimmie, what's the matter?' She says, 'Otis died.' And it broke my heart, because she had let me hear his music."

Asked which songs associated with Tennessee have inspired him, he cited Elvis Presley's cover of "Mystery Train," written by West Memphis, Arkansas, native Little Junior Parker, and in the country vein, Roy Acuff's "Wreck on the Highway," which he laughingly described as "the cosmic end of hillbilly." (From memory, he sang a few lines: "When whiskey and blood run together . . . I didn't hear nobody pray.")

Once a year, Stuart makes a point of visiting Lester Flatt's grave in Sparta, where the guitarist once lived. "I dog him for being down there restin' and me out here killin' it on the road," he jokes about his former mentor. On a serious note, he believes in honoring the past. "I come from the South," he said, "so you know, ultimately, I was taught that thing about respecting your elders. The people that raised me in country music, truthfully, were some of the master architects and pioneers. To disown and disavow that and walk away from those teachings would be walkin' away from a real piece of my soul — probably the *bottom* of my soul."

Before deciding to join the *Grand Ole Opry*, Stuart met with two of its leaders, Acuff and Minnie Pearl, both of whom have since passed away. "I wanted *their* endorsement before I went over and talked to the corporate table," he said. "Minnie put her hand on mine, she says, 'Don't you think we've outgrown that word "hillbilly" a little bit?' And I considered that. I understand the slang. I understand how it's a bitter word with a lot of those old country cats, but to me it's a term of endearment and respect."

Lester Flatt's protégé hopes to forge his own niche, building on the past and innovating into the future. With the proliferation of artists in today's country music world, "you'd better have a place where you put yourself," said Stuart. "And I just *proudly* stand up in the hillbilly division of country music."

Country

WHEN I ARRIVED AT WAYLON JENNINGS and Jessi Colter's compound in Brentwood, a suburb south of Nashville, the iron gates leading to their white stucco house were open and the guardhouse unmanned. With its perquisite manicured lawns, Brentwood has evolved into a kind of Elysian fields for country musicians, where its stars repair from the road in the lap of luxury.

With some trepidation, I rang the bell. A voice summoned me to come on in. Somewhere inside was the man who had once developed a reputation for being one of country music's "outlaws," a renegade with a penchant for making music on his own terms. Instead of being met at the door by a liveryman, Waylon and Jessi themselves cheerfully greeted me (as they have probably done to an endless stampede of press people). We walked through the living room, where stood an enormous gilded harp (which Jessi plays), and into the kitchen.

Waylon *looked* pretty much the way I had expected: he could have been his own roadie. He was of solid build, with roughly-shorn facial hair, and wore a black T-shirt emblazoned with the name of a casino in Gardnerville, Nevada, where he likely had performed. On his wrists were two hefty braces, which he wore for treatment of carpal tunnel syndrome, from too much picking and strumming. As I fumbled with my tape recorder, I couldn't help wondering how the interview would go. Would Waylon be "lonesome, ornery and mean," as he sings menacingly in one song, or still in the drug-induced fog that had once engulfed him? Would he respond to my questions with oblique, one-word answers?

I needn't have worried, for as soon as the tape recorder was switched on, he proceeded to talk nonstop for two hours straight. He carefully considered each question and politely expanded on each subject raised. In person, Waylon was a gentle host, and a gentleman. Only once did he get a little ruffled, when I asked whether he thought people ever perceived of him as a "redneck." First coined in the 1830s, this term originally referred to a farmer or outdoor laborer with a sunburned neck, but in modern usage it has come to mean — often derogatorily — a poor, rural Southern white.

We had been talking about what it was like to go from a little town on the Texas Panhandle to performing in front of ten or twenty thousand people, all "yelling and whooping and wanting to touch you." His description reminded me of Merle Haggard's live version of "Okie From Muskogee," in which a member of the audience can be heard screaming "Ya-hoo!" I suggested that even though Haggard is often perceived as a redneck, perhaps he is simultaneously the opposite of a redneck.

"No, not quite," said Waylon said, politely disagreeing. "He's like the rest of us. Some-how you revert back to that in a lot of ways. That guy that hollered 'ya-hoo'? You know what, I've met him many times and I've seen that look on myself many times, too. A lot of that 'ya-hoo' is to hear his own voice. Like with me, a lot of times where I'd say something mean, they thought I was the guy that went in and sat down, with my back to the wall, you know, and grabbed the waitress, kissed her, and threw her over in the corner and punched out the bartender, and waited for somebody to come in so I could kill him. Well, that's the image.

"People that meet me and know me know that I'm not a mean person — there's not a mean bone in my body. But that guy hollerin' 'ya-hoo' is just like them people right down in front who to this day will tell you that me and them used to get drunk together. That's funny, because I never drank. I never did like whiskey. Course, I was higher than a kite on somethin' else. But that was my big brag."

I told Waylon that, although I was raised in the North, my maternal grandparents farmed milo and soybeans in West Tennessee, and that when I used to ask my grandmoth-er if she was a redneck, she would be insulted. Waylon said her reaction might have been on account of my being a Yankee.

"Well, it's that accent," he said. "You say it with . . . you know, it's like, I don't know if you want to use this one or not but like one time, Miles Davis, we had the same manager, and Miles, I was at his house one day with my manager [Neil Reshen] and he was talking, he was laughing, he said, 'Neil, that new white roadie you hired me called me a mother-fucker.' He said, 'Now I don't mind being called a motherfucker, but when he said it, it had too many r's and an Irish accent.'

"Now that might be what's pissing your grandmother off — your accent, and the way you say 'redneck'. Because, see, I'll call myself a hillbilly, and I'll call myself a redneck, but I don't want no other sonofabitch that's not from around here, that ain't one, calling me that. It's like you can get your ass kicked."

I told Waylon that he seemed to be more of a philosopher than a redneck, like his friend, Will Campbell, the author (*Brother to a Dragonfly*) and preacher who once worked as his roadie.

"That's a compliment, that you put me in the same word with Will," he said. "But you're right, I know what you're talking about. When I write a song, a lot of times, I'll go back to my roots. And my roots are as redneck as anybody. And I still have a lot of that in me. I have to fight it every day of my life. I can't help it, because you know what? I grew up that way.

"I quit school, and I went back and got my GED, but I'm really self-educated as far as that goes. I had to learn all these things through bad experiences and good experiences. But it's like I said, that guy [who yelled] 'ya-hoo,' now I could never do that, see? When I

Luttrell, Tennessee's own **Chet Atkins** works the soundboard at RCA's Studio B while a clean-, cut **Waylon Jennings** looks on. The year is 1965, prior to Waylon's "lonesome, on'ry and mean" phase; *Rolling Stone* now calls him a "weathered country legend." Atkins is known for his mellow fingerpicked guitar. Courtesy of the Country Music Foundation.

got into drugs, one of the things they helped me overcome was shyness, because I was very shy and backwards and awkward when I was growing up.

"What I am is a self-made man. I really am. It comes through, and I know those people trust me. Because they know that whether I am now or not, I have been, and that's where the audiences are. That's what country music is all about."

I ASKED WHETHER HE THOUGHT MANY SOUTHERN MUSICIANS had black mentors, like Jim Dickinson's yard man Timothy Teal. Waylon recalled growing up in Littlefield, Texas, and delivering ice to a beer joint in the black section of town.

"I was the only white boy that was welcome in Jaybird's Dew Drop Inn," he said. "In the back there, on a Saturday night, they could get on with it! Now, I learned from a guy who called himself Chuck Berry Jr., and he was a long, lanky ol' boy. Had two gold teeth in front and he got them put in there and had four-leaf clovers worked out of them, you know? And he borrowed two dollars from me one time and I didn't see him again for 20 years, almost.

"He's the one who taught me to move the strings up where I could bend them, and use a banjo string for the little E, that made the strings loose where you could play that bluesy stuff, you know? And when I was 16, he taught me. Played it upside-down backwards. He used open tunings. To me, as I remember back, he was the most wonderful guitar player in the world."

One day, while Waylon was napping, a visitor dropped by his house in Brentwood. "They said there was a guy here, a black guy, came to the door that said he was an old friend of yours. I don't know how I knew, [but] I said, 'Did he have gold teeth in front?' They said, 'No.' But what had happened, he had been in prison and they had taken them out, you know?"

The two reunited, and Waylon put him up in a down-town Nashville hotel. "I got him a guitar, and let him rock 'n' roll for about a week and he disappeared and I ain't seen him since. They said he partied and had women all over that place. But I said 'go ahead,' I said, 'You got a whole week to have a good time now.' And I haven't seen him since."

Then I repeated Dickinson's comment: that white people can't play the blues, but play at them.

"He's full of shit," said Waylon. "Ask him to go listen to Tony Joe White ["Polk Salad Annie"]. Tony Joe White's one of the best blues guitar players and singers there is in the world, and Hank Williams Jr. can hang in with anybody singin' blues. But you know what that is? Love for it. That's what music is. It's what you learn, it's what you feel, what you love to do. Chips Moman wrote a song one time and I recorded it, but I had said it before, that it wasn't a matter of I had my music, it was a matter of my music had me. And I had no choice."

Waylon paused.

"Every once in a while I think, man, this road, I'm tired of it. But I get off of it two weeks and I'm walking the floor and don't even know what's wrong, you know? And Jessi even notices it before I do. But I'll never quit. I'll be in it somehow, somewhere, maybe not as good, but I'll do something in music."

(Over the past year, Waylon has cut back his touring schedule for health reasons.)

Growing up in Texas, a young Jennings heard musicians like **Bobby "Blue" Bland** over the radio. A native of Rosemark near Memphis, Bland sings mostly rhythm and blues and borrowed his trademark, throat-clearing "squall" from Rev. C.L. Franklin, Aretha's father, who preached in Memphis. Ernest Withers/Panopticon.

WHEN WAYLON WAS A KID, HE TUNED IN TO A MIDNIGHT SHOW broadcast from Shreveport on KWKH. "They had a thing called Stan the Record Man and No-Name Jive," he said. "That's what rock 'n' roll was called before it was called rock 'n' roll. He called it no-name jive. Isn't that great? And it was Bobby Blue Bland, Fats Domino, all of them people."

Country music and blues are related, he said, because the vocal phrasing and bending guitar strings are virtually impossible to transcribe on paper. The two forms both have to do with "the same man singing the same song about the good and the bad times, the woman he wants, and the woman he's got, and the one he can't keep." Both also share the same "singalong thing." Country singers often borrow from the blues, he said, citing Hank Williams' covers of "Lovesick Blues" and "My Bucket's Got a Hole in It" as examples.

Waylon once wrote a book called *Unsung Songs and the Reasons Why* consisting of songs or pieces of songs he'd written down in the middle of the night or when he was high. "I looked at them afterwards, and it didn't mean shit unless you sung them, you know? If you sung them they were funnier than hell," he said. "Like I told somebody the lyrics to a new song over the phone and it didn't get to him. And then I come out and sing it to him, and they just flip out over it. 'Where did that come from?' And I said, 'Well, I told you the lyrics.' 'Well, I didn't get it,' you know?

"A song is a circle," he added. "And it's up to you where the end is. You can overdo it, you can under-do it."

AFTER ARRIVING IN NASHVILLE in the mid-1960s, Waylon found himself succumbing to what he describes, in one of his recent songs, as "The Hank Williams Syndrome." Many country fans believe that Williams, who died at age 29 in the back of his Cadillac, is the greatest country singer of all time. A few months prior to his death on Jan. 1, 1953, the Alabama native had been fired from the *Grand Ole Opry*, whose management had lost patience with his drinking and carousing.

"You hear all these wild stories about him," he said. "It was such a short span of time that he was even on top, but he left such a legacy. I mean, some of these stories are not true at all, some of them

He lived only 29 years, but **Hank Williams** has inspired countless musicians — for better and worse. The Alabama native wrote the memorable "Long Gone Lonesome Blues" while fishing on the Tennessee River (it became a number-one hit). He died a few years later outside Knoxville in the backseat of his Cadillac while being driven to this show in Ohio. Courtesy of Hatch Showprint.

are made up. Like that one — it was a joke — about a guy who loved Hank Williams so much that he got mad at his wife because she wouldn't run around on him because he thought that Audrey had run around on Hank, you know? And he wanted to be just like him, right down to the fine-tooth comb. We were all that way a little bit. You know, you thought everything else was boring-sounding."

Waylon is skeptical that Hank took pills solely to treat a congenital back problem. "That's the best trick in the world to get drugs — talk about a bad back or something like that," he said. "I mean, I don't want to be settin' here passing judgment. Because when I came to town, I thought that was part of it, you know? If Hank did it, so you ought to do it, too. You hear those stories and they sound so big and romantic.

"And since then, I've seen people that tried to be like me, and they missed the point, the whole thing. There's a guy right now that's having problems. He loved my music and I was one of his heroes and now he's in all this trouble with drugs. You can't help but feel a little guilty. If I can help him now, I would."

Waylon believes his drug odyssey was triggered by the transition from being a young musician working his way up, to stardom. "When you're on the road, you get into a different mode. You're a little bit above society's rules, and it's disorienting and everything but that's where a lot of the drug things come in. It's not normal for a guy that grew up in a town of 2,000 people to get out every night and have 10,000 people yelling and whooping and wanting to touch him, you know? That's what you're looking for, and it means a lot in the beginning. That's acceptance. But as far as the drugs are concerned, there's no real excuse for it. There's really not. Except stupidity, maybe."

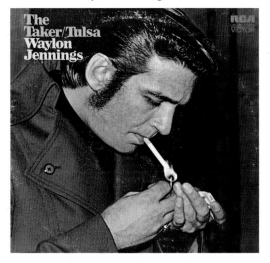

WAYLON SAID THE FAMOUS *Wanted: the Outlaws* album — the first million-seller in country music history — consisted mostly of repackaging and "sweetening" songs that had been recorded a decade earlier. As for the title, he only considers himself an outlaw in the sense of someone working outside the system.

He readily admits, however, that when he started recording in Nash-

Hoss — shown here in his salad days — reportedly refused to sing in Swahili on "We Are the World." He feels overlooked by country radio.

ville he "messed up their little playhouse." "They" are the country music powers-that-be — the establishment — and what he calls the "Johnny-come-latelies," rock producers who switch to country and "start producing records like they're going out of style." The same handful of musicians and producers are making most of today's records and, in his opinion, driving the music into the ground. To Waylon, contemporary country music consists mostly of "imitation and regurgitation."

"They like to do it assembly-line and tell the singer what to sing, and the record companies are notoriously bad about this. I heard one talking the other day, on the air, about this 'controlled composition,' which gives a writer 75 percent of his writing. They penalize him 25 percent for writing his own songs. And they're making some long excuse. And it ain't nothing but stealing. And I don't put up with it. I make them give me all my money. And they don't like that."

Now in his sixties, Waylon feels blacklisted from country radio because of his age. But he is proud of having stood up for his rights. "When I came here," he recalls, "you had to use their studios and pay them to use their studios and engineers. If I left nothing else for people, the thing that I created for this town was that there's always one more way to do things, and that's *your* way, and you have a right to try it at least once."

To Jennings, who once played bass with Buddy Holly, country music is not just one form but a synthesis of many styles. Sometimes it is viewed as a Southern phenomenon, but Waylon doesn't see it that way, noting that many of his concerts take place in the Midwest. "I think country music was probably born out of the Depression," he said. "I know when I was growing up, every other house had somebody playing guitar or fiddle or piano: that's what you did on the weekends."

He believes that anybody can make country music, regardless of their background. He remembers watching a TV show pairing the Welsh pop singer Tom Jones with Little Richard, one of rock's inventors. Jones "hung right in there with him," he said, adding, "It doesn't matter where you're from. It matters where you're from *mentally*. That sounds corny, but it's true."

WAYLON JENNINGS WAS RAISED IN THE CHURCH OF CHRIST and thought about becoming a preacher ("almost stunted my growth"), but he became disenchanted with what he viewed as the church's hypocrisy. Singing is allowed in the church but no instruments.

"God probably loves music too, and He wouldn't have given us talent, if He hadn't wanted us to use it," he said. "But [the preacher is] sitting there talking from a pulpit, with carpet on the floor, the people are sitting in a bunch of chairs, the wonderful big benches, which basically are the hardest things I ever sat on in my life, in church for two hours, you know — drove me a little nuts. And he's speaking through a *microphone*. But something like a musical instrument, he thinks is bad.

"Well, I mean, in the Bible, the man after God's own heart was David, you know, and his music. I think music, without words, could be one of the greatest ways to worship in the world. Now I'm not a real religious person or anything, I'm not getting off on this kick. But I think music is the only really true communication instrument in the world, because you can get all kinds of people together under one roof."

Jessi and **Waylon** have been together for 25 years, which Waylon says is doing pretty good by Music City standards. In 1996 they released *Right for the Time* on the Texas-based Justice label. *Old Dogs* is in the works with Bobby Bare, Mel Tillis, and Jerry Reed.

JESSI COLTER, WHOSE MAIDEN NAME WAS MIRIAM JOHNSON, borrowed her stage name from her father's great-uncle, Jesse Colter, a counterfeiter by trade. However, she has followed a different path.

Earlier, Waylon had described his wife of 25 years as spiritual, not religious. "I can't find that faith or that feeling that she has," he said. "So I tell everybody she's got a direct line to God and that don't put me in too bad a shape, you know?"

Jessi and I moved to the back patio and let Waylon get on with his errands, or whatever an "outlaw" does in his spare time.

"I believe in the New Testament experience," said Jessi, who grew up in Phoenix, Arizona. Her mother was a prominent Pentecostal minister there, and Jessi became the church pianist at age 11. Growing up in a mostly Mormon place, she learned to cope with being a minority, and developed inner strength, confidence, and a sense of individuality.

To this day, Jessi loves the old hymns. Her favorite song is "It Came Upon a Midnight Clear," which she is as likely to sing in July as she would in December. Capitol Records was once "shocked" when she cut an album, *Miriam,* consisting solely of spirituals. "It's almost like [singers] can mention anything else," she said, "but if you mention *God,* you hear, 'Well, uh, uh,' you know? And it just burned me — it irked me — that you couldn't also give of the very essence of yourself and have it accepted. It kind of made me stubborn creatively."

The record companies have never really understood what to do with Jessi. Even in the 1970s, when she had a number-one hit with "I'm Not Lisa," they couldn't decide whether to call her country or pop. These days, Jessi travels with her man, singing love songs past and current. For some time, she has also been writing "things of a spiritual nature" which have yet to be recorded.

"I've got some ideas in my mind that are coming together," she said, adding that she hopes "one or two" of her songs will someday find their way into the congregation. "I don't know just how it's gonna come that I'll be received. The truth of the matter is, without God and the spirit of God that moves all things, what is life anyway? Music comes from the spirit, and I think if it gets disconnected from that, it's gonna lose some strength and get old."

On a visit to Jerusalem, Waylon and Jessi discovered that many Biblical phrases which appear to be allegorical, such as the "eye of the needle" and the "valley of the shadow of death," are actually based on real places. She was surprised to find that Waylon often knew more about Holy Land geography than she did, even with all her religious upbringing. It was then that she realized how much Waylon "believed and understood."

Women In Nashville Music

By Stephen L. Betts

In 1986, with the disheartening *Urban Cowboy* era mercifully dead and buried, Nashville began to recover by looking — with some reverence — to its more colorful past for that elusive "next big thing." Along with the earliest chart appearances of neo-traditionalists like Dwight Yoakam and Randy Travis, the year was notable for the ascendance of format-shattering acts like the cerebral Lyle Lovett, renegade Steve Earle, and fringe-festooned chanteuse k.d. lang. While their chart action and country radio airplay may have been minimal, these artists proved to be among the few true pioneers in country music at the time, understanding not only what it had been but also what it could become. The jury is still out on whether the same holds true for this decade's biggest acts, but a handful of this decade's non-mainstream artists have at least cemented Nashville's growing reputation as an eclectic music center.

The kind of attention Nashville attracts during the boom periods is more challenging to its female artists. In early Music City history, women like Dolly Parton, Tammy Wynette and Patsy Cline were among the few who emerged victorious from struggles associated with the misconception that they were merely "girl singers." They made it possible for women of the '80s and '90s to focus on the message in the music, without the extra baggage of titillation, insipid cuteness, or otherwise inappropriate lyrical content.

Emmylou Harris, evolving artist, comes from Hank Williams' home state of Alabama and her voice is nearly as haunting as ol' Hank's.

Perhaps that's one reason Nashville has become such a desirable place for women to live. Emmylou Harris moved here from California in 1983. Former disco diva Donna Summer also took up residence in Music City and began collaborating with veteran songwriters such as Harlan Howard. Howard likewise figured in the career of another Nashville transplant, Nanci Griffith, a Texas native who spent the better part of her teenage years performing in smoke-filled bars.

When she moved here in the '80s, Griffith became a Music City fixture. She has had a country sensibility throughout her career but still remains primarily identified as a folk singer. Before signing her first major label deal with MCA, she released four albums on the then relatively unknown Massachusetts-based Philo/Rounder label. *Last of the True Believers* featured two songs that became genuine chart hits for Kathy Mattea, "Love at the Five and Dime" written by Griffith, and "Goin' Gone," Mattea's first number-one record.

Rounder is also home to the massively successful Alison Krauss, who stunned Music City when she snagged four trophies at the 1995 Country Music Association awards, including Female Vocalist of the Year. Krauss has managed to sell nearly two million albums with very little cooperation from country radio, the mainstream artist's lifeline.

(continues)

Rounder also played a significant role in the early Nashville career of Irish-born singer Maura O'Connell. Destined initially to take over the family fish shop, O'Connell instead left Ireland to tour the U.S. with traditional Irish musicians DeDanaan. While her upbringing included exposure to everything from light opera to Frank Sinatra, O'Connell cited the early works of Emmylou Harris, Bonnie Raitt, and Nashville native Carlene Carter as inspiration for the new phase in her career. In 1987, she made the move to Music City and signed with Warner Bros., where she eventually recorded three acclaimed albums. Today O'Connell has her own label, Permanent Records, and has led the charge of Celtic artists involved in various Nashville-based projects.

THE TYPE AND FREQUENCY OF AN ARTIST'S AIRPLAY is the subject of constant scrutiny in the executive offices of Nashville's record labels. "Adult Album Alternative" radio stations like Nashville's "Radio Lightning" have recently been invaluable to Emmylou Harris' career. Her Grammy-winning 1995 *Wrecking Ball* wowed the critics, confounded some fans, and, understandably, completely escaped country airplay. Produced by Daniel Lanois (known for his work with rock icons U2 and Bob Dylan), this is Harris' most experimental record to date, with covers from sources as diverse as Jimi Hendrix and Lucinda Williams. While she's always been counted on to dig up unlikely material (on previous albums she has recorded songs by everyone from the Louvin Brothers to Townes Van Zandt), *Wrecking Ball*, with its murky, slurred vocals and spare rhythm tracks, challenged listeners to think of Emmylou as an evolving artist, something her fans and critics had always known about her.

Perhaps the most genuinely "country" artist to emerge in the '90s is singer-songwriter Iris DeMent. Although she has since relocated to Kansas City, DeMent was born in Arkansas, raised in California, and came to Nashville in 1990. Her own unique brand of plaintively sung Americana is predominantly acoustic old-time country music with minimal production. She has earned raves for her three albums on Warner Bros. (the first of which appeared initially on Rounder), and caught the attention of artists like Merle Haggard, who recorded her intensely beautiful "No Time to Cry," featuring Iris on piano, for his album, *1996*.

Like the vast majority of women in country music today, Iris has little use for the fringe and cowgirl accoutrements of yesteryear. She does, however, seek to revere the sacred names of Loretta Lynn, Mother Maybelle, and Kitty Wells. These women blazed their own trails and made it possible for those working today to take a more substantial role in the development of country music.

Stephen L. Betts is a researcher and writer for Jim Owens & Associates, which produces shows for TNN. He also contributes to *Country Song Roundup* and *New Country*. His mother made hats for Minnie Pearl.

GILLIAN WELCH IS A YOUNG SONGWRITER who has just begun to make it big with a pure clear voice and simply crafted songs harking back to the Carter Family and Stanley Brothers. Fittingly, *Revival* is the name of her first CD; it was nominated for a Grammy in the contemporary folk category but lost out to veteran rocker Bruce Springsteen.

Several years ago, I called her in the drizzling rain from a pay phone on Nashville's Elliston Place. Without hesitation, she suggested that we meet at Vandyland, which serves plate lunches on Nashville's tony West End, across the street from the venerable Vanderbilt University. Somehow, this juxtaposition — basic, yet refined — seemed to fit her experience to date.

I first heard Gillian and her partner David Rawlings purely by luck when they opened for Johnny Cash at a street fair outside Nashville. Then, a couple of days later, the Bluebird Cafe's Amy Kurland suggested that Gillian would be a good person to interview for a young songwriter's perspective. At the time, Gillian was in her mid-twenties.

Considered one of Nashville's most talented songwriters, **Gillian Welch** grew up in California and studied music in Boston, where she met her partner, guitarist David Rawlings. Photo by John Patrick Salisbury, courtesy of Almo Sounds, Inc.

Their music has been termed everything from "traditional folk" to "American primitive," while she herself prefers the unassuming (and slightly tongue-in-cheek) "that songwriter stuff." *Billboard* called Welch's vocals "as straight as a Kansas highway" and noted her "uncanny sense of craft and an unflinching eye for detail that is totally contemporary." Her fellow songwriters concur. In Paul Kennerly's opinion, she possesses "more soul than Otis Redding," and Matraca Berg, who co-wrote "Strawberry Wine" for Deana Carter, said that the first couplet of "Barroom Girls" gave her a mean case of writer's block: "Oh the night came undone like a party dress/And fell at her feet in a beautiful mess."

In a publicity photo, Welch's straight black hair is pulled back, she wears a plain print dress, and an expression that belongs to the Dust Bowl era. Over lunch, she told me about her *real* life. Born and raised in southern California, where her parents worked for the *Carol Burnett Show,* Welch earned a degree in photography at the University of California at Santa Cruz. After graduating, she worked as a freelance photographer and in a custom color lab, and played in bands on the side. One day, she decided that "that was backwards" of what she wanted.

"So I applied to the Berklee College of Music, and got in, and sold my Mustang to pay for the tuition," she said. The Boston-area school has a reputation for its solid jazz, rock, and classical programs. Gillian, on the other hand, was one of only a handful of country and bluegrass students. "We were a very tight little band of irregulars," she said of her partners in rhyme.

She studied ear training and songwriting, and also met David, a native Rhode Islander who helps "finish" and arrange her songs, in addition to playing lead guitar and singing harmony. (Gillian sings lead and plays rhythm.) She scouted Nashville on a couple of school-sponsored trips and liked what she found.

"I heard that the music community was very open, more so than Los Angeles or New York, and that the real moving parts of it — the publishing houses and the record labels — were more accessible." she said. "For one thing, most of them are on the ground floor. It's kind of a stupid logistical thing, but it really makes a difference. You can point to a little house over there and go, 'That's Almo Irving Publishing,' and you can walk in the door, you know?

"And I don't know if you can do that in L.A. I mean, I lived there until I was 17, and I don't know where any of that stuff actually happened. It just never was quite as visible to me. Except for, like, the big building shaped like a record needle, whatever that is — Capitol or something." (Actually, Capitol's circular building is meant to resemble a stack of records.)

George Jones once proclaimed that "it's hard to get a contract in this town unless you got a cute little butt, blue jeans, and a black hat on," but gender discrimination doesn't strike her as a problem in Nashville. While "the old school" is still around, she thinks "that's kind of changing." She didn't have to worry about racial discrimination, she added jokingly, because being white in Nashville, "I fit right in." (Actually, Music City is less homogeneous than commonly perceived, with a black population of 25 percent.)

After graduation, Welch took the plunge and moved to Nashville. To get by, she worked as a temp, "but I can't type or, like, do *anything*." She just couldn't hack a regular job. "I mean, that's one of the reasons that I think I was so clearly committed to making it in music," she said, laughing.

Next, she got a job as a cleaning lady at a bed and breakfast on the outskirts of town. After being promoted to innkeeper, she began spending half the week at the inn and Thursday through Sunday playing music. Eventually, the 20-hour days infringed on her songwriting and she began to feel "out of the loop." She didn't want to settle for nonmusical jobs and end up getting "sucked into the straight world."

So she borrowed some money from her family, joined the ranks of the unemployed, and scraped by for six months, playing an occasional party gig and doing odd jobs. By the time the six months were up, she had successfully secured a songwriting job at a small but prestigious publishing house.

At first, she and David performed three or four nights a week at writers' nights around town. These ranged from enjoyable ones presided over by friends like Stacy Earle and Stephanie Smith, to the more mundane at Bogie's, Guido's, and the Silver Dollar, and a few "too horrible" to even remember. "It's not so much the venues as the people who run them," she said. "Some of the guys who seem to be able to stick with it and do it for years are total bores, and the emcees can be really abrasive and rude."

The benefits of performing regularly, however, outweighed any of the more "terrible, tedious evenings" which she and David had to endure. When she moved to town, Welch had only written four songs, and she is still a slow worker. On the writers' night circuit, she packed two years' worth of experience into four months.

Publishers attended her shows and began asking her to drop by their offices. She made friends and professional contacts who in turn placed calls on her behalf to arrange additional interviews. After a flurry of meetings with some 20 publishers, she hired a lawyer to help her negotiate a deal.

In early 1994, she began cranking out about a dozen songs a year for Almo Irving, which represents Nanci Griffith and other songwriters outside the commercial country mainstream. She works out of her rented house, developing several songs simultaneously. "I like to think that it's quality over quantity," she said. A bluegrass aficionado, she brings her songs to those musicians whom she admires, while Almo Irving pitches them to the more lucrative country acts. "Orphan Girl" was first recorded by Tim and Mollie O'Brien, a brother-and-sister duo, and then picked up by Emmylou Harris. Trisha Yearwood and Kathy Mattea have cut her songs as well.

Appropriately enough, Welch often focuses on strong independent women. "It used to be a joke among my friends that all my songs were about women who hit the road," she said. "One of them said my first album should be called *Screw You, I'm Outta Here*." She often comes up with song ideas and imagery while traveling, "particularly in automobiles." For instance, the backdrop for "Wichita" is a filling station.

Speaking of vehicles, she bought an old Ford pickup to replace the Mustang whose sale put her through music school. Her Southern accent is coming along nicely, and she isn't feeling a great deal of tortured-artist angst about her life and career. "Without sounding hokey," she said, "this has been a really great couple of years for me — probably the best. And I really like living here."

Despite her success, Welch's goals remain comparatively simple: pay the rent and keep her truck on the road. "Actually, someone has offered to give me a really cool old gas stove. I can't remember what brand it is, but it's pink," she said. "I would really like a house to go with it. I'm tired of renting apartments."

Appreciating Lefty

by Gil Reavill

Country music inspires strong passions — both for and against. The favorable kind are on display in virtually every country music concert and during Nashville's yearly Fan Fair. The average country music audience is fanatic on the approach to rabid.

But there are also a lot of disbelievers, to whom country music is simple, unsophisticated, even crude. These people think of redneck as a term of disapprobation (they "nix hicks," as *Variety* would say), and applaud the apostasy of k.d. lang, who went from calling herself the reincarnation of Patsy Cline to totally disavowing country music in general and Nashville in particular — a case, say the disbelievers, of a girl coming to her senses.

The first time I listened to country music it was forced on me. I was working on a dairy farm in Wisconsin, and the owner, Jim Marquardt, played it for his cows — said it increased milk production. Once, when I tried to change the dial to my favorite rock station, he insisted that his Holsteins preferred country.

"Either country or classical," he said. "They don't like rock and roll." Eventually I realized that he was really talking about his *own* musical tastes. Marquardt played the accordion and loved polka music.

But maybe there was something to it after all. A university study published in the 1990s did indeed establish that dairy cows are soothed by music. Judged solely on the basis of milk production, bovines prefer Mozart to the booming dynamics of Beethoven — and country to rock and roll.

The study had nothing much to say about human musical preference, but that summer on Marquardt's farm, I began to develop a taste for country music. I have met up with country's detractors for just about as long. I've always thought that if they would just give the music a chance to work its charms, they might be able to appreciate it too. Perhaps there are those who do not actively dislike country music but might not know where to start.

What hooked me was the music's unapologetic embrace of narrative. Indeed, country has become the primary refuge for the storytelling impulse in American music. Narrative songs used to be wildly popular, with Tin Pan Alley churning out thousands of homiletic mini-stories. With the rise of rap and alternative rock, popular music has either parodied, twisted, or abandoned the story song.

Except for country. A classic example is "The Long Black Veil" by songwriters Danny Dill and Marijohn Wilkin, who in the 1950s pioneered what came to be known as "the Nashville Sound." William Orville "Lefty" Frizzell (1928-1975) made it into a big hit in 1959; the song rescued the Texan's sagging career and figured heavily in his decision to move to Music City.

"The Long Black Veil" is based on the real-life murder of a New Jersey priest, and tells an elemental, wonderfully succinct story. In the song, a man is accused of murder, and when the judge asks for his alibi, the suspect remains silent, "for I had been in the arms of my best friend's wife." Innocent of murder, guilty of adultery. After his execution, his lover makes repeated tearful visits to his grave, shrouded with a "long black veil" to protect her identity and grief.

LEFTY FRIZZELL Sings JIMMIE RODGERS SONGS

"MY ROUGH AND ROWDY WAYS"
"BLUE YODEL No. 2"
"BLUE YODEL No. 6"
"LULLABY YODEL"
"TRAVELIN' BLUES"
"MY OLD PAL"
"TREASURE UNTOLD"
"BRAKEMAN'S BLUES"

PRICE $1.25

PEER INTERNATIONAL CORPORATION
SOLE SELLING AGENT
SOUTHERN MUSIC PUB. CO., INC.
1619 BROADWAY NEW YORK 19, N.Y.

Lefty Frizzell and **Jimmie Rodgers**, two of country music's greatest stylists. Both had Tennessee ties: Rodgers made his first recordings in Bristol and, several decades later, Frizzell belonged to the Opry.

One of country's great stylists and innovators, Lefty could never leave a note without twisting it "four ways to Sunday," as he liked to say. He influenced just about every country singer who came after him, from the great George Jones (whom the producers almost sent home from his first recording session for sounding too much like Frizzell), to modern-day stars like Randy Travis and Dwight Yoakam.

I discovered Lefty about the time of the birth of my daughter and played him incessantly. "Always Late (With Your Kisses)" became her lullaby; she listened to it virtually every night until she was over a year old.

(continues)

My wife Jean is one of those gentle skeptics who is not quite as enthusiastic as I am about the power of country. At times she has gone so far as to suggest (blasphemy!) that Lefty's music might be a tad hokey, or that the sound of George Jones' voice is the exact definition of "corny." I have tried to persuade her that the sentimentality of country music is all just surface mush, and that there is an underlying bedrock that redeems it. I am not sure she has been convinced, but the constant dosage of Lefty has made my daughter, at least, a big fan.

This might serve her in good stead when she starts to listen to music on her own, because one of country's virtues is that it can function as a door leading to other kinds of music, from old-time to Western swing to bluegrass.

"The Long Black Veil," for example, takes its cue from traditional folk ballads that have been a staple of American music since European immigrants brought them here. Perhaps more than any other kind of contemporary popular music, country connects to the roots of American song. Other kinds of music seem increasingly and sometimes boastfully deracinated, as if they had been invented anew with each offering.

Country music is proud of its roots, and that comes across in many of the songs. What you hear when you listen to country's Golden Age troubadours — singers like Lefty, Hank Williams, Loretta Lynn, or Faron Young — is the voice of the people, sounding pure, high, and fine.

There is an egalitarian quality to country music that can be mistaken for bumpkinhood, but if attended to closely, can summon up that elusive figure, Everyman. It speaks against artifice and privilege. Country can be sentimental and willfully naïve, but at its best it can replenish a faith in the basic, all-people-created-equal ideals of democracy.

In today's Nashville, as country music gets ever more sleek, sophisticated, and commercial, some of this egalitarian quality can be obscured or, worse, rendered as just one more element in the act, like a rhinestone jacket that can be taken off after the show. When you see the stadium extravaganzas of Garth Brooks (whom some people have taken to calling "the Anti-Hank"), you have to realize you are a long way from Lefty and more than few steps toward Elton John.

But the real thing still comes along from time to time, in the voice of Willie Nelson, or when Steve Earle or Emmylou Harris or Dale Watson crank up to play. And you can always go back to the greats, to Lefty and George Jones and Ernest Tubb. When you hear it, you know it — that's pure country.

Gil Reavill is the author of *Manhattan* and *Hollywood,* both published by Compass American Guides. He also writes screenplays.

EVERY SEPTEMBER, THE HARLAN HOWARD BIRTHDAY BASH convenes somewhere in Nashville. One recent year, it took place in a giant fenced-in parking lot overlooking downtown, on the fringe of Music Row. Since the 1950s, "the Dean of Nashville songwriters" has had 4,000 different versions of his songs recorded here, including such classics as "Busted," "Heartaches by the Number," "I Fall to Pieces," "She's Gone Gone Gone," and "No Charge." (For the record, the song that he *wishes* he had written is "Bridge Over Troubled Water.")

His wife Melanie refers to the Michigan native as "a factory worker," although it once took him nine months to write a single line. Now in his seventies, he continues to use the same formula. Armed with coffee, cigarettes, felt-tip pen, and legal pad, he first scribbles down the words and then creates a melody. Howard said his writing is not as "frenzied" as it was back when he first arrived in town, too broke to open a checking account, but he maintains that his "batting average" has improved — and he became a country music hall of famer in '97.

Those who turned up to pay their respects and perform a few songs included Brooks and Dunn, Kim Carnes, Jack Clement, Lucinda Williams, Emmylou Harris, and John Hartford. In the audience were songwriters, industry people, and music lovers. While the head honchos sat up front near the stage, I stood in back and chatted with Jack Chiniski, who has driven buses for everyone from Clint Black and the Bellamy Brothers to the Dead. In short, the Howard bash was Nashville through and through: a marriage of creative genius and palm-greasing.

In the parking lot after the show, I collared songwriter Stephen Allen Davis and talked with him about the profession's demands and compromises. We sat on the hard top at stage right and almost got run over by a truck. In the interest of journalistic accuracy, I pointed out that it was a Studio Instrument Rentals truck.

"Yeah," Davis said, enjoying the digression from the standard rote questions ("where are you from," "who influenced you," etc.) "SIR is the, uh, code word for these boys."

The native Nashvillian now hangs his hat near Boulder, Colorado. In his songs, he has a knack for viewing life in an insightful if unconventional way, as is the case with "Jesus in the Back of a Cadillac," a song from his *The Light Pink Album* (1995) in which Christ is depicted "sucking down a rootbeer and a corndog."

Davis grew up listening to the blues on Nashville's WLAC and used to go to bed with the radio under his pillow. Then in 1968, when Davis was just 17, the station's legendary deejay "Hoss" Allen broke his "Take Time to Know Her," which had been recorded by soul great Percy Sledge.

Davis believes that his singing and songwriting were virtually predetermined. "Whatever I do evolved around my voice," he said. "It has a very bluesy kind of a feel to it, so anything I sing, even if it's 'Howdy Doody,' man, it's gonna sound soulful." He was heavily influenced by R&B classics like "Hit the Road, Jack," "Cool Jerk," and "Respect," as well as by the Beatles. Although country music can be soulful, it's not soul *per se,* he said.

Iron City native **Melba Montgomery** has sung duets with everyone from Gene Pitney to Charlie Louvin. George Jones describes her as a "down-to-earth, hardcore country singer." Harlan Howard wrote her biggest solo hit, "No Charge" (1974), about parental love. Courtesy of the Country Music Foundation.

"When I think of soul music, I think of Wilson Pickett, not Little Jimmy Dickens, you know? That's soulful, but not what I think of as soulful."

Davis views Nashville as a "creatively dangerous town," adding that while he enjoys writing hits and making money as much as the next guy, "I'm more into the art than I am into hit songs." Fed up with Nashville's "politics and money aspect," Davis moved West in 1991. "I find that when people ask you how you're doing here, they don't mean 'Is your life in a good place and are you in contact with a higher power' or anything like that," he said. "It's more like, 'Who's cut your song, who are you writing with, how many songs do you have on this album,' and stuff like that.

"Making money is a fine thing to do — I'm totally into that," he adds. "But when it just gets into some dumb-ass shit like a lot of the songs are, and trying to come up with the next hook that's gonna make you a lot of money . . . I mean, I like hooks, but when they're just stupid, what the hell, man! But that's part of it."

When I mentioned that Boulder is supposed to have a vibrant music scene, he replied, "I wanted to be *away* from a scene so I could do my music. Like a scene fuckin' makes me crazy. I don't want to be in a scene. I like to be by myself. I come to a scene every now and then and it's OK. Like this thing tonight, you know? It's great, I saw a lot of old friends and stuff like that. But I used to love hanging out at this shit. Now it's like, you know, I got through it and do it because I *want* to."

Notes From a Tobacco Farmer's Daughter

by Kathy Chaffin

My first memory of a country music song was a little boy's version of Hank Williams' "Hey Good Lookin'." There is no way I could ever forget it, having heard it over and over and over again.

I was probably ten years old that summer, which would have put my cousin, Doug, at the age of four. His parents were helping my family prime tobacco that day, and he was jumping up and down in an empty tobacco sled belting out the chorus. If he sang it once, he sang it a hundred times; and each time he sang it, I'd start to laugh. This usually meant a reprimand from Arizona, a tobacco-chewing, overall-wearing woman who tied tobacco leaves onto the sticks. My job as a hander was to "hand" her neat bunches of leaves as fast as I possibly could.

It was a boring job, and I usually tried to make it more exciting by daydreaming about what Arizona would look like in a dress, or by paying attention to what everybody else was doing. On this particular day it was my cousin that kept me distracted, and if I pause and remember, I can still hear those words echoing through the patch of trees where we worked. *(continues)*

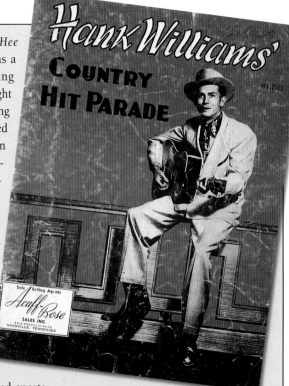

That evening I watched *Hee Haw* with my family. Even as a young girl who knew nothing about growing old, I had to fight back tears when Roy Clark sang "Yesterday." Many years passed before I heard him sing it in person at The Crosby Clambake in 1986. That time nothing could stop the tears. If Buck Owens had only been there to sing "Tall Dark Stranger," I would have been convinced I had died and gone to heaven.

My Uncle Ralph taught high school horticulture for 30 years. He loved flowers and spent hours working in the greenhouse in his back yard. He also loved sports and politics and became the first mayor of his small town. I remember Uncle Ralph as a devoted family man. He and my Aunt Doris raised two daughters and, in time, they made the inevitable transition to grandparents with two more little girls to love.

It rained on the fourth day of spring, in 1993 when my aunt and cousins were joined by relatives, friends, and my uncle's former students to bury the man they loved and admired. I left the cemetery that day regretting that I had never taken the time to get to know him better.

Two years after his death, my aunt told me something about my uncle that I never knew. He was a Randy Travis fan, and not just your everyday fan who bought tapes and went to concerts. My uncle did that and more. He once drove from bookstore to bookstore to buy a book on Travis, and my aunt recalled with a smile how excited he was when he found it. His family shared his excitement and enrolled him in the Randy Travis Fan Club. Uncle Ralph preserved the newsletters in a scrapbook that followed Travis' career.

The first page of the bulging, rust-colored scrapbook features a photograph of a young Travis with a "thank you" and an autograph in black magic marker. Nestled in the corner of the plastic cover are membership cards for Ralph Kurfees and his granddaughters, Carrie and Stacy; a ticket stub from a 1991 concert at the Charlotte Coliseum; and a pin proclaiming the wearer a member of the Randy Travis Always and Forever Fan Club.

The second page features photographs taken outside the coliseum at a 1988 Charlotte concert and a review in the next day's newspaper with the headline, "Travis Hits Home . . ." A feature article dated October 16, 1988 chronicles Travis' singing career from a local fiddler's convention at age nine to the amateur talent competition at Lib Hatcher's club that launched his career. Then a January 21, 1989 clipping lists "Deeper than the Holler" as the number one country single that week. These are followed by page after page of newspaper and magazine clippings. A niece in Florida and a sister in Pennsylvania contributed articles from out of state.

In 1992 my uncle had to start a second scrapbook to keep up with Travis' phenomenal singing successes and early acting appearances. One of the last entries before he died was a newspaper photograph of Randy Travis presenting the Country Music Hall of Fame Award to George Jones at the 1992 Country Music Association awards show. The Randy Travis scrapbooks didn't end with my uncle's life on March 21, 1993. The family he left behind continues to add to it as a tribute to the fan they loved.

FOR YEARS AFTER MY MOTHER DIED IN 1985, I'd think of what I would say to her if I could see her one more time. So many things were left unsaid. Then one night, five years after her death, I dreamed that I accompanied my critically ill grandmother to a grand hotel in the mountains where she was to make the transition to the afterlife. It was one of those dreams that are so real you wake up not convinced it was a dream. My Mama was standing out in front of the hotel when we walked up. I was so happy I broke out into song. I should tell you that I really don't sing well, but in this dream I sounded every bit as good as Kathy Mattea when I sang to my mother: "Where have you been? I'm just not myself when you're away."

I sang the chorus over and over, and woke myself up.

My daddy played country music on his truck radio when I was a little girl. I didn't pay much attention to the words. All I knew was that the songs made me feel safe. And today, they still do.

Kathy Chaffin is a journalist living in Mocksville, North Carolina.

Soul

STEVE CROPPER STARTED OUT listening to country music. He went on to write songs for some of soul's greatest singers, including Otis Redding. A few years ago, the guitarist was inducted into rock's hall of fame. To Cropper, music all boils down to "sounds," pure and simple. He describes himself as "a ballad man" — fittingly, "Unchained Melody" has always been one of his favorite songs.

Tall **Steve Cropper** and a playful **Otis Redding** (center) loom over Stax vocalists Eddie Floyd ("Knock on Wood"), Sam Moore ("Hold On! I'm Comin'"), and Arthur Conley ("Sweet Soul Music"); trumpeter Wayne Jackson holds the camera. Courtesy of Steve Cropper.

Cropper is best known as the guitar voice bending, wailing, and scratching as it propelled Booker T & the MGs — the epitome of Memphis '60s soul — through the band's funky instrumentals. "Green Onions," the group's first hit, was released in 1962, three years after Cropper graduated from high school. According to legend, "Green Onions" was a fluke: the biracial group was rehearsing at the Stax record studio and the jam session just happened to get recorded.

I asked him to analyze his staccato comping during the first few bars, just before Booker T. Jones' organ comes in. Were those identifiable

The Five Royales were a big early influence on Steve Cropper, particularly the R&B group's guitarist Lowman Pauling.

chords, or what? Chuckling, he explained that "I was really more into making *sounds* out of a guitar than I was actually *playing* one. I'm a self-taught musician. I had influences and a few lessons here and there along the way, and people showing me licks and trading licks and stuff like that. But I'm pretty much a self-taught guy."

Cropper compares his style to that of Bo Diddley, the influential rhythm-and-blues guitarist who enjoyed making sounds purely for sound's sake. "And he was big on the tremolo, which I love," Cropper said. "The song 'Bo Diddley' was one of my favorite songs when I was a kid learning to play, one of the earlier songs that I learned, and it was really just a rhythm thing."

Cropper also credits Lowman Pauling, songwriter and lead guitarist for the Five Royales (a band that used to spend time in Memphis), for a lot of his guitar licks as well as his overall style. "They were famous for 'Dedicated to the One I Love,' which is a Shirelles cover, but they had the original hit on it," he said. "Some of their other songs were 'Think' and 'Say It' and 'Monkey Hips and Rice.' I still got their albums at home and listen to them every now and then. I thought [Pauling] was great. He died a couple years ago. But he really influenced me. I got to see him live one time in Memphis, and I liked the way he mixed his rhythm with his leads. And it was always interesting to me, the way he did that.

"Nowadays, on every record, there's like three, four, maybe five different guitar parts, you know, being played on a record. When I was comin' up, there was a budget for one guitar player [laughs]. There was not enough *money* to hire five. So I had to learn how to mix rhythm with lead, until the later years of Stax, and then we actually did have a lot of records where there were two guitar players on the date. [But] it was very difficult for me for a long time to learn how to play with somebody else.

"And I got a lot of work in the '70s when I moved to L.A. I mean, when people heard that I was living there, I got call after call after call to play sessions. Well, there was always one other, or maybe sometimes two other guitar players on the date, and I'm going, 'Why did they call me if they've already got a guitar player?' Because I still didn't really know what it was to play with other guitar players. All I did was step on 'em. Because I cover all the bases."

———

I MET CROPPER AT HIS TRAVEL AGENCY IN A CONVERTED HOUSE on Nashville's Music Row; he specializes in booking musicians' tours. On his wall are framed copies of his four songs that have become million-plus sellers, and a collage of photographs taken at a "Free Soul" concert in Chicago where the MGs shared the bill with blues guitarist and fellow Stax artist Albert King, who played while smoking his briar pipe. He especially likes the collage, presented to him by Murphy Dunn, for its shot of Al Jackson Jr., the MGs' late drummer.

Cropper continues to work behind the scenes, writing songs, playing sessions, and producing. In 1994, the MGs cut *That's the Way It Should Be,* their first recording in decades, and toured with Neil Young. Now in his mid-fifties, "The Colonel" also periodically hits the road with the Blues Brothers, of which he is an original member. In Nashville, he is a member of the Northwest All-Stars, along with Billy Preston, the Rascals' Felix Cavaliere, and Grand Funk Railroad's Mark Farner.

Raised on a farm in Dora, Missouri, about 200 miles "straight up Highway 63" from Memphis, Cropper spent his formative years in nearby West Plains. Although he didn't come from a particularly musical family, a couple of his aunts played piano, and his fiddling uncle had an extra guitar that he seldom used. "I used to get it out and, you know, it had strings missing on it, but I used to like hearing the tone of it."

On Saturday nights, his family sat around the radio and listened to the *Grand Ole Opry.* When he was nine, the Opry's traveling show came through town, headlined by Minnie Pearl, Rod Brasfield, and Little Jimmy Dickens. "I remember getting to see June Carter, and I think at that time she was about 13 years old," he said. "The Carters were just kind of breaking her in and bringing her out there — which is real interesting."

West Plains was also home to Porter Wagoner and the Rhodes family, whose early TV show ran in Memphis for years. Cropper's father once told him that he remembered hearing Dusty Rhodes fiddling at pie suppers when he was just six or seven years old. "Spec Rhodes was a very famous comedian who later, I think, joined the Opry, after the Rhodes family sort of split up," Cropper said, "and Slim died, I guess in the '60s, slipped in a bathtub, busted his head. But his nieces and family, and his daughters . . . Donna sang background on the *Ralph Emery Show,* and Sandy sang with Charles Chalmers and on a lot of Memphis hits; and they were out with Liza Minelli and people like that.

"We've always kind of considered Memphis a melting pot for a lot of different kinds of music," he added, "bluegrass, Ozark music, stuff that came over from Arkansas and up the Mississippi. And Memphis just sort of being on the river there in a central location, that's where it all happened. I mean, nobody can really explain it all, but it's interesting that out of that came all these great records in the '60s. Out of the Delta, blues, farmers and all comin' in there and bringin' their influence."

When Steve was in the fourth grade, his family moved to Memphis. He remembers being "intrigued" by the black church music broadcast over WDIA. "I used to listen to that stuff every chance I got," he said.

He didn't start playing guitar until he was 14, while attending Messick High School. Like the rest of the student body, he was mesmerized by Dick Clark's dance show on TV, as well as by black rhythm and blues. Chuck Berry, Little Richard, and "even the slow stuff like the Platters," influenced Cropper's style. His favorite, though, was Bill Doggett's "Honky-Tonk," featuring guitarist Billy Butler. "An incredible record," he said. "Where I grew up, in Memphis, it was, if not *the*, it was the first one or two songs that you learned on guitar."

These days, Cropper mostly listens to contemporary music, but he still remembers all of his old favorites, such as "Annie Had a Baby" by Hank Ballard and the Midnighters, and now and then he'll give one of them a spin.

In 1967, all the MGs wrote "Slim Jenkin's Place" about a soul-food joint near the Stax studio; on the flip side, the group covered the Young Rascals' "Groovin'." Cropper left in 1971 after new management became more interested in albums than 45s.

CONSIDERING HIS ILLUSTRIOUS CREDENTIALS, talking with Cropper is a daunting proposition. Solidly built, with a beard and ponytail, he possesses a no-nonsense, almost businesslike manner. A picture in *Guitar Player* magazine made him look somewhat menacing, but in person he couldn't have been more accommodating.

While working for Stax, Cropper co-wrote with the label's soul singers, turning out such classics as "Knock on Wood" (with Eddie Floyd) and "In the Midnight Hour" (Wilson Pickett). His biggest seller is "(Sittin' On) The Dock of the Bay," a collaboration with Otis Redding. The two recorded the song days before Redding's fatal plane crash in 1967;

Cropper later added the sound of breaking waves to the beginning. At Stax, he produced the Staple Singers, Rufus Thomas, and Eddie Floyd. Since then, he has worked with a diverse range of artists, including José Feliciano, Yvonne Ellman, Tower of Power, Jeff Beck, Poco, and John Prine.

Cropper started working for Stax co-founder Jim Stewart when he was in high school. Stewart was building a studio in Brunswick, a small town northeast of Memphis. Then Stewart's sister, Estelle Axton, mortgaged her home to make a down payment "on this old theater that was gonna go out of business," Cropper said, referring to the Stax building on McLemore, "and I was involved in that. I worked with her some in the record shop, and I wound up going over there and pulling seats out of the place, you know, putting up baffles and really helped build that studio, with Chips Moman and Jim Stewart.

"And I was just a kid, and they probably didn't think I'd ever amount to anything, and probably Estelle Axton believed in me more than anybody. I just sort of worked my way on up."

In those days, Cropper wore many hats. "I've done it all," he said, laughing at the memory. "From janitor to you-name-it, you know? I mean, I was the tech copy boy at Stax, and I went and mastered the records, most of them with Scotty Moore, or some of them in New York with Tom Dowd. I would take the records to the plant, a place called Plastic Products — they were in Memphis, and then they moved [some operations] down to Mississippi.

"And I used to drive down there, put the records in the vat, you know, and quality-control those things, go down there and pick them up in three days, and get trunkloads of records, and go out and try to sell them, you know. Take them to the radio stations and try to get them played. So I do all that stuff along with playing on them, helping produce, and helping write some of them. So I was just kind of in there."

For Cropper, Memphis in the '50s was a special time in the music industry. The people who were manufacturing, distributing, and selling records "wanted to record the stuff they were selling," he remembered. Estelle Axton's Satellite record store adjacent to Stax became the nerve center. Cropper said, "People would come by and say, 'I write songs, how do I get anybody to listen to them?' Or, 'I sing, how do I get somebody to listen to me?' And she could do that."

Booker T & the MGs was an interracial group — Cropper and bassist Donald "Duck" Dunn are white, Jones and Jackson black — but they were all just "big buddies" and didn't really care what people thought. Back then, they took segregation for granted because it was a way of life and "nobody really explained it to us."

When they first met in the mid-1950s, "it was just common that black people rode in the back of the bus," he said. "I mean, there was no fuss about it, you know? It was just the way it was . . . . We were kids and very naïve, and we didn't know anything was wrong and, you know, we treated everyone equal. There was no tension or anything. That all came later, with all the marches and burnings and shootings and all that, and all of a sudden everybody went, 'Oh, wait a minute, what is this?' I think only after all of the movements did white people generally get an idea what the hell was going on."

When recording guru Jerry Wexler first heard the MGs, their music "knocked my dick in the dirt," he wrote in *Rhythm and the Blues*. Later, he brought Wilson Pickett from New York, put him in a hotel room with Cropper and a bottle of Jack Daniel's, and told them to write. The session yielded "In the Midnight Hour."

"The [Stax] rhythm section had developed a method of building ad hoc head arrangements," wrote Wexler. "Nothing was written down. I'd watch them come in the morning, hang up their coats, grab their axes, and start to play. If they didn't have a session or a song, they'd ad-lib, developing chord and rhythm patterns until something blossomed. It was effortless, easy as breathing. The feel was real, right, and tight in the pocket."

The band had formed in 1962, when Cropper was 19 or 20. After the unexpected success of "Green Onions," they quickly organized a tour. Sometimes, he recalled, when they pulled up to a motel, "they would just say, 'No,' you know? 'You guys are together, you can't do that.' So we'd go on somewhere else. And a lot of towns we'd have to stay in a black-owned motel. They didn't care, you know? They needed the money, and it was fine. And we didn't care, either. It wasn't something that bothered us, like it does a lot of people.

"Every now and then, maybe down in the South, some people would look at us a little funny, and I think whenever we would go through a few places, not to name names but . . . Alabama and stuff . . . we would be a little more cautious about how we handled situations. Sort of the old theory, 'won't start nothing, won't be nothing.' So we were on the lookout for stuff like that, but for the most part, we were fine, and there was never, that I can ever recall, any incident that caused any hardship on anybody."

After Stax was sold to Paramount in 1968, Cropper initially thought "it seemed like it was gonna be a lot of fun, there was a lot of work going on." But he soon found that whereas the early Stax had been singles-oriented, "when we got into the corporate thing, they wanted almost the same number of albums." At one point, he recalls working on seven simultaneously. Before Paramount took over, "our whole lives were built around having these big chart singles, that's all we wanted," he said. "We had a chart with a thermometer: how many singles we had sold and all that sort of stuff, you know. And we were trying to reach the eight million mark. We were all working towards that. It was just like one big happy family. It was great."

Cropper soon became frustrated with the new management approach, which translated into more studio work and fewer performances. Booker T. left Stax in 1969, and Cropper soon followed suit, starting his own label at Columbia. Out of loyalty to Stax, he agreed not to compete with his former employer. He continued to produce several Stax artists, write songs with Mack Rice ("Mustang Sally"), mix for Al Bell, and play sessions for David Porter. "So I didn't really leave the womb completely," he said.

Then his contact at Columbia quit a few months into the deal and moved to RCA, bringing Cropper. A three-year "nightmare" ensued in which the company was "more interested in me producing their artists than they were [in] promoting and selling the records of the artists that I was producing." On the bright side, he was "shuffled" out to

Los Angeles. "I really started liking that California atmosphere because there were a lot of musicians out there, and I got to be on a lot of sessions, like Ringo Starr, stuff like that," he said. "And that's when I made the decision: I want to move to California."

I asked Cropper what was expected of him at those L.A. sessions where several other guitarists were present. Was he supposed to play rhythm, lead, fills? "Well, nobody really knew," he replied with a smile. "It's sort of like, you know, just create this giant train wreck and we'll see what to do with it. And I'm not putting them down, or the producer — I think some of the producers didn't really know what to expect.

"But my style is pretty much based as much on the holes I leave as the notes I play. Well, if I'm playing with another guitar player, he's filling all my holes, you see? So it's kind of taking away from what I'm good at. And so it took me a long time to learn how to play with other musicians.

"And I have always been the type of musician that, really and truly, I listen to all the musicians, but I'm more in tune with the singer. I listen to what the singers are doing, and playing fills and weaving in around the singer, picking up where he leaves off and kind of keeping the melody going and stuff like that. And in L.A., I had to learn a different style, a different approach to that [and] not only listen to the singer, [but] everybody else, too, and what they were gonna play, and try to stay out of their way."

Cropper spent the 1980s in California and then returned to Tennessee, but not to his old Memphis haunts. This time around, he decided to try his hand at Nashville, his current home and the place he calls his "hub."

One might well wonder how one of soul's premier guitarists ended up in what is traditionally viewed as a country music town.

It happened like this.

Cropper's good friend Mentor Williams, a songwriter whose credits include Dobie Gray's "Drift Away" (one of Cropper's favorite songs) and Alabama's "When We Make Love," lived near Cropper in L.A. and occasionally came to Nashville to make demos. Cropper began spending more time in Music City — four or five months a year — and "commuting" between California and the Third Coast (one of Nashville's sobriquets).

Eventually, Williams landed him a publishing deal, "so I came in here and tried it for a while," he said.

"I tried writing country for a while, and you know, I think I can write country. With the right breaks and the right songs, I think it can happen. I haven't spent a whole lot of effort at it [but] I still write a lot. I've got songs on [blues guitarists] Jeff Healey and Robert Cray, different people. So I enjoy doing it." He doesn't, he adds, "work at it 18 hours a day like I used to."

In person, **Steve Cropper** isn't as nasty as he looks. Lately, "the Colonel" has been working in the movies, appearing in *Blues Brothers 2000* and co-writing the soundtrack to *Vampires* with fellow MG "Duck" Dunn. Courtesy of Steve Cropper.

Cropper is awed by the technical proficiency of Nashville's session players, although their fast guitar runs don't do much for him. "I've played on a lot of country sessions," he said, "but to compare myself with these country pickers here, I mean, I'm a Volkswagen compared to these Ferraris that they got on these records. I never had those sights, I never had that goal in my life, to be that good of a musician, you know? I just like making records."

Many of these "Ferraris" have told Cropper that they love Memphis soul and were influenced by it, "even though they can play rings around it," he said, chuckling. "They're very versatile. I mean, they could probably play my licks better than I can!"

On the day we talked, things were hectic at Cropper's office. Workmen were hammering away on three new studios in the basement, and *Songwriter* magazine was moving in upstairs. Through it all, the self-described "new slum lord of 16th Avenue" remained calm and congenial. He clearly enjoyed talking about his life's milestones, such as the Blues Brothers' reunion at a surprise party for Dan Akroyd that "just literally blew him away." Recently he rubbed shoulders with James Brown and ZZ Top at the Super Bowl halftime extravaganza.

Cropper has certainly covered all the bases, but now it was time to get back to business.

"I'm a happy camper, what can I say? Everything's working out real good. I still miss the old days, and I miss havin' those chart records like that; and you know, we all still miss Otis Redding. There'll never be another one like him. I kinda miss that, but you know it was a lot of work — it was just seven days a week, full bore. I'm getting too old to do that. But I like to keep my fingers in different projects. I still get offers from time to time. We'll do some more. It was fun working with the MGs and making that record, and we'll do another one."

———

NOW IN HIS FIFTIES, MABON "TEENIE" HODGES was raised on a 200-acre farm in Germantown, which has since metamorphosed into a Memphis suburb and Tennessee's 11th-largest city. On this day, Teenie was kicking back in the Peabody Hotel's lobby bar, nursing a cold and sipping a snifter of Courvoisier. Wearing a tan sleeveless vest, the photographers' kind with lots of pockets, he looked poised for a trek through the urban outback. A black leather purse was slung over his shoulder. Teenie lit the filter end of a cigarette — clogs it, he told me, to keep the fiberglass out of your lungs.

The first song Teenie remembers hearing is the old country standby, "I'll Be There (If You Ever Want Me)," which was co-written and recorded by Ray Price. He received his first songwriting credit for "I'll Take What I Want," cut by Sam & Dave and released in August 1965. But his personal theme song could just as well be "It's Nice To Go Trav'ling" ("but it's oh, so nice, to come home"), because Hodges is a dyed-in-the-wool Memphian. People say that it's hard to make a living at music in Memphis, and that musicians who want to make money go to Nashville — Memphians care more about making music for its own sake. Hodges politely disagreed with this theory.

"People are not here because they want to make music," he said. "People are here because they want to be here. It's a better place to be than Nashville, or Jackson, Tennessee, which is smaller than Memphis, [or] Los Angeles, New York, Detroit, Chicago . . . because of the — what do you call it? — the economics.

"Because I know if I only play so many days, that I can take care of my expenses, you know. Other than that, I don't see anything. My family's here is the only reason I'm here. But I've lived in different places, also. [The cost] was 10 times higher. But I still like Memphis. I like the people."

Hodges is best known as the rhythm guitarist in singer Al Green's band. Together, they wrote such classics as "Take Me to the River," "Love and Happiness," and "Here I Am (Come and Take Me)." In the '70s, Teenie was once voted second-best guitarist, after Jeff Beck, in a poll of 200 of his guitar-wielding peers. When Green became a pastor and moved into the gospel field, Hodges and three of his brothers formed the Hi Rhythm Section, named after their former record

Teenie Hodges (foreground) has supplied his guitar and songwriting talent to many soul greats, including the late O.V. (Overton Vertis) Wright of Leno, Tenn., best known for his rendition of "That's How Strong My Love Is." More recently, he has recorded with Otis Clay, Ann Peebles, and Trudy Lynn. In this shot, NBA great Earl "the Pearl" Monroe and George Clinton of Parliament/Funkadelic admire Teenie's watches. Courtesy Colin Escott/Showtime Music Archive.

label. If you saw *The Firm*, then you've heard the Hodges Brothers (at least subliminally) playing Teenie's "I Sho Do" in a bar scene. (And Bonnie Raitt included the song on *Longing in Their Hearts*.)

While Hodges likes Green's gospel music, he believes the reverend is "not bein' as bad as he could be" ("bad," here, meaning very good). He felt downright "embarrassed" for Green after hearing his duet with Bonnie Raitt on their remake of "Let's Stay Together." On the other hand, he considers the Arkansas-born singer "the most creative stylist I've ever seen." He also defended Green's conversion to religious music, which he deemed a sincere effort. Some have cynically suggested that Green's Full Gospel Tabernacle is little more than a tax shelter, but Hodges said that those who really know Rev. Green know that

Originally from Forrest City, Arkansas, soul singer **Al Green** — shown here relaxing on Beale Street — was developed by Memphis bandleader Willie Mitchell. At Hi Records, Green and Teenie Hodges co-wrote classics like "Take Me to the River" and "Love and Happiness." Green now oversees the Full Gospel Tabernacle. Photograph by Erica Lansner.

this isn't so. Even in the early days, Teenie said, Green insisted on recording at least one gospel song on every album. For a long time, Green boycotted the secular songs which brought him fame (and letters from female fans begging him never to marry), but now he covers his old songs, having decided that God and love are not necessarily incompatible.

I went to the Sunday service at Green's church, out in the boondocks south of town. I arrived several hours early and busied myself repacking the car. All of a sudden, Al Green screeched up in a shiny red sports utility vehicle and hopped out. He wore a black suit with rows of silver studs, shades, and that irrepressible, 1,000-watt smile. The church was large, and the audience comprised both regular attendees and fans from his secular days.

In his sermon, he stressed that "the wages of sin is death" (Romans 6:23) and urged his congregation to repent. "If you do anything outside of what the Book says, and outside of what God says," he intoned, "you do it *at your own risk*." Green pranced all over the church, and by the end, he had jumped up on the pulpit. He testified, and even sang a little. Although the subject was sacred rather than secular, and his vocal range a tad lower than it once was, he still had the same passion.

———

OLDER BROTHER LEROY NICKNAMED TEENIE at the ripe old age of six months, when he was relatively small but had a big stomach. "He thought I was gonna be fat, I guess," Teenie said, "but to somebody's surprise. . . ." His voice trailed off, and he laughed softly. Today's version is decidedly lean but *not* mean.

Hodges' parents came by way of Arkansas to Germantown, where Leroy and a pair of twin sisters were born. After moving to Tennessee, Mrs. Hodges added Teenie and his twin sister, and six other siblings. In all, she gave birth to a staggering four sets of twins (one child died at birth), including seven kids over one four-year stretch.

Teenie heard his first live music at Blackfish Lake, Arkansas, where he was staying with an uncle. The harmonica player, James Cotton, was in town. Only nine, Teenie wasn't permitted to go inside the club, so he watched through the window. A few weeks later, Teenie watched B.B. King play at the same place.

"I'd heard B.B.'s record, but I hadn't heard James Cotton," he said. "James was just *wonderful*, but I'd never heard of him before. 'How could he be that good?' I'm thinking. If someone is good, you should hear them on the radio. But it wasn't like that. I'd never heard James Cotton. But I think he's from West Memphis, Arkansas, right across the bridge." (Cotton actually comes from Tunica, Mississippi.)

Willie Mitchell, a Memphis bandleader, arranger and producer at Hi Records, where Green recorded his classics, told *The Downtowner* magazine he first met Teenie on a country store porch in Germantown when Hodges was 15 or 16. "I was getting some gas, and he was stroking a guitar," he said. "I thought, 'This guy's got to have some talent somewhere because nobody plays the guitar that wrong! And he's just sitting there sweating, drinking a big ol' soda, no shoes on. I put him in my car and carried him home with me. I put him in the band, and he stayed with us five years." Teenie still wears overalls to gigs, although his guitar, a black headless Steinberger, is decidedly uptown.

Mitchell's recollection of that epochal encounter prompted me to ask Teenie for his take on the old Furry Lewis line, "Memphis women don't wear no shoes":

PZ: What does that mean?

TH: It's being country.

PZ: Not like country music, right?

TH: No! Country is, like, rural, I should say. You know, out in the country is not being country-western, black, or Indian. It's just country. You lives in the country, you are considered country.

PZ: So country is not a racial thing, right?

TH: No, no . . .

PZ: It's anyone that lives in the country . . .

TH: Yeah . . .

PZ: That sounds nice. Maybe I should move to the country.

TH: [laughs] I know *I* should. I'm goin' to. . . .

Despite his casual attire, Teenie was already a professional when Mitchell "discovered" him. At just 14, Gene "Bowlegs" Miller had recruited him for a Kenny Brothers session on the Goldwax label. The trumpeter and bandleader had quite a surprise in store for Teenie. "I wasn't a bass player," Teenie recalled, "but I could play it, you know, and he had asked me to do the session, and when he came to Germantown to pick me up, he called and said he was coming. Said, 'But do you have a bass?' I said, 'For what?' He said, 'You gonna play bass.'"

Miller and Mitchell were among Hodges' biggest musical influences. At first, Mitchell doubted whether Teenie could play guitar, but a couple of years later "he hired me, on something real fluky," he said. "And then Willie set me down and taught me chords — scales, more or less. And Isaac Hayes and Marvell Thomas would drive me crazy telling me chords to play and telling me, 'Don't change your fingers.'

"And a guy named Simeo Evans and Vernon someone — both of them were from St. Louis, trombone player and a baritone player. And they just instilled into me, it doesn't take this much. But it was giving me a headache! I could take it for maybe a week, and then I would just have to say, 'I can't come tomorrow, I've got a headache,' you know, from them telling me so much. Also Tommy Lee Williams, who taught me how to count, and is on *Perfect Gentlemen,* the Hodges Brothers/Hi Rhythm album. I was 22 years old, so he was the last person to teach me."

A high school teacher named Archie Bradley provided Teenie with his only formal training. "I had an hour rest period, and I went to his classroom, and he had a vacant period for his classroom that day. For 45 minutes he taught me as much as . . . it was, like, *ten years.*"

———————

IN TEENIE'S OPINION, MARKETING IS THE KEY TO SUCCESS in the music business, which explains rap's popularity. "Anything the media feeds you, you will accept," he said. "If it's marketed, it will sell. It's that simple." Rappers have been smart enough to get their money "on top," he added. "If R&B artists could do the same, it would be no comparison to the wealth of the artists."

Hodges feels somewhat jaded by his treatment at the hands of the industry. He's still trying to collect his royalties from Cream Records, which bought Hi in 1977. To avoid the same problem, he formed his own company, Velvet Recordings of America. He owns the rights to his own music, and only seeks distribution deals. "They know better than to try and take this away from me," he said, adding that since becoming his own boss, "I've never starved, and I've made 99 percent more or less money than I make now. It doesn't make a difference. God determines my destiny, nobody else."

——————

TO HODGES, THE "SOUL" MUSIC THAT HE MADE at the Hi and Stax labels should really be called pop; it also contains elements of blues, rock, and jazz. Each of the various forms simply requires "a different technique."

It's the emphasis on melody, Hodges said, that makes Memphis music special. (As we talked, the Peabody's player piano worked through the dulcet changes of "Moonglow"!)

"In Memphis, we play with more of a melody. I mean, the music, not the singer necessarily. The music itself is saying a melody: that, if you play this song, you've got to follow this melody. Whereas certain songs you can just change all the way through, *this* song you've got to play a melody. In Memphis, people write songs with melodies. On the instruments. Each instrument has its own definite melody."

He adds, "There are only so many notes in the scale, so anything you play, it's only so many notes on any instrument. So those are the only notes you can play and nobody will ever play a note that hasn't been played, unless somebody creates something with another note on it, or some other notes — say, to create a note called Z . . . [laughs] . . . which *is* no such thing."

Hodges' favorite guitarists are the three Kings — Albert, B.B., and Freddie — as well as Albert "Ice Man" Collins, and Jimi Hendrix, who "did so much with it." Locally, he likes Thomas Bingham and Mitchell Stokes — Green's current guitarist — and from out of town, Larry McCray, and Donald Kinsey of the Kinsey Report.

Teenie loved Elvis "from the very first recording," but he suggested that, perhaps, the King gets too much credit. "Who can say who deserves it? I can't judge. As far as I'm concerned, my kings are Little Richard and Chuck Berry. The king, to me, is the one who started a fad. It's not someone who came in during the fad."

So, I asked, who started the fad?

"What's his name?" he said, snapping his fingers. "The guy killed in the plane crash."

"Buddy Holly?" I replied, a little incredulously.

"Right — Buddy Holly."

"You think he started it?"

"Buddy Holly, Chuck Berry, and Little Richard," he replied, without losing a beat. "They were the first — that *I* heard."

Jazz in Memphis

by Peter Zimmerman and Frank Stewart

Over the years, the Memphis area has produced an astonishing number of first-rate jazz players. Saxophonists George Coleman, Hank Crawford, and Frank Strozier all attended Manassas High, and other Bluff City natives include trumpeter Booker Little, clarinetist Buster Bailey, bassist Jamil Nasser, and drummer Jimmy Crawford. While many have left town for better work opportunities in New York and L.A., the local jazz scene continues to be well represented by the likes of Fred Ford, Jim Spake, Charlie Wood, and Herman Green.

Jazz is often associated with blues. The Memphis version also owes much to the local church influence, which might explain the city's pedigree of talented pianists, including Jimmy Jones, Harold Mabern, James Williams, Donald Brown, and Mulgrew Miller. Most would agree that Phineas Newborn Jr. (1931-1989), born in Whiteville, Tennessee, but raised from infancy in Memphis, was the city's greatest keyboard talent.

For instance, Gene Harris called Newborn "the greatest thing that ever happened to jazz." A shy, slight man who never said a bad thing about anybody, Phineas was influenced by Art Tatum and Bud Powell. His virtuosic style was at once cerebral and emotional. He drew from all different periods of music, from ragtime and stride to bebop and beyond, and his work reflected the whole history of jazz as well as other genres. In his rendition of Billy Strayhorn's "Lush Life," for instance, he quoted from Ravel's "Sonatine."

As for his chops, he has been described as "genuinely a two-handed pianist." (On one cut, in fact, he used only his left hand!) "Phineas possesses a beautiful touch and produces striking contrasts of upper and lower register, with fine delicate runs in the high notes backed up by a solid bass line," wrote Claude Carriere. "He also creates some breathtaking parallel lines with a two-octave gap between [his] left and right hands."

Aside from the piano, Phineas also played vibes, trumpet, tenor and baritone saxes, and French horn. His greatest albums are considered to be *Please Send Me Someone to Love* and *Harlem Blues*, both recorded in 1969 with bassist Ray Brown and drummer Elvin Jones.

I asked Newborn's stepson Frank Stewart to write the following piece:

———

I WAS SEVEN IN THE LATE 1950s when my grandmother received a letter telling us my mother had a fiancé called Phineas Newborn. The only other Phineas I had heard about was a fella named Barnum, and he ran a circus, so Phineas couldn't be but so bad. I was living in Memphis, Tennessee, where my mother and Phineas came from. The letter was a call to adventure — I was to go to New York to meet him.

I had no idea what a jazz musician was, let alone what jazz was. The only music I knew about was gospel (and that only on Sundays), R&B, and blues. R&B was on the radio, blues was all around; in Memphis you only had to walk out the door of your house to find someone with a mouth organ or an old piece of guitar.

By the time I arrived in New York, Phineas was a hot commodity. He took me on his engagements at clubs like the Vanguard, Birdland, and the Five Spot, and introduced me to Count Basie, Charlie Mingus, Roy Haynes, Paul Chambers, Oscar Pettiford, and a host of others. When Pops (Louis Armstrong) first heard bebop, he said, "They sound like they playing Chinese music." That's how I felt about Phineas' music.

I was seven and Phineas was

Although trumpet wasn't **Phineas Newborn**'s first instrument, this particular job — at Hamilton High School in 1956 — did have its perks. One of the greatest piano players in jazz history, the Whiteville native possessed the unique combination of technique, creativity, and warmth. Jim Cole/Mississippi Valley Collection.

around twenty-seven, but to me he seemed about nine: a little strange but a lot of fun. He took me swimming at 2 o'clock in the morning, to the movies to watch the same film three times in a row, to countless toy stores. He had been on the road since the age of 11; I guess I represented the childhood he never had. We sure tried to make up for lost time.

He may have acted like a child around me, but Phineas definitely wanted to be his own man. He grew tired of having others make money off his talent and tried to break his management contract and become a self-contained entity. The music industry of the time wasn't ready to let go of such a successful property; so they made it very difficult for Phineas to make a living. Our family life suffered, but no one suffered more than Phineas. This struggle was more than he could bear and led to a breakdown. He was institutionalized on many occasions, but he never stopped playing, and he recorded more than a dozen albums.

He died on the porch of his mother's house in Memphis. His influence lives on.

Frank Stewart's photographs appear in Wynton Marsalis' *Sweet Swing Blues on the Road* and Lolis Elie's *Smokestack Lightning*. He is based in Brooklyn, N.Y.

Music is in a continual state of becoming.
~Aaron Copland

New Acoustic

WHEN I CALLED EDGAR MEYER AT HIS HOME in Nashville and asked how he was doing, he pondered the question for a moment, then chuckled.

"Um . . . just on the edge," he said.

That is an apt description of just where Meyer keeps himself and his musical laboratory. He may be the finest classical bass player of our time. In fact, some musicians have theorized that he is the best of *all* time. One thing is certain: no one with a Southern accent has ever played this unwieldy instrument as encyclopedically as Meyer. And if anyone could shatter the myth of the hayseed Tennessee musician, it is Edgar Meyer.

He was raised in Oak Ridge, a small city in East Tennessee where the atomic bomb was developed. As Meyer points out, Oak Ridge is no hick town, boasting more PhD's per capita than any other place in the country. Growing up in this think-tank environment, Meyer's music became informed by his early fascination with mathematics.

His bass-playing father first tried his son out on the violin, starting him at the ripe old age of four. "I had actually been wanting to play the bass since I was two or three," Meyer told *Strings* magazine. "I hated the violin when [my dad] started me on it." He finally switched to bass when he was five. These days, the violin is his favorite instrument, but at that point, he told me, he wanted to be exactly like his father.

As a youngster, Meyer devoured jazz music, listening to the greats for hours on end. His father, who had once played with the big bands, said that when they brought baby Edgar home from the hospital, a Count Basie record was spinning on the turntable. Later on, Meyer's taste became more eclectic, including such singers as James Taylor, Stevie Wonder and Luciano Pavarotti. Like his friend Mark O'Connor, who follows later in this chapter, he has also drawn inspiration from the Indian violinist Lakshminorayana Shankar. Formally, he studied at Indiana University with the bassist Stuart Sankey.

What makes Meyer unique is not just his technical prowess but his ability to play in a variety of musical settings. Although he has a classical background, he has chosen to dabble in jazz and bluegrass. For a time, he played on some Nashville country sessions but ultimately decided that he preferred a longer format than the customary three or four minutes. In addition, although he likes drums, he prefers not to work with them.

*I have often heard
people speak of the
mannerisms of
musicians as
affectations adopted
for mere effect; in
some cases this may
be so; but a true artist
can no more play
upon the piano or
violin without putting
his whole body in
accord with the
emotions he is striving
to express than a
swallow can fly
without being
graceful.*

~ James Weldon
Johnson

Classically trained bassist and composer **Edgar Meyer** of Oak Ridge delves into many other styles, including bluegrass and jazz. His recent *Uncommon Ritual* has been described as "American chamber music." Photo by Jim McGuire, courtesy of Sony Music Corporation.

"Most drum instruments overlap the bass very severely in terms of the frequency content," he said. "So what ends up happening is the bass becomes an extension of the drums. Which is the way that a lot of music works, and that's wonderful, but it's not necessarily the way that I want to use the instrument most of the time."

Meyer said that, aesthetically, he has spent over half his life (he is in his thirties) within the confines of classical music, a genre that for the most part does not use drums. There is percussion in the orchestra (and modern pieces are often written with it in mind), but the heart and soul of what most people call classical music are compositions from the 17th, 18th, and 19th centuries, most of which do not employ the drum. That music — the older, classical mode — is the sound that he says he carries in his head.

Meyer believes that what most people identify with, and are moved by, is the emotional sound of the drum. From his viewpoint, most people, when listening to non-pitched instruments like drums, respond to rhythm only and not texture. Although difficult, he said, it would be nice to try and accomplish what drummers can do — without using drums.

I mentioned to Meyer that I had once seen Arthur Taylor, the great jazz drummer, play an extended and quite melodic solo on "The Man I Love." "By the same token, I can make the bass sound like a drum," he replied. "It turns into a pretty limited use of the instrument, but it's fun to aspire in that direction."

His particular bass, which is slightly smaller than most, was built by Giovanni Batista Gabrielli in 1769. Meyer's father had admired it before Edgar was born, at which time it was not for sale. Meyer bought it when he was 23. He has spent years developing what is regarded as near-perfect intonation, not an easy task on a six-foot, 35-pound "monster" (as one 19th-century composer described the standup bass). The four 42-inch strings each hold some 50 pounds of tension, requiring a considerable amount of strength.

Meyer is regarded as particularly adept in his bowing technique, which he displayed on Kathy Mattea's "Where Have You Been," voted the Country Music Association's song of the year in 1990. He has also worked with the likes of Vince Gill, Lyle Lovett, and Mary-Chapin Carpenter. However, he has never quite been able to find a meaningful niche for himself in country music. "I think the only satisfactory role for someone in my frequency range in that music is a pretty conventional one," he said. "Of course, I was called to do a lot of projects and be the novelty guy, but that's what I was — a novelty guy."

Meyer feels that it is hard to divide music into clean-cut genres in the same way that people might trace their genealogical lineage. Such an approach "holds some water, but it's leaky," he said. In his own music, for instance, some influences — such as mathematics and nature — do not come from any particular musical place. Rather, he sees musical inspiration as an infinitely complex process that cannot be fully analyzed and set down.

Meyer said that being a musical chameleon is not difficult per se, adding, "It's not the genre-skipping as much as the repertoire-skipping, so if it was only one classical program and one . . . nonclassical program, going back and forth wouldn't be too hard." What *would* be difficult, he explained, would be to do his own classical concerto one night, then a duo program with progressive jazz banjoist Béla Fleck, followed by a trio with bluegrass-influenced musicians like Jerry Douglas and Russ Barenburg. That would be a difficult scenario, if for no other reason than the sheer number of programs he would have to lug around in his head.

His fundamental approach to "repertoire-skipping" is to be consistent musically. As Meyer puts it, he doesn't try to be classical Edgar and bluegrass Edgar: "I keep the same values, and a lot of the same ways of playing." He bridged this gap on *Appalachia Waltz,* a best-selling record (labeled classical) on which he collaborated with cellist Yo-Yo Ma and O'Connor. His latest, *Uncommon Ritual,* features Fleck and Mike Marshall on mandolin.

My own first exposure to Meyer's playing was accidental. I saw him play on the *Lonesome Pine Special,* a TV show in Kentucky on which he shared the bill with Ray Brown and Victor Wooten (see pp.154-155). To my surprise, Meyer was more than holding his own with this master of the jazz bass. During the astonishing finale, the two men fingered the notes on each other's bass strings while continuing to pluck their own.

Later, a friend played me some cuts from Edgar's out-of-print MCA recordings. On "Strollin' (With My Moose)," Meyer walks his bass and overdubs himself on synthesizer, then takes a funky bowed solo in the upper registers, climaxing with a difficult run of high notes. Next came his version of Henri Wienawski's "Caprice in A Minor," on which he shows his arco technique to furious effect — yet playing in a completely different style.

Like Meyer, **Jimmy Blanton** (1918-1942) came from East Tennessee. Duke Ellington hired him on the spot after band members heard him at an after-hours club in St. Louis; two years later, at age 23, he died from tuberculosis. Blanton revolutionized the jazz bass by playing horn-like melodic lines with incredible facility, in addition to supplying rhythm. Courtesy of the New York Public Library.

Sometimes Meyer's on-stage dramatic flair has raised eyebrows. A reporter from *The Wall Street Journal*, for instance, noted his "free-wheeling movements (including occasional Elvis-style pelvic thrusts)." Meyer himself downplays the significance of his body language. When I mentioned that I had seen him play a program at Lincoln Center — he is a member of its Chamber Music Society — alongside two other bassists and that they looked stiff and starchy compared to his more animated movements, he cautioned not to put too much stock in the visual aspect of his performances. "I mean, it's fun to watch people, but the big thing is how they *sound*," he said. "I used to move around a lot more. More often than not, the players that I really love don't move a lot."

Meyer considers himself part of an extended "family" of musicians who modify traditional string band music, casting it in a more progressive mold and adding eclectic influences. Among its members are Mark O'Connor and Jerry Douglas, who plays the Dobro, a brand of resonator guitar; the mandolinist Sam Bush, and violinist Darol Anger, known for his work with the Turtle Island String Quartet. "Traditional instruments played in an uptown fashion," is how banjo player Bill Keith describes new acoustic, adding that its practitioners, like those in jazz, tend to use more minor, augmented, and diminished chords.

The music has been given several names. Anger came up with "newgrass," a takeoff on bluegrass which has gained common parlance. However, Meyer said that O'Connor, for one, "would jump to the other side of the road" if that term were applied to his music, since he sees his roots as being in old-time and not bluegrass. Now there is even a band called Psychograss, led by Nashville-based guitar virtuoso David Grier.

Trying to define what makes it "acoustic" (or "new," for that matter) is problematic, according to Meyer. "Do you call Jerry and me acoustic if we plug in when we play?" he asked. Even electric music usually depends on acoustic drums, he said, and even an acoustic musician like himself also creates purely electronic music in his home studio using computers and other high-tech equipment.

"By the time you record acoustic music," he observed, "you're heavily invested electronically. For the convenience of discussion, we'll just say [it's] music that can be done in its best form with just the instruments in the room. With [the band] Strength in Numbers, that was always the case. We would always do these outdoor gigs where we were loud as hell, but the very best way to hear the band was in a small room — I mean, like a living room. So I would look at that as an acoustic band."

Meyer feels that the sound produced by acoustic instruments is more complicated and "unmanageable," yet at the same time more pleasing, than the sound of electric instruments.

As for naming names, he thinks that the practice of dividing music into genres can be useful to a certain extent. "There's no denying that when you really take a couple of steps back and get an overview, you can see some rough divisions. But they start to fade in the more detail you look at things. And ultimately there's a lot of blurring [and] a lot of . . . things that don't neatly fit. And in fact, the more detailed you look, I would actually say that not very many things fit very neatly."

Would musicians prefer not to be categorized at all?

"I would say it's not really that one would aspire one way or the other. I mean, I *personally* — outside of just being able to exist professionally — I really don't *care*."

I asked Edgar Meyer for his take on the future of acoustic music and got an earful:

"One of things that happens in music, as I perceive it, [is that] people try to look for what the next thing is, or the superior thing, or what the cool thing is. [But] it's almost never like that. Usually in music you have 15 things coexisting and they tend to coexist a hundred years later. [Trumpeter] Wynton Marsalis may try to redefine what jazz is, and try to create a pure, unbroken thing straight from New Orleans — and this is only meant with great respect for him because he's accomplishing a lot of great things — but, it's not that simple. And, you know, his disregard of, for instance, all the white guys in the '70s — Chick Corea, John McLaughlin, and the whole bit — isn't going to make them go away. They still are musicians of equal stature to anyone that Wynton is placing up on a much higher pedestal.

"And so what's gonna happen [is] there's a perception now that jazz has been narrowly defined and we now know what it is. I would say that [in] 20 or 30 years we'll be back to the same old mess. What I'm saying is, there's gonna be acoustic music, there's gonna be electric music, there's gonna be everything in between, and they're both gonna keep going *just* fine.

"And if nothing else, just as a historical curiosity it would go on for a damn long time, but there's such an interest, for instance, in classical music. You know, there are fifteen different ways to do things, and one of the things now is, if you play music from the 15th, 16th century, you try to do it on exactly the instruments that they did it on and exactly the same way.

"So if there's any of that kind of interest ever, you know, there's many lifetimes worth of acoustic music that people will study just in retrospect and will continue to play just in that way. So . . . music is not like telephones and TVs where you throw out the old one because the new one's better. You're gonna keep the old one *and* the new one. And they'll both be there."

UNOSTENTATIOUSLY BUT CONFIDENTLY, JERRY DOUGLAS PLAYS the Dobro, a guitar with a vibrating disk mounted inside the body under the bridge. His instrument lends itself to bending notes and using a slide, he said, which gives it more of a bluesy, "vocal quality" than conventional guitars.

It wouldn't be a stretch to compare his blistering speed and accuracy while working through the changes of a country song like "If You've Got the Money, Honey" to, say, jazz pianist Oscar Peterson's rendition of "On Green Dolphin Street." Watching Douglas on stage, one wonders how a human being can possibly move his fingers so quickly, much less conceive such a torrent of improvisation — and then nail the notes so flawlessly and with such beauty.

The answer is practice. (*continues on page 158*)

Victor Wooten and Alison Brown

by Peter Zimmerman

Victor Wooten grew up in a Virginia military family. He started playing bass at age three and opened for Curtis Mayfield and War a couple of years later. Alison Brown's parents are West Coast lawyers, and she matriculated from Harvard and UCLA before deciding to become a full-time banjo picker. She has formed a "contemporary folk" label, Compass Records, which released Wooten's solo bass project, *A Show of Hands*, and recently, *What Did He Say?* Although they come from different backgrounds, Wooten and Brown agree about the importance of diversity in music, and both fuse different kinds of music into their own special hybrids.

Vic Wooten doesn't necessarily consider himself a new acoustic musician since, he says, "I play mostly electric stuff," although he does get a chance to play with some of the people who fall under that label, including Meyer, Douglas, and O'Connor. Nor is he a jazz musician, as music magazine pollsters have pigeonholed him due to his mostly instrumental collaborations with Béla Fleck's band. Victor's brother Roy, aka "Future Man," is also a Flecktone.

"I wouldn't say that I don't like labels," he said between sips of fresh orange juice, "but as soon as you call it something then it's in that box, and I try to get outside of that box. To me it's all just music — just like we're all people."

Conversely, when music is labeled, "people may not approach it as honestly," he said. If he had to label his own music, he would prefer to call it "fusion," not in the '70s sense, but in that he likes "to fuse a lot of musics together."

Since all musicians use the same 12 notes, there is nothing new under the sun. "What difference does it make which music came first?" he asked. "It's almost like asking which race showed up first. Everything that's here is as important as the rest. The fact that it's here shows that it's important, to me . . . But I think all the different styles of music come from each other. It's a circle, rather than a line with a circle and an end."

When we spoke, Victor was running late for a sound check at Tramps in New York, where he and his wife live when they're not in Nashville. He wore a Clifford Brown Jazz Festival shirt, named for the great jazz trumpeter. He described Nashville as a low-key, safe, inexpensive, and relatively friendly place.

As a black living in a "white-bread" town, Wooten feels that he has experienced a certain degree of racial discrimination, but no more than elsewhere. "Prejudice nowadays," he said, "is not so much on the level of the Ku Klux Klan anymore — the original boys in the hood, you could call them — it's an underground kind of thing."

Despite Nashville's reputation as a country music town, he views it as a musically diverse place, hosting everyone from rappers Count Bass-D and rocker Peter Frampton, to soul singer Jonelle Mosser, whom he started out with when he first moved to Music City in 1988. He points out that Nashville is the home of the Fisk Jubilee Singers and of black harmonica player DeFord Bailey — an early Opry star who is curiously absent from country's hall of fame.

"There's all kinds of music in Nashville," he said. "I just see the very big possibilities of growth, and that excites me — that's why I'm glad that I'm there. It's gotta explode one day."

I told him about my encounter with blues guitarist Larry Lee, who would rather grow tomatoes than cut records. He replied:

"Most of us would consider 'on the wall' working a job that we hate, going there every day, but making enough money to have our nice plush apartment. This guy's just living simply, playing music. No one knows who he is, he just plays for the sheer enjoyment of playing and he loves to grow tomatoes. To me, that's as 'on the wall' as you can get. It can happen.

"Make the kind of music that you want to make, and if it sells, that's an added bonus. What's most important to me is being able to do what I love to do."

———

"When I write tunes I like to come up with a melody that I hope is going to be somewhat memorable," Alison Brown said, "that you can maybe walk away from it and have it in your head."

So when one critic described her music as easy listening, she didn't object. "It's probably ridiculous to say it, but I kind of like some easy listening music, and I think that the reason that I do is that I like melodic music," Brown said.

"And I think that that comes from my bluegrass background because, when you

(continues)

think about it, bluegrass music is all melody and not a lot of rhythmic variation. I mean, everything is either a two-beat or a four-beat, or a three occasionally, but the thing that really distinguishes bluegrass tunes is the melody more than rhythm.

"And so I find when I write, I tend to go for melodies just because I like them, and easy listening is obviously very melodic, too. So looking on the bright side of that comment, I mean, I can see what he means."

When Brown was six, she was not opening for Curtis Mayfield. She spent her teen years near San Diego, where her parents are attorneys. As a child she learned guitar; and it wasn't until two years later later that she switched to the five-string. Meanwhile, Brown attended Harvard, earned her MBA at UCLA, and worked for Smith Barney for two years.

But underwriting sewer bond issues bored her, and those melodies just wouldn't give her any peace. When the market crashed in 1987, she gave up on investment banking and spent six months writing songs. Then lightning struck in the form of fiddler Alison Krauss calling out of the blue and inviting her to join Union Station. She spent three years with Krauss, during which time she recorded her own, Grammy-nominated *Simple Pleasures,* followed by *Twilight Motel* and the eclectic, world music-inspired *Look Left* and *Quartet,* which sound more like jazz than bluegrass. Her most recent effort, *Out of the Blue,* ventures into samba and bossa nova.

Since no one quite knows how to market Brown, she has ended up in the new acoustic camp.

"A lot of the people in the field sort of start with a bluegrass background," she said, "but then look to other influences, or maybe, you know, just other things that they were exposed to growing up."

"I mean, I didn't grow up in Tennessee, but growing up in Connecticut and mostly in California, I heard a lot of different kinds of music and I think that that just sort of rubs off on you. So when I started to write music, I found out that it didn't come out as, you know, Earl Scruggs banjo tunes, but had other aspects to it as well — which all fit within new acoustic music — jazz and pop influences."

Brown said she has been particularly influenced by Tony Trischka, dubbed "the Nietzsche of the banjo," whom she saw when she was seven. Her other influences include mandolinist David Grisman, mainstream jazz players like Cannonball Adderly, Bill Evans, and Wes Montgomery, and the "sex jazz" records of Lee Ritenour and Nathan East.

Like Wooten's, her music is instrumental. "It never occurred to me that music needed to have words," she said. She is heartened by the emergence of female bluegrassers, such as Lynn Morris and Laurie Lewis. She is forever experimenting with ways to make her flathead 1938 Gibson Mastertone sound mellower.

Unlike the guitar (and similar to the drum), the banjo has 100 moveable parts, including various brackets, bolts, rods, and bars inside the neck and tailpiece. "I like to tinker with the sound of the instrument," she said.

Brown's heavy-duty academic credentials make her something of an anomaly in the country music world, but she said that most people are curious rather than resentful. Compass currently has 15 musicians on its roster, and about twice as many releases.

"I've learned way more about the record business than I ever really thought I would, or probably that I ever should know to be an artist," she said. "I mean, you really learn the underside of the business and why contracts are written the way they are and how record companies operate. Sometimes it makes you want to move to the woods.

"But definitely as a result of that I'm much better able to fend for myself than your average Joe. I try to share that information with other artists so they can create situations for themselves that are as favorable as possible."

Douglas took up the mandolin at the advanced age of five and a couple of years later discovered the guitar. But it was a *Grand Ole Opry* package show in Youngstown (near his hometown of Warren, Ohio) that turned out to be what he calls the "pivot point" in his musical career. That was the first time he heard Flatt & Scruggs, and he remembers being "turned on" by the sound of Uncle Josh Graves, the band's famous Dobro player. He proceeded to buy one and learn how to play it. Today, in his thirties, Douglas has practically cornered the market on Nashville Dobro. When you need Dobro, call Jerry. Like Edgar Meyer, he is capable of playing in a wide variety of styles, although he is steeped in bluegrass.

I spoke with Douglas at Bristol's Paramount Theater about an hour before he was due to perform solo. We smoked cigarettes by the back door while he compared the Dobro with its kissing cousin, the National steel guitar. Both were developed in the 1920s by the Dopyeras, five brothers originally from Czechoslovakia. Although both were intended for Hawaiian music, then in vogue, country musicians soon adopted the Dobro, while Delta bluesmen picked up the National steel.

DOUGLAS WAS VIRTUALLY WEANED ON BLUEGRASS. His parents were originally West Virginians; and they moved to Ohio in the early 1950s so that his father could work in the steel mills instead of the coal mines. His father's band, the West Virginia Travelers, got its name "because everybody in the band was in the same boat as him and moved from West Virginia to find work."

Growing up in the '60s, Douglas listened to the Beatles, the Byrds, and the Stones, and he noticed how these rock bands had borrowed harmonies from earlier country acts such as the Everly Brothers and the Louvins.

While in high school, Douglas took a summer off and moved to Washington D.C. to play with the Country Gentlemen, along with Doyle Lawson. A year later, he moved to Lexington, Kentucky, to work in banjo player J.D. Crowe's band, along with guitarists Ricky Skaggs and Tony Rice.

Three years later, he relocated to Nashville and joined Buck White and His Down Home Folks, now called the Whites. Due to his precocious talent, Douglas arrived in Music City with a job already lined up.

"I moved to Nashville with a job, which is rare," he admitted. "People come there wanting to be a country music star, and some of them make it and some of them wash dishes. Some of them do both."

But Douglas has spent precious little time washing dishes. After working with the Whites for eight years, he turned his attention to making records full-time. Since he is regarded as the most accomplished Dobro player around, he can pick and choose whom he works with. He has put out several of his own records and a stunning collaboration with Edgar Meyer and guitarist Russ Barenburg called *Skip, Hop & Wobble*. He also produces other artists, including the Irish-born singer Maura O'Connell. "I'm just juggling a whole lot of things right now, see what wins out," he said matter-of-factly.

In his opinion, country music has been going through a slick commercial phase, just as it did in the '60s. The same musicians play on everybody's records and the resulting sound has become somewhat "formulaic," he said. This commercial trend subsided during the traditionalist movement of the early '80s and, in turn, the music "covered a broader spectrum."

"But, you know, it's great," he added, choosing not to dwell on the negative. "Different groups of players pull different things out of each other. You try to mimic each other in a way. You try to have some common thread running through, taken from each other — the musicians, I'm talking about — in the room."

Douglas said he would be hard-pressed to name his favorite song, but he tends to like those with strong melodies. "I'm a melody player," he said. "I play a lot of melody and work from the melody when I play. I'm bound to that."

So how, I asked, would you describe your own music?

"Well, I don't know," he said a bit reluctantly. "I'm basically a blues, country blues, bluegrass, punk, disco player." He laughed, and then, on a serious note, added, "I'm an acoustic musician. That's a pretty broad range of music, but I prefer acoustic, playing acoustic."

SEATTLE-BORN FIDDLER MARK O'CONNOR WASN'T CONTENT to become a legend in his own time; instead, he managed to become one even *before* his time. Still a few years shy of 40, O'Connor has already played on hundreds of Nashville record sessions. At age 12, he won the junior division of the National Old-Time Fiddling Championship (held in Weiser, Idaho). By the time he was 22, he had won the competition's open four times and opted to "retire," as his label's press release delicately puts it. However, his winning streak stretches back even farther: he won his first contest, a classical/flamenco guitar competition at the University of Washington, at 10.

I had known about O'Connor's prowess for a few years. (Once I gave a tape of his New Nashville Cats to my mother, but new acoustic wasn't exactly her cup of tea — Chet Atkins and the Rolling Stones are more to her liking.) Then on a visit to Nashville, I went to see Alison Krauss in concert at the refurbished Ryman Auditorium. Since I'm Magic Johnson's height and the regular seat was too cramped, I asked the usher to reseat me and moved to a portable folding chair behind the balcony. By my side sat a man whose face looked familiar, but I couldn't place him. I noticed that, although he appeared to be concentrating intensely, he wasn't tapping his feet. This struck me as somewhat odd, because the repertoire was upbeat bluegrass and the beat infectious.

During the intermission, some of the audience approached the stranger to say hello and ask for autographs. I finally realized he was Mark O'Connor, only not wearing his trademark fedora.

I introduced myself and a month or so later caught up with O'Connor and his PR man Ray Crabtree in Nashville. We met at a macrobiotic eatery called Slice of Life on the cusp of Nashville's Music Row. In between bites, he held forth with authority and enthusiasm on a wide range of subjects, all at least tangential to music.

In new acoustic music, traditional instruments are played in an uptown fashion. "When I first came on the scene, they ran," says fiddler **Mark O'Connor**, who moved to Nashville from Seattle. "But I convinced them. I said, 'Man, give this sound a chance and people will like it.'" Photograph by Tim Campbell.

He spoke animatedly about Bach and Paganini, new age and jazz, and the fringe elements of commercial country, which once served as his bread and butter. O'Connor is not particularly fond of categorizing music. "I try to break down label barriers," he said. Indeed, he does appear to transcend them, synthesizing traditional musical forms with modern ones, from pre-Celtic to fusion and beyond.

Although America is a relatively young country, it is O'Connor's opinion that it has spawned more different types of traditional music than any other country in the world. Further, he noted that we call the people who pioneered these forms "traditionalists" even though, ironically, they were considered innovators in their own time. The late John Coltrane's music is labeled "mainstream" today, for instance. Back in the late 1950s and '60s, "he was so forward-looking he was freaking everybody out," O'Connor said, until people finally "accepted him as, like, God, you know, of the saxophone."

Likewise, he said, "you probably figured Bill Monroe as a traditionalist. Well, let me tell you, when he first came on the scene, he turned some heads! [In the] 1930s, they were going, 'What in the heck is that, he's got accordion and banjo and this high singing and this three-part harmony and those solos that were slightly more virtuosic than before.' And then you think about Bob Wills. Well, he's traditional country, but he actually fused hillbilly music and jazz together, something unheard of! I mean, *now* we consider that our *tradition*."

On the difference between violin and fiddle, O'Connor maintained that they are essentially one and the same. Fiddle is simply a slang word for violin, "like calling a guitar an ax," he said. "There are some stylistic differences that require adjustments in technique, as in all styles of music. But functionally speaking, it's the same."

O'Connor's fiddle sound has sometimes been described as "contemporary," an adjective which he dismisses as misleading as "traditional." Regarding Nashville producers like Chet Atkins, Owen Bradley, and Jimmy Bowen — all accused of excising country music's hillbilly roots and thereby homogenizing it — O'Connor argued that Atkins and Bradley are themselves from East Tennessee, where hillbilly music originated. (Bradley, who died in early 1998, actually came from Westmoreland, in Middle Tennessee.)

"Now, Chet, he *loves* fiddle music," he said. "He is just adamant about fiddle music. But he took the fiddle off of country records and added soupy strings, because they thought they could get more radio programming. What you're talking about is the commercialization of a musical art form, and to be honest with you, I disagree with a lot of it.

"If you want to blame the commercialization of Nashville music, you can start with the radio. They're demanding it, and what they want turns the whole music scene."

In terms of his own recordings, O'Connor refuses to pander to radio. Take his CD titled *Heroes,* which he made primarily "for musicians and music fans," hoping that they would be "emotionally moved by it." Beaming, he notes that there wasn't a single bad review out of a stack three inches high. "I don't think that's probably ever happened in the history of music; and so, it's all downhill from here," he jokes. "That was like the pinnacle."

Heroes typifies O'Connor's syncretic approach to music. It is a tribute to O'Connor's favorite fiddlers, the ones who influenced his development as an artist. He tracked them all down and brought them into various studios across the country. You can hear his fiddle in the right speaker and his mentors' in the left. A stickler for detail, O'Connor wrote his own liner notes, explaining the significance of each artist and how they personally affected him.

On one track, L. Shankar, who toured with John McLaughlin's group Shakti, plays his own invention, an electric, ten-string double violin. Stéphane Grappelli jammed with O'Connor on Fats Waller's "Ain't Misbehavin'" — which the jazz stride pianist taught Grappelli back in 1939 — and Charlie Daniels, whom O'Connor admires for his "attitude," participated on "The Devil Comes Back to Georgia," featuring cameos by Johnny Cash and Marty Stuart. (A music video of the latter showed up on "Beavis and Butthead," O'Connor noted with amusement, and went to number two on VH-1.) O'Connor also pairs up with Jean-Luc Ponty (fusion), Doug Kershaw (Cajun), and a range of country fiddlers, from Texas Shorty and Benny Thomasson to Kenny Baker.

Although Mark O'Connor hails from the Northwest rather than the South and didn't grow up in a musical family, the rest of his background is decidedly country. His father was a construction worker, and his mother, a housewife, "spent every available cent on music and records for us," he once told *People.* "We had a stereo system," he added, "but my parents didn't have a bed. They slept on boxes."

Born in 1961, he took up classical guitar at age three and by 11 had added violin, banjo, and flamenco guitar to his skills. When he was 12, O'Connor's career went into overdrive. After hearing him practice, country legend Roy Acuff, himself a fiddler, promptly thrust him onto the Opry stage.

"That was a big, big night for me," O'Connor said. "The following Monday I made my first album. They told me I could have anybody in Nashville play on it. So I just picked two of my favorite players out of the hat. And they got them." (For trivia buffs, he chose Norman Blake and Charlie Collins, one of Acuff's Smoky Mountain Boys.)

While he could hardly be described as a Nashville booster, at times he feels compelled to defend what has become his hometown for the past 15 years. Nashville has a lot more to offer than just commercial country music, he maintains, citing pop's Amy Grant, gospel's Michael W. Smith, and electric bassist Victor Wooten as examples of its diversity.

Roy Acuff (1902-1992), at the microphone, gave Mark O'Connor his first leg up at the Opry. Pictured with his band in the mid-1930s, Acuff grew up north of Knoxville in Maynardville — as did honky-tonk singer Carl Smith ("Hey, Joe"). From the left, "Brother" Oswald Kirby, Jess Easterday, Acuff, Rachel Veach, and Lonnie "Pap" Wilson. Courtesy of Les Leverett.

Like New York and Hollywood, the nation's other major recording centers, Music City is often maligned as little more than a commercial hit factory, while some of its greatest assets exist in obscurity. "Never lose sight," O'Connor said, "that in L.A., man, [Jascha] Heifetz was teaching violin there! You don't immediately think about that when you talk

about the L.A. music scene, but that's a *scene* — that's incredible! Same with New York, same with Nashville."

He admits, however, that like many musicians who come to Nashville, he knew full well that it offered professional opportunities. The commercial gigs helped him pay the rent and bought time to work on his own personal music, his "artistry."

These days O'Connor, whose ideas were once scorned by local music industry, has practically — but not quite — become part of the establishment. In addition to touring, he teaches at Vanderbilt University's Blair School of Music, and serves on the advisory board of the Nashville Community Music School, which offers fifty-cent music lessons to underprivileged young people (jazz bassist Smith taught at Tennessee State in Nashville). He composed music for a children's video version of *Johnny Appleseed*. For years, major country artists like Randy Travis have recruited him to play on their albums. Now he has become so busy that he often must turn down work in order to have time to pursue his own projects.

Things have not always been so good. Initially, Nashville was fairly reluctant to have its boat rocked. "I tell ya," O'Connor said, "I think it's really unbelievable that an alternative-type musician like me can make that big of an impact in that commercial mainstream world. When I first came on the scene, I mean, they *ran,* and they were really scared. But I convinced them. I said, 'Man, give this sound a chance and people will like it.' "

Every summer, Mark O'Connor leads a weeklong fiddle camp located along the banks of the meandering Harpeth River, a half hour's drive west of Nashville. Aside from fiddling, the only distractions in this rustic, sparsely populated area are some lonely ceremonial Indian mounds that predate DeSoto's sighting of the Mississippi. One recent year, 153 fiddlers attended, arriving from 35 states and six foreign countries.

At the time we talked, O'Connor was excited about the upcoming camp, headlined by fiddlers from Mexico, Morocco, and Norway. Past guests have included Danish violinist Svend Asmussen and Claude "Fiddler" Williams, who played with Count Basie and Nat King Cole (not to mention jamming with a seven-year-old Charlie Parker). "In 1936, he was voted guitar player of the year by the *Down Beat* jazz readers' poll, but he doubled on violin," O'Connor said. "He's the last survivor of that era — a swing violin player, living in America, a walking legend and history book from Kansas City."

When O'Connor started teaching at Vanderbilt, the school's dean, Mark Wait, was quoted as saying, "Blair shouldn't be limiting itself to the strictly defined classical tradition. We need to make music schools relevant to the world in which our students live." In his class, O'Connor has opted to focus on playing by ear, and downplays the importance of reading music. "We'll have some theory," he told *The Tennessean,* "but I'm bent on having fun with music. I'm not going to take away from their more serious studies, but if the students want to get serious, I'll get as serious as they want."

This, coming from the fiddler who, according to *Strings* magazine, "set the technical standard" at a Carnegie Hall concert with Itzhak Perlman, Isaac Stern and Midori — three of the world's greatest living classical violinists!

O'Connor laments the dearth of academic settings in the United States for studying traditional fiddling. Jazz has been a music school staple for decades, he points out. Country music's "ambassadors" have been remiss in teaching their art, having concerned themselves with making hit records and "appealing to the masses" over the radio. He finds it remarkable that a traditional music curriculum hasn't been developed in Nashville, which he dubbed "Fiddle Central." He asks: "How in the world do we expect to train musicians from nonmusical families about this music?"

Part of the problem lies in the fact that, in previous generations, fiddlers were often born into musical families and learned their trade from a relative. This practice, however, is gradually changing, O'Connor said. "For the first time, at my fiddle camp and now at my class at Vanderbilt, I'm seeing yuppie moms and dads bringing their little kids for an alternative in music learning. Real exciting, I think."

INSTEAD OF VIEWING MUSIC AS SO MANY MONOLITHIC GENRES, O'Connor believes musicians are a sum of their various cultural influences and experiences. In bluegrass, for example, there is a pronounced blues strain, both in the bass lines and in many of the chord progressions, while the fiddling is rooted in the Scots-Irish tradition.

"The Irish and Scots had their own form of blues called the 'air,' their own sad air, which was a music that didn't have any metronomic time," O'Connor added. "It was just a beautiful plaintive melody, played with a variety of expression according to the soloist on any given performance."

He still dreams about the Shetland Islands, where he attended a fiddle festival in the late 1980s. A musicologist named Tom Anderson showed him some fiddle tunes that had been composed more than 500 years ago and written in the old quarter-tone scale. "On the fiddle, of course, you can play them because of the fretless finger board," O'Connor said.

Anderson, who died a few years ago, feared that this old music would be lost to posterity: "He had the capacity to realize that if he went to school and learned how to write down the music, he would save it. And he did."

Quiet yet headstrong, the late **Bill Monroe** possessed more than a little testosterone, and was known for refusing to eat crow, particularly at the hands of the fairer sex (Wanda Huff, for example, once accused him of striking her with a Bible). After a bout with cancer in the 1970s, he turned to religion but seldom proselytized. Music, not money motivated him. "We're here to help each other," the Kentucky native once told a fellow musician. Fittingly, his funeral was held in Nashville's Ryman Auditorium, former home of the *Grand Ole Opry*. Courtesy of Hatch Showprint.

The late Bill Monroe shared Anderson's desire to preserve traditional music, and tried to teach tunes to O'Connor whenever their paths crossed. On those occasions, he recalls, Monroe would pull him aside and say, "Oh, I got a good number for you, Mark. This will be a *powerful* number for you on the fiddle."

Prior to Monroe's death in 1996, O'Connor had told me, "you know, once he's gone, there will be nobody else like him."

O'Connor probably hopes that, one day, the same will be said of him.

This photograph of the late **Roy Acuff** with Louis Marshall "Grandpa" Jones is on display at the museum in Maynardville, Acuff's hometown. The King of Country Music entertained Opry audiences and overseas troops with his yo-yo tricks and by balancing the fiddle bow on his chin. He also ran for governor on the Republican ticket in 1944 and 1948. Jones, a Kentuckian, became a senior citizen in his early twenties as part of his stage act; his wife Ramona plays old-time fiddle.

It is an inexpressible pleasure to know a little of the world,
and be of no character or significancy in it.
~ Richard Steele (1672-1729)

Destinations

Since most of Tennessee is sparsely populated — three quarters of its
population live in four of its 95 counties — a small amount of advance planning geared
toward your specific musical interests will help you make the most of your visit. This is
especially true if your proposed itinerary includes not only the twin tourist meccas of
Nashville and Memphis but a sampling of the smaller cities, towns, and rural stretches as
well. The following is a description of the best music-related sites, festivals, and venues in
East, Middle, and West Tennessee, with a select list of useful numbers, accommodations,
and restaurants. If you're planning to travel the back roads, pick up DeLorme's *Tennessee
Atlas & Gazetteer*, $15, tel. 207-865-4171.

Where you will end up going depends on what kinds of music you like. Generally
speaking, old-time and bluegrass predominate in East Tennessee, and country and new
acoustic in Nashville; blues and soul (and Elvis) are the norm in Memphis, and gospel
flourishes throughout. Most music festivals — those with professional musicians — and
amateur competitions ("conventions") take place in the summer. Spring and fall are also
good times to visit, not to mention less crowded. In the winter, which is often cold and
dreary, musicians tend to hibernate, and although clubs in the big cities stay open for
business, the more isolated areas will have considerably less to offer.

East Tennessee lies within the Eastern Time Zone, while Middle and West Tennessee
are on Central time. In other words, Nashville and Memphis are an hour earlier than
Knoxville and Chattanooga. The area codes for East, Middle, and West Tennessee are 423,
615, and 901, respectively. Lists of useful phone numbers and addresses for all three sec-
tions follow this chapter.

East Tennessee

East Tennessee remains largely undeveloped, at least from the standpoint of a musical tourist. There is, however, plenty to do here. Music permeates the mountains and valleys of East Tennessee, perhaps more so than any place in the state. British song collector Cecil Sharp, who passed through southern Appalachia around 1915, described "a community in which singing was a common and almost as universal a practice as speaking." Now as then, the challenge is *finding* the music. Some of the best music in East Tennessee takes place at "pickin' parties" — informal jam sessions held in the homes of amateur musicians and their friends. However, if you don't have several months to ingratiate yourself with a local musician and get invited to one of these parties, there are still plenty of other accessible venues.

Even though music lovers often focus their efforts on Nashville or Memphis and overlook East Tennessee, this region's 33 counties attract more general tourists than either Middle or West Tennessee. Mostly they come for the scenic attractions, such as the Great Smoky Mountains National Park and Cherokee National Forest, the state's top two tourist destinations. And while singer/songwriter Dolly Parton's theme park is the fifth most-visited place, Dollywood is the exception to the East Tennessee rule: the best music is found in its small towns and hollows. Despite the region's relative obscurity, the musicians here have played a major role in the development of old-time, gospel, and bluegrass — even blues and R&B. This heritage is well worth exploring, to say nothing of the area's historic sites and staggering scenic beauty.

Bristol, Johnson City, and Kingsport are northeastern Tennessee's three largest population centers, forming a triangle which is known as the Tri-Cities. This lies within a five-county region (including one in Virginia) that has half a million residents and is called "upper East Tennessee." Tennessee's northeasternmost city, Bristol (pop. 25,300) actually straddles the border with Virginia. Its main thoroughfare, State Street, bisects the states north-south, with Tennessee to the south. The two Bristols run separate governments and

In the late 1940s, **Curly King and the Tennessee Hilltoppers** (above) and Virginia's Stanley Brothers became the house bands on WCYB's *Farm and Fun Time;* guests included Flatt & Scruggs and Mac Wiseman. A native of Bristol, Virginia, King's given name was Cecil H. Crusenberry. He preferred country and western to bluegrass, and the Hilltoppers featured steel guitar and crooning vocals. Apparently the group made no records, although some radio transcriptions have survived. Courtesy of Richard Blaustein/Archives of Appalachia.

municipal systems, and the beautiful old neon sign on State reads, somewhat schizo-phrenically, "Welcome to Bristol, VA/TN: A Good Place To Live."

Several years ago, Bristolians formed an organization called the Birthplace of Country Music Alliance (BCMA) which strives to promote the area's musical heritage. The 1927 Bristol Sessions, which took place on State's south side (as Tennesseans are wont to point out), is where two of country's biggest names were first recorded; hence, the "birthplace" moniker.

That historic year, a Victor talent scout named Ralph Peer placed an ad in the local paper inviting all local music talent to show up for a recording session. The Carter Family drove down from Virginia's Clinch Mountains, and Jimmie Rodgers hopped a train from Asheville, North Carolina, where the Mississippian happened to be yodeling at the time. Maybelle Carter is called the Mother of Country Music, and her guitar style has influenced generations of country pickers.

A.P. Carter wrote and collected classics such as "Keep on the Sunny Side" and "Little Darlin' Pal of Mine" (whose melody Woody Guthrie borrowed for "This Land Is Your Land"). Together with Sara — A.P.'s wife and Maybelle's cousin — the Carters are considered country's "First Family."

Rodgers, meanwhile, is country's Father and, as of 1961, its first hall of fame inductee. The songs he recorded in Bristol and later in his career reveal a black blues influence (as do those of A.P. Carter, who learned tunes and guitar runs from Kingsport's Lesley Riddle). Somewhat paradoxically, Rodgers' singing has in turn been the major influence on country standard-bearers like Tubb, Frizzell, and Haggard. Peer also recorded the Stonemans, Blind Alfred Reed, banjo player B.F. Shelton, and an assortment of string bands, gospel quartets, and old-time fiddlers — "an almost perfect cross-section of early country music," according to Charles K. Wolfe.

In the 1960s, developers razed the three-story brick building where the sessions took place. A commemorative plaque in the parking lot of a Rite Aid pharmacy at the corner of State and Anderson marks the spot. The alliance more than makes up for this loss of a national landmark — after all, you can't *hear* a building — by sponsoring half a dozen concerts a year at the 1931 Paramount Theater on State, featuring top names like Doc Watson and Bristol's own Doyle Lawson. Tim White, an alliance member who plays banjo and paints signs for a living, has created a mural a few blocks down State which depicts the sessions' main players, including Victor's Nipper the Dog — the one with his ear cocked to the Victrola. Pickers congregate here on Tuesday nights when the weather is warm. On Thursday mornings, jam sessions occur at the Star Barber Shop (1003 W. State, just over the Virginia line), and proprietor Gene Boyd cuts hair when he isn't busy fiddling around.

North of Kingsport in Maces Springs, Virginia, the Carter Fold Music Barn holds its two-day festival in early August and offers live music on Saturday nights. Next door stands A.P.'s general store, now a museum, which is open for a few hours before the Saturday performance. Down the road, a homecoming and all-day singing is held in July on the grounds of the white clapboard church where A.P. and Sara are buried (Maybelle's grave is near Nashville). A museum devoted to Jimmie Rodgers is located in Meridian, Mississippi.

Bristol's most famous musical son, Tennessee Ernie Ford, spent the better part of his career singing spirituals and hymns. Early on he worked at Bristol's WOPI radio station. His 1955 cover of "Sixteen Tons" (written by guitarist Merle Travis) sold a million copies in three weeks, an unheard-of figure back then. Based in California, Ford hosted a national TV variety show for six years, and then returned to Bristol to record his *Comin' Home* album at the Anderson Street United Methodist Church where he sang as a child, using his relatives for the backup choir. Sacred music became his trademark — *Hymns* went platinum in 1963 — along with a pet expression: "Bless your pea-pickin' heart." Ford's small boyhood home at 1223 Anderson Street, now owned by the Bristol Historical Society, is open by appointment. Few of the original furnishings remain, with the exception of a clawfoot bathtub where Ernie used to splash around as a boy. His church is a few blocks away.

Ford's former employer, WOPI, still broadcasts from the ground floor of Grand Guitar, a guitar-shaped museum with regional musicians' instruments, clothing, and paraphernalia, located southwest of town, just off Interstate 81. The station's *Jamboree* was an important early radio show; today, the real thing — early country and bluegrass — is played on the weekends, while weekdays are given over to easy listening. On the museum's second floor, a map of musicians who have come from within a 100-mile radius of Bristol fortifies the small city's "birthplace" status. To name just a baker's dozen: Roy Acuff, Kenny Chesney, Harlan Howard, Jim & Jesse, Patty Loveless, Loretta Lynn, Jimmy Martin, Molly O'Day, Dolly Parton, Earl Scruggs, the Stanley Brothers, "Pop" Stoneman, and Lulu Belle Wiseman.

Bristol has a long tradition of music-making — accompanied by heavy partying. In the 1890s, for instance, an open-air dance floor

Blountville fiddler **Nora Cross** tapped her bare feet so enthusiastically that the windowpanes rattled. Courtesy Bud Phillips.

was erected in Flat Hollow (near today's intersection of Mary and Piedmont streets) catering to "the town's rednecks along with girls and women of questionable repute." Upset by the moonshine and brawls, as well as the early disco's location at the edge of a large expanse of bushes, a local "supermoralist" purchased this particular site, according to local historian Bud Phillips, "but the 'sinners' simply bought more plank and moved their playground to the backside of Furnace Bottom."

In a somewhat parallel development, the Hickory Tree store between Bristol and Bluff City used to hold jam sessions in the 1970s that attracted top-notch musicians like Ricky Skaggs and Keith Whitley. The tradition ended after the management tired of removing condoms and beer cans from the parking lot. These days, the picking and grinning commences nearby on Thursdays and Saturdays at the Clifton Brothers produce stand, located on highway 421 south of Bristol.

Sullivan County also produced the "Two Charlies Who Match." Charlie Hopkins and Charlie Carrier were both born on Hatcher's Creek in 1870. Both their parents were named Jim and Sarah, and both their wives, Minnie. One's sister married the other's brother. In their youth, both worked at logging camps and covered territory from North Carolina to the Great Lakes. It is said that one could stand more cold weather, and that Charlie Carrier could set you straight.

The Bristol International Raceway & Speedway sponsors the Goody's 500, a NASCAR circuit race which is immensely popular among East Tennesseans and a good place to take in some local color (and pieces of disintegrating tire). The BIR, with its 36-degree banks, is nicknamed "the world's fastest half-mile." During Race Week in late August, you can inspect the cars close up and get your favorite drivers' autographs. Since the world's largest battery manufacturer, Exide Corp., recently relocated to Bristol, the cars aren't likely to run out of juice. In September, Bristol holds its Autumn Chase Festival, featuring a hot-air balloon race and country music.

If you're a nature lover or fisherman, try the Holston River valley. "Surely the Lord never made a more beautiful place," enthused John Sevier, aka Nolichucky Jack, who settled here in 1771 and later became Tennessee's first governor. The setting looks Alpine, with mountains towering in the distance and cattle lowing in the foreground — quite different from a West Tennessee Delta landscape.

———————

SOME OF THE GREATEST "HILLBILLY" MUSICIANS have come from the mountain hollows and small rural communities around Bristol. In fact, one could make a compelling argument that this area is where the hillbilly myth first took root back in the 1920s. Born near Johnson City, Charlie Bowman fiddled for the Hill Billies, whose stage antics portrayed the mountaineer as "a comic or laughable character" and may have inspired cartoon strips such as "Snuffy Smith" and "L'il Abner." Bowman also co-wrote "Nine Pound Hammer."

Mountain City's blind fiddler, George Banman Grayson, joined forces with Florida's Henry Whitter in 1923 — four years before the Bristol Sessions — and recorded "Lee Highway Blues," "Handsome Molly," and other classics that musicians still practice today. Bluff City's Fiddlin' Dudley Vance won championships from Tennessee to Oklahoma and Florida, and his Tennessee Breakdowners were well-known throughout the Southeast.

These and others, such as old-time singer Clarence "Tom" Ashley and fiddler Uncle "Am" Stuart, all trekked to the Mountain City Fiddlers' Convention held in 1925. Stuart, who came from Morristown, had learned most of his tunes shortly after the Civil War. Though 74 at the time, he hooked up with the Hill Billies at the convention and proceeded to tour the vaudeville circuit for his last few years. Mountain City (pop. 2,169) still holds its annual fiddlers' convention in the summer, as does the little town of Laurel Bloomery (see the old-time chapter), which lies north on highway 91 towards the Virginia line.

The even smaller community of Shingletown (pop. 30), where shingles were once manufactured, is between the two places, tucked away a few miles east of 91. Here, next to a quaint white church, stands (barely) Heird Reid's DAVI SON'S CASH GRO., which his wife Hazel's family has owned for over a century. The small building is patched together and sided with various rusty old signs; inside, the floors and shelves (and their contents) slope improbably. Jam sessions commence on Friday nights, and when you need a break from the picking, you can sit on the bench outside, smoke or spit tobacco, and compare turkey-hunting notes. Not long ago, a photograph of the store appeared in *National Geographic's* cover story on Appalachia. The ensuing furor seems to have died out, and things are now settled back to their old slow pace.

East of Mountain City toward Bristol lies picturesque Shady Valley, the home of Jesse Jenkins' undeveloped cranberry bogs and an old river-rock and wormy chestnut schoolhouse. In inclement weather, avoid highway 421, with its steep switchbacks over the Holston and Iron mountains. Back in Bristol, for a souvenir of your trip to the hollows, pick up a pair of Pointer-brand overalls, made locally by William King Clothiers. They're available at Don's Men's Shoes, 626 State.

For the past century, Heird Reid's wife Hazel's family has owned and operated the general store in Shingleton, off the beaten path between Mountain City and Laurel Bloomery. Jam sessions commence Friday at quitting time. Perry Walker. Above: An old store receipt.

To the Fiddlers by Governor Bob Taylor

EN ROUTE, April 24, 1899
My Dear Fellow Sawyers:

Experience teaches us that first impressions are the more lasting. Next to the impressions which I received from a dogwood sprout or twig of a weeping willow, when I was a barefooted boy, are the impressions which were made upon my young mind and heart by the fiddlers. The tunes they used to play got tangled in my memory and they are just as vivid there today as are the faces I used to know and the incidents and happenings of the happy days gone by.

I can see Polk Scott and Sam Rowe just as plainly now as I actually saw them when I was a ten-year-old lad at the old log schoolhouse that stood by the bubbling spring. They played at the "exhibition" at the close of our school; and I have never heard any sweeter music since. Sam's big brown whiskers rolled and tumbled in ecstasy on his fiddle, as he rocked to and fro, with half-closed eyes, and, with whizzing bow, reveled in the third heaven of "Arkansas Traveler." Polk's black mustache swayed and flopped like a raven's wings, as he soared amind the grandeurs of "Natchez Under the Hill."

They were the "Paganinis" of the mountains; they were the "Ole Bulls" of our humble society; they were the royal "Remenyis" of our rural, rollicking festivities; they were big-hearted and genial; they were noble fellows, and so are all fiddlers to this good day. Their melodies were the echoes of nature's sweet voices. In every sweep of the bow there was the drumming of the pheasant or the cackle of a hen or the call of Bob White or the trill of a thrush. Sometimes I could hear a whippoorwill sing; sometimes a wild goose quack, and a panther yell; now and then the cats would fight, and the music was always mellow with "moonshine."

When I grew a little larger I used to slip out from the smiling roof of "home, sweet home," and cut the pigeon wing with the rosy-cheeked mountain girls, until it seemed that my very soul was in my heels. I still have fond recollections of every fiddler who played at the old-time country dance; and when I hear those sweet old tunes, even now it is difficult for me to keep my soul above my socks.

So far as I am concerned, I am a worshipper at the shrine of music. The classics of Mozart and Mendelssohn are grand and glorious to me, but I cannot be persuaded to turn my back on the classics of plain country fiddlers. The old country tunes were handed down from the days of the Revolution, and every one of them breathes the spirit of liberty; every old jig is an echo from the flintrock rifles and shrill fifes of Bunker Hill; every "hornpipe" is a refrain from King's Mountain; "Old Granny Rattletrap" is a Declaration of Independence; "Jennie, Put the Kittle On," boils over with freedom; "Jaybird Settin' on a Swingin' Limb" was George Washington's "favoright," and "Gray Eagle" was Thomas Jefferson's masterpiece; "Leather Breeches" was the Marsellaise hymn of the old heroes who lived in the days of Davy Crockett.

No wonder the fiddlers are so patriotic and brave. I never saw a real, genuine fiddler who would not fight; but, mind you, I have quit fiddling.

When I grew large enough to cast sheep's eyes at the girls, when love began to tickle my heart and the blood of the violets got into my veins, I began to draw the bow across the vibrant strings of the fiddle to give vent my feelings, and I poured my spirit out through my fingers by the bucketful. I swapped spirit for smiles at the ration of sixteen to one; I exchanged clogs for compliments, and jigs for sighs and sentimental exclamations. No ordinary mortal ever felt the raptures of a fiddler; the fiddle is his bride, and the honeymoon lasts forever.

I fiddled and I fiddled and I fiddled, until youth blossomed into manhood, and still I fiddled and I fiddled. Politicians sneered at me as a fiddler; but the girls said it was no harm, and the boys voted while I fiddled, and the fiddle won. There is always some old sour and tuneless hypocrite abusing and denouncing "us fiddlers." I have heard them say that they never saw a fiddler who was "any account," and I have known good men who sincerely believed that fiddlers were dangerous to communities. There never was a greater error of opinion. There is no more harm in wiggling the fingers than there is in wagging the tongue, and there is a great deal more religion in a good, law-abiding fiddle than there is in some folks who outlaw that divine instrument. There is infinitely more music in it than there is in some hymns I have heard sung by old dyspeptics who denounce it. Music is music, whether it be the laughter and song of the fiddle or the melodies of the human voice; music is the hallelujah of the soul, whether it comes through fiddlestrings or vocal chords. Happy is the home in which fiddles and fiddlers dwell, and nearest to heaven is the church where fiddlers and singers blend their music in hymns of praise to Almighty God.

I have heard cultivated musicians laugh at the country fiddler, and call his tunes "rag music;" but the law of compensation governs in this realm, as well as in every other, for the country fiddlers laugh just as heartily at the sublimest efforts of high-class musicians. Neither can understand the other. To the noteless and untutored fiddler the grandest efforts of the greatest orchestra are the senseless hieroglyphics of sound; to the cultured ear the simple melodies which dance out from the bosom of the fiddle and the soul of the fiddler are but the ridiculous buzzings of bumblebee discord.

But there is no reason why the virtuoso and the fiddler should fall out. Let the nightingale sing in his realm, and let the cricket sing in his. We will all play together on golden fiddles in the "sweet by and by."

Yours truly,
Robert L. Taylor

DRIVING SOUTH FROM BRISTOL towards Johnson City, take the left fork on highway 19E to Elizabethton, where Slagle's Pasture, open Saturday nights, offers some of the best music in upper East Tennessee. The local favorites are Jim & Jesse, who actually come from Virginia. The town's T.N. Garland makes dulcimers out of gourds. Continuing southeast, 19E leads to the town of Roan ("rone") Mountain, where the Birchfield family's Roan Mountain Hilltoppers have been making music the old-fashioned way, complete with washtub bass, for generations. Front man Bill Birchfield's robust laugh sounds like the nine-pins in *Rip Van Winkle* that "echoed along the mountains like rumbling peals of thunder."

Elizabethton is a historical hotbed, the main attraction being its 1882 covered bridge spanning the shallow Doe River. The Watauga Association's constitution drafted here in 1772 established the first majority-rule system of American democratic government; the site is now marked by a pagoda and a tree stump. Three years later, down the road at Sycamore Shoals, Richard Henderson's Transylvania Company cut the largest real estate deal in U.S. history. Over Chief Dragging Canoe's objections, the Cherokee tribe sold the pioneers 20 million acres of Cumberland River watershed, including much of Kentucky. Elizabethon is also the birhplace of Samuel Powatan Carter (1819-1891), the only American to serve both as Navy admiral and Army general. Moody Aviation, based at the municipal airport, trains missionaries how to fly in Appalachia's turbulent skies.

In June, a rhododendron festival is held at Roan Mountain State Park, site of the world's largest indigenous stand of Catawba rhododendron (roughly 600 acres). Explorer and botanist André Michaux discovered this species while exploring the area in the 1700s. He also christened the buttercup, crabapple, and lily of the valley.

Elizabethton, Roan Mountain, and Piney Flats north of Johnson City were stops along the 220-mile trail to the 1780 battle at King's Mountain, South Carolina, where a group of pioneers led by Bristol's Gen. Evan Shelby (whose son, Isaac, became Kentucky's first governor) killed or captured Ferguson's entire Royal army. According to Thomas Jefferson, this feat "terminated the revolutionary War with a seal of our independence." You can hike or drive the overmountain trail, which begins in Abingdon, Virginia, and reenactments take place in September.

THE SECOND OF THE TRI-CITIES' THREE URBAN CENTERS, Johnson City (pop. 51,600) is home to what is arguably the area's preeminent live music venue, the Down Home club, as well as one of the nation's only accredited bluegrass programs, at East Tennessee State University. Located at 300 West Main and open Wednesday through Saturday, the Down Home is perhaps the closest you will come to a picking party without actually crashing one. Wednesday's "Open Hoot" is a good place to check out the local songwriting talent. Top acts often pass through, including the Osborne Brothers, Del McCoury, J.D. Crowe, and the Nashville Bluegrass Band over a recent three-month period. On any given night, you might hear Mississippi blues, zydeco, or New Orleans-style jazz. On a recent visit, I saw a local guitarist named Reese Shipley perform there. He looked and sounded like he could have belonged to Django Reinhardt's Hot Club of France, as the band ran through everything from "Ain't She Sweet" and "Sandman" to "Back in the Saddle Again." Accompanying Shipley on old-time fiddle was Dr. Richard Blaustein, a Brooklyn emigré who now teaches at East Tennessee State's Center for Appalachian Studies.

Jack Tottle, who authored the Bible of the mandolin (*Bluegrass Mandolin*, Oak Publications), runs the center's bluegrass and country music program and hosts *Bluegrass Heartland* on the college's WETS radio station. The ETSU Bluegrass Band has toured the Soviet Union and Poland, and its alumni include country singer Kenny Chesney and pickers Tim Stafford, Adam Steffey, and Barry Bales, all of whom have played with the precocious Alison Krauss. *Down Around Bowmantown*, an LP on the center's Now and Then label, features field recordings made in Washington County over a 50-year span.

On campus, the Carroll Reece Museum exhibits some gorgeous antique instruments. You can easily while away a few days at the Sherrod Library just listening to the Archives of Appalachia's seven reel-to-reel tapes of WCYB-Bristol's *Farm and Fun Time*. Some of the biggest names in bluegrass, such as Flatt & Scrugg's Foggy Mountain Boys (whose one-time fiddler Benny Sims lives here) and the Stanley Brothers, got their first exposure on this late-1940s radio program, playing for free in exchange for advertising their upcoming shows. There are those who maintain that, based purely on WCYB's contributions, the bluegrass capital of the world belongs in Bristol, rather than Owensboro, Kentucky, where the International Bluegrass Music Association is based. Johnson City also once served as headquarters for Jim "Hobart" Stanton's now-defunct Rich-R-Tone records, the first independent to record bluegrass acts such as the Stanleys, the Bailey Brothers, the Payne Family, and Wilma Lee and Stoney Cooper.

This area served as the backdrop for "The War of the Roses," the 1886 gubernatorial race between brothers Robert and Alfred Taylor, featuring fiddle-offs between the two. They grew up in nearby Happy Valley, near the confluence of the Watauga and Dee rivers. While governor, Bob lived in a house on South Roan Street called Robin's Roost from 1892 to 1897 (as did Alf, from 1900 to 1903).

LOCATED A FEW MILES WEST OF JOHNSON CITY on highway 321, Jonesborough is Tennessee's oldest town, established in 1779. Old-time and country jam sessions take place behind Mauk's Pharmacy on weekends. The history museum on Boone Street contains an impressive cast-iron cauldron, once used for rendering lard, and antique quilts with colorfully named designs like "Drunkard's Path," "Flying Swallows," and "Halls All Around." In October, the National Storytelling Festival, which includes music, attracts some 9,000 people, nearly three times the town's local population. Early in his career, Andrew Jackson relocated here from South Carolina and was admitted to the bar in the town's then-log courthouse. A plaque with the Ten Commandments has been affixed to today's marble version; down the steps are stocks with a working padlock. Elihu Embree published his *Manumission Intelligencer* here in 1819, but the nation's first abolition journal proved to be a short-lived venture. In the 1830s, during the heyday of stagecoach travel, Main Street was a major horse refueling center between Knoxville and Abingdon, Virginia.

CONTINUING WEST TOWARDS GREENEVILLE ON 321, you see picture-perfect farms with alternating rows of corn and tobacco. Exit at Chuckey for the Rheatown store, which sponsors occasional jam sessions. This road also leads to the site of David Crockett's birthplace, now a 60-acre park featuring a replica of the Crocketts' cabin and an exhibit exploring his legacy. The man who once proclaimed that he could outspeak any man in Congress "and give him two hours' start" was born in 1776 by Limestone Creek, a tributary of the Nolichucky (and not on a mountaintop as asserted in Disney's "Ballad of Davy Crockett"). Standing on a bluff overlooking the rushing Nolichucky and surveying the land where Crockett started out can be a bone-tingling experience. Still, one can't help but wonder what he'd make of the power walkers on his old stamping grounds.

Quaint Greeneville's offerings tend to be more historical than musical — unless you stretch musical to include the frantic warbling of native son and world-champion tobacco auctioneer Sandy Houston. The town is built upon the legacy of Andrew Johnson, who ran a tailor shop here and went on to become governor, U.S. senator and, following Lincoln's assassination, the 17th president. Johnson is the only president ever impeached, and he was acquitted by just one vote. His tailor shop, home, and grave can be viewed, as can his library, at nearby Tusculum College.

Davy Crockett's Common Sense

We lived in the back-woods, and didn't profess to know much, and no doubt used many wrong words. But we met, and appointed magistrates and constables to keep order. We didn't fix any laws for them, tho'; for we supposed they would know law enough, whoever they might be; and so we left it to themselves to fix the laws.

I was appointed one of the magistrates; and when a man owed a debt, and wouldn't pay it, I and my constable ordered our warrant, and then he would take the man, and bring him before me for trial. I would give judgement against him, and then an order of an execution would easily scare the debt out of him .... My judgements were never appealed from, and if they had been they would have stuck like wax, as I gave my decisions on the principles of common justice and honesty between man and man, and relied on natural born sense, and not on law, learning to guide me; for I had never read a page in a law book in all my life.

~ *A Narrative of the Life of David Crockett of the State of Tennessee* (1834 autobiography)

In the 1780s, when Tennessee still belonged to North Carolina, Greeneville served as the capital of the so-called Lost State of Franklin. This group of pioneers passed its own laws regarding taxes, militia, and courts and distributed the first political pamphlets west of the Alleghenies. During the Civil War, East Tennessee delegates met at the Greeneville Union Convention seeking to remain in the Union after the state had already seceded. Their efforts were in vain, and Confederate troops under Gen. Felix Zollicoffer's command soon occupied East Tennessee.

Northeast of Greeneville at Bull's Gap is a tourist complex dedicated to comedian Archie Campbell, nicknamed "the Will Rogers of the *Grand Ole Opry*," or just plain "Grandpappy." To the south, opera singer and actress Grace Moore grew up in mountainous Cocke County, near Del Rio; to the east, in Cosby, is Jean and Lee Schilling's well-regarded dulcimer shop, Mountain MusiCraft.

Thespian and singer **Grace Moore** (1907-1947) grew up in Slabtown. Mountainous Cocke County is also home to the 1767-vintage, three-level Swaggerty's Fort, near Parrottsville.

DOUBLING BACK NORTH TO THE VIRGINIA BORDER, you'll find the best music venue in Kingsport (pop. 42,200). The Beechwood Music Center, located in Fall Branch (south on I-81, north on highway 93 to Baileytown Road), features a May festival and an October jamboree, as well as Overalls Nights and afternoon gospel programs. On the outskirts of town, Warriors' Path State Park holds a folk festival in July. The town also has its own Appalachian Barber Shop Quartet. It's the hometown of composer Kenton Coe; the bluegrasser Doyle Lawson lived here for a time, as did bluesman Brownie McGhee. Eastman Kodak's large plant dominates the town, spewing out the steam of industry.

THE FIVE COUNTIES BETWEEN KINGSPORT and the Big South Fork National River and Recreation Area are among the state's most remote. In order to ferret out the music here, you will truly need some time to beat the bushes. The counties all border Virginia or Kentucky to the north. With the exception of Campbell County, which is bisected by Interstate 75, the roads are secondary at best. Travel often takes longer than it would appear on the map, so budget some extra time.

Sneedville, the guitarist Jimmy Martin's hometown, sponsors its Clinch River Run and bluegrass concert in early June. Parallel to the river, the Clinch Mountains run northeasterly into Virginia, whence came the Carter Family and the Stanleys. Bassist Billy Greer, who plays for Kansas, the album-oriented rock group, hails from Surgoinsville. Sunday mornings in historic Rugby (see next page), Christ Church Episcopal cranks up its 1849 rosewood harmonium.

Despite these fairly slim musical pickings, East Tennessee's northwestern quadrant may still be worth a detour. Named for a famous passage through the mountains, Cumberland Gap National Historic Park offers 50 miles of trails in three states. The museum at Lincoln Memorial University in nearby Harrogate houses 25,000 Civil War artifacts, including the cane that Lincoln carried to Ford's Theatre.

In Hancock County, the mysterious Melungeons — sort of Tennessee's Basque people — were formerly thought to be a frontier mixture of whites, free blacks, and Native Americans. However, recent evidence indicates that the Melungeons, who have dark hair and olive complexions, descended from a group of shipwrecked Portuguese and Turkish sailors.

This photograph of coon skins drying on a shed was taken along Newman's Ridge in Hancock County, home to the dark-haired Melungeon people, whose origin is unknown. Perry Walker.

Thelma Frogges runs a package store just down the road from the restored settlement of Rugby, established in 1880 by Thomas Hughes, an English Christian Socialist. To the north lies the wild Big South Fork recreation area. Perry Walker.

Also in Hancock, one of the country's last cooperages makes buckets and churns from wooden slats without using nails or glue. Lovers who drink from Rogersville's Ebbing and Flowing Spring at full "tide" — from a trickle to 500 gallons a minute in under three hours — will marry within the year. Fiddler Tammy Rogers is a native, and the Bailey Brothers, who bridged the gap between 1930s close-harmony duets and 1940s bluegrass singing, came from the nearby hamlet of Klondike.

Farther east lies Rugby, a class-free cooperative founded in the 1800s by British social reformer Thomas Hughes. Browse in the 7,000-volume library, specializing in Victoriana. A trail beginning at Laurel Dale cemetery — the colony was destroyed by the 1881 typhoid epidemic — leads down to the "gentlemen's swimming hole" on the Clear Fork; ladies are now welcome as well. Historic Rugby has some nice, restorative Victorian cottages for rent, and Thelma Frogges' little store down the road can supply you with a six of Bud. Senator Howard Baker once practiced law in Huntsville and spent his free time taking nature photographs of this rugged area.

THE COUNTY SEAT OF WARTBURG, EUPHONIOUSLY NAMED after the German castle where Luther hid, was once home to a piano factory run by Heinrich Dieterich Wilheim Waltersdorf, who in 1848 emigrated here by a combination of ship, train, stage, riverboat, and hoof. Today's musical offerings consist of the Rocky Fork Jamboree on Flat Fork Road, holding forth every Friday night for the past 15 years, and Bruce Greene's combination music store and barber shop, a block down from the town square. The town is also the shoving-off point for the Obed Wild and Scenic River, whose numerous rapids — including one stretch called "Ohmigod!" — are for experienced canoeists only; the visitors center is worthwhile.

East of town, one of Frozen Head State Park's peaks is perenially enshrouded in snow, hence its name. James Earl Ray once made license plates nearby at the century-old Brushy Mountain State Prison in Petros. Ray was convicted of killing Rev. Martin Luther King, Jr. in 1968 outside a Memphis motel room. As of this writing, a gravely ill Ray has been re-canting his story claiming that the assassination was a conspiracy. Back in Wartburg, prisoners pull weeds and paint columns at the courthouse.

One night, while driving north on highway 116 and rubbernecking at the prison, I missed the Frozen Head campground turnoff. The road climbed higher and higher, passing through a number of small communities, all mysteriously unmarked. The next day, a ranger told me that, "you wouldn't want to knock on doors at night" to get directions. Once driven by timber, coal, and moonshine, the local economy has now diversified into marijuana growing. During Halloween, the locals block the road by felling trees and burning bridges. Bring your own jumper cables.

THE MUSEUM OF APPALACHIA, SET ON A FARM NEAR NORRIS, is the brainchild of John Rice Irwin, who has painstakingly collected a quarter million artifacts. Sixteen miles north of Knoxville, this site is a repository for East Tennessee musical knowledge and trivia. You can learn about obscure yet influential folks like Cas Walker, the colorful Sevier County politician, businessman, and radio and TV personality who gave Dolly her first chance, and programs such as the *Mid-Day Merry-Go-Round*, broadcast over WNOX-Knoxville. The museum's Fall Homecoming in October features some 100 acts, including Charlie Acuff, Roy's cousin (who fiddles lefthanded), and Crossville's Lantana Drifters, an old-time swing band. Carlock Stooksbury, an unofficial staffer, demonstrates how to play the mouth bow and Jew's harp.

The Acuffs (and honky-tonk singer Carl Smith) grew up to the east in Union County's Maynardville. Along highway 33 is a museum devoted to Roy, who started out on the medicine-show circuit, joined the *Opry* in 1938, and stayed at it until his death in 1992. The sign on his dressing room door read: "Ain't nothin' gonna come up today that me and the Lord can't handle."

Famous for his renditions of "The Great Speckle Bird" and A.P. Carter's "Wabash Cannonball," he is considered the King of Country Music (as opposed to its Father, Jimmie Rodgers). His music came from "our people and our places," Acuff wrote in his autobiography. "To me, it's just country — hillbilly if you wish, and I don't mind that because I am and it is. Anybody who tries to make much more than that out of it is just making it far too complicated."

Guitarist Chet Atkins — whom the museum deems "the most influential man in Nashville" — grew up just down the road from the Acuffs in tiny Luttrell. The self-described "shy, quiet kind of guy" has produced numerous classics, including Eddy Arnold's "Make the World Go Away," Skeeter Davis' "End of the World," and Jerry Reed's "When You're Hot, You're Hot." Over the years, he has worked with everyone from Hank and Elvis to Les Paul and Jim Reeves, and this is just a short list.

The nearby Norris Dam was completed by the TVA in 1936 as the centerpiece of its massive rural electrification program. On the third Friday in August, the Big Ridge State Park on Norris Lake sponsors its annual bluegrass and gospel festival. Southeast toward Knoxville, the national laboratory at Oak Ridge manufactured uranium 235 for the first atomic bomb in what is now the world's oldest graphite reactor. Free, self-guided tours are available Monday through Saturday. The American Museum of Science and Energy, open daily, is also in Oak Ridge.

KNOXVILLE, TENNESSEE'S THIRD LARGEST CITY AND FIRST CAPITAL, sits in a wide valley between the Cumberland and Great Smoky Mountains. Here, the Holston and French Broad Rivers merge to form the Tennessee. The city (pop. 167,000) is also home to the University of Tennessee, with some 26,000 students. Three interstates meet here, making it an axis for the entire East Tennessee region: driving to either Bristol or Chattanooga takes two hours.

The Laurel Theater/Jubilee Community Arts is one of the town's best venues for bluegrass, old-time, and folk. Jubilee features a Harp Sing (see below) on the second Sunday of each month, and offers courses in everything from English country dancing to T'ai Chi. Concerts are also held at the Bijou and Tennessee theaters, the latter of 1928 Moorish design. For music on Saturday nights, try David's Cider Barn on Clinton Highway (also, Thursday mornings at True Value Hardware on Chapman Highway, and Friday nights at Benfields', south on highway 321 to Morgantown Road). Large shows take place in UT's Thompson-Boling Arena, which seats 26,000. The 17-day Dogwood Arts Festival is held in April, and the Festival on the River kicks off on Memorial Day weekend. For a debriefing on Knoxville's music, stop by Bud Brewster's Pick 'n' Grin music store at 106 Gore. For music listings, check Friday's detours! section in the Knoxville News-Sentinel. WIVK plays country music.

Knoxville has a rich musical legacy. In the 1840s, W.H. and M.L. Swan's songbook, Harp of Columbia, was published here, providing instruction in shape-note singing. Sacred Harp music, with each of its four parts equally "eventful," differs from most choral music in which the soprano voice is dominant. All-day singings and singing schools, an out-growth of the Sacred Harp tradition, influenced country musicians like Kirk McGee and A.P. Carter and paved the way for the development of modern gospel music. Today, the shape-note method is still practiced in some of East Tennessee's rural churches. (For more information, ask at the Jubilee Center.)

Starting in the late '30s, black gospel's Swan Silvertones held court, sponsored by a local bakery. The group's lead vocalist, Claude Jeter, influenced many later singers, including Al Green. WNOX's *Mid-Day Merry-Go-Round* fostered the early careers of Molly O'Day, Pee Wee King, Mac Wiseman, Johnny & Jack, and a legion of other country artists. The best place to familiarize yourself with this seminal radio program is the Museum of Appalachia in Norris (see p. 182); especially daunting is a list of musicians who started out in Knoxville, compiled by Acuff band member Harley "Sunshine Slim" Sweet (known to show up at WNOX with his fiddle wrapped in a paper bag).

For many years, the legendary Arthur Q. Smith — possibly the greatest country song-writer of all time — eked out a living in Knoxville, selling his songs for $25 and some-times bartering them for booze. He stationed himself at the Three Feathers Bar and Grill across the street from WNOX. He allegedly wrote Hank Williams' "Wedding Bells" and worked as his manager for a spell, but after the two went on a binge in Little Rock, Hank's wife Audrey fired him. Twenty years after his death in 1963, Ricky Skaggs had a number one hit with Smith's "I Wouldn't Change You If I Could." Born James Arthur Pritchett in Georgia, Arthur Q. should not be confused with Fiddlin' Arthur Smith of West Tennessee (or, for that matter, with Arthur "Guitar Boogie" Smith of North Carolina).

A young North Carolinian named Don Gibson wrote "I Can't Stop Loving You" in a sweltering trailer outside Knoxville. Other local products include singer Con Hunley and the comedy team of Homer and Jethro, and writer Cormac McCarthy, whose *Suttree* is set in Knoxville.

The University of Tennessee was founded as Blount College in 1794, two years after Knoxville became the territorial capital, and two years before Tennessee became a state. Even Michael Jackson could fill only half of UT's enormous Neyland Stadium, and when 92,000 rabid orange-and-white-clad football fans *do* regularly fill it, Neyland technically becomes the state's fifth-biggest city. "Rocky Top," The Vols' fight song (also one of five of-ficial state songs), was written by Gatlinburg resident Felice Bryant and her late husband Boudleaux; the Bryants also created "Bye Bye Love," "Wake Up, Little Susie," and "Take A Message to Mary." The whole town, even McDonald's, is festooned in the university's col-ors, orange and white, inspired by the daisies which once grew on campus. Even the Sun-sphere in World's Fair Park between campus and downtown takes on an orangy hue (officially it's "gold").

EAST FROM KNOXVILLE, FOLLOW HIGHWAY 441 TO SEVIERVILLE, the Sevier ("severe") County seat. In front of the courthouse stands a sculpture of a young Rebecca Dolly Parton, guitar in hand. A few miles down the road in Pigeon Forge (pop. 3,000) is the singer's epony-mous theme park, which she bought in 1986 (it used to be called Silver Dollar City).

Dollywood is a good, clean, well-run place to take the family, albeit a bit pricey (roughly $20 a day, per person). The park attracts some two million visitors a year. In addition to its Appalachian theme and the ubiquitous rides and cotton candy, country's top names perform May through October at the park's Showcase of Stars concert series. Dolly herself presides over the opening-day parade in late April. The fall harvest festival takes place during October.

Get your bearings at the "Rags to Riches Museum" which chronicles the life and career of this petite (in most places) blond (-wigged) singer, songwriter, and actress, who grew up in nearby Locust Ridge. Some of her vital measurements are provided — she's five feet tall and 110 pounds, wears size 5 shoes, and has a 19-inch waist. Regarding her much-ballyhooed bust size, which is not proffered, she has observed that God wouldn't have given her such an ample figure "if he hadn't wanted people to notice them." They certainly did, when she played Miss Mona in *The Best Little Whorehouse in Texas.*

In "Kentucky Gambler," an early classic, Parton suggested that "when you love the greenback dollar, sorrow's always bound to follow." In this case, Whitney Houston's remake of Dolly's "I Will Always Love You" must have caused her great pain. Now in her early fifties, Dolly runs an empire (wigs, cosmetics, film production) worth at least $100 million. Despite her success, Dolly remains philosophical. In a recent *McCall's* interview, she declared her belief in the hereafter. "This life is the hard part," she said. "After that it's pie."

Catering to busloads from middle America, live music clubs and theaters have sprouted up along Dollywood Boulevard on the town's north side. For example, Chattanooga native James Rogers' *High Flyin' Country* serves up equal parts patriotism and Christianity at the Music Mansion Theater. (Rogers, who has opened for Alabama, Roy Clark, and Glen Campbell, said he likes the town's "family atmosphere.") At the Dixie Stampede, you can eat dinner and "be dazzled by a professional group of entertainers and artists at the same time." Singer T.G. Sheppard of Humboldt and others have their own theaters. In addition, Pigeon Forge's five malls offer some 225 outlet stores.

Dolly Parton, who grew up poor in the Smoky Mountains, has hugged Mick Jagger and curtsied before Queen Elizabeth. She has a house in Nashville but spends a lot of time in a Winnebago with her longtime, low-profile husband Carl. This photograph of her warbling was made at Dollywood, her theme park in Pigeon Forge. James Barringer.

————— ■■■■■ —————

DOLLYWOOD IS THE MAIN BENEFICIARY of Great Smoky Mountains National Park, located just 10 miles south on highway 441. The park's nine million visitors make it the busiest in the country and four times more popular than any other attraction in Tennessee. Between the two parks lies the neo-Alpine village of Gatlinburg, where you can ride Ober Gatlinburg, advertised as America's largest tramway. After you've practiced your putting at Hillbilly Golf — located at the first traffic snag — or your driving at Rebel Yell Racing, stop by Possum Jones Kuntry Kookin and pile on.

A few miles inside the park entrance, get your bearings at the Sugarlands visitors center. The Smokies, split between Tennessee and North Carolina, offer 900 miles of trails, including a segment of the Appalachian variety. At the park's Cades Cove, music is featured prominently at the old-timers days held in May and September. You might hear songs like "Wild and Reckless Hobo," recorded in the '20s by early country star George Reneau, who was known as the Blind Minstrel of the Smoky Mountains.

————— ■■■■■ —————

THE AREA BETWEEN THE SMOKIES AND CHATTANOOGA IS "INDIAN" COUNTRY. Since few historical records of it exist, we don't know much about Native American music other than that it was melody-based, used a diatonic scale, and was played on flutes, water drums, and rattles. Its impact on the pioneers' music has been debated.

The wide Tennessee River valley between Maryville and Chattanooga was once home to the Cherokee people. Near the little town of Vonore (north of Madisonville) is the former village of Tanasi ("tah-NAH-see"), from which the state and river derive their name. The current spelling of Tennessee first appeared on Lt. Henry Timberlake's 1762 map. Tanasi (the word's meaning is unknown) briefly served as the Cherokee capital in the 1720s; today it lies beneath the waters of Tellico Lake, the result of the TVA's damming of the Little Tennessee River. From Vonore, follow state highway 360 south and go straight at the fork to the black marble monument located 300 yards west of the submerged capital. A mile or two farther on stands the headstone of Oconastota, the great 18th-century Cherokee warrior, surrounded by columns inscribed with the tribe's seven clans.

Back in Vonore, the Sequoyah Birthplace Museum pays homage to the inventor of the Cherokee syllabary and provides information about Native Americans, particularly the Cherokee. This tribe, which migrated from the Carolinas and points north, once dominated East Tennessee; by 1721, it controlled an area comprising 125,000 square miles over eight Middle Atlantic and Southern states. In the decades following the American Revolution, treaties reduced its holdings east of the Mississippi to a mere 12,000 square miles. The Removal Act of 1835, championed by Andrew Jackson, dealt the final blow, requiring that all Cherokee move west to reservations in Oklahoma.

Visiting just prior to the "removal," the painter George Catlin met with Chief John Ross and in his diary noted "the unassuming and gentlemanly urbanity of his manners, as well as the rigid temperance of his habits, and the purity of his language." The tribe's last council was held in 1838 at Red Clay, due east of Chattanooga, and now a state historical area. It was from here that 15,000 Cherokee departed — at bayonet point — along the infamous Trail of Tears. *The New York Observer* reported in 1839 that "even aged females, apparently nearly ready to drop into the grave, were traveling with heavy burdens attached to the back — on the sometimes frozen ground, and sometimes muddy streets, with no covering for the feet except what nature had given them."

Thousands died of starvation and exposure. A few, led by Tsali, fled to the mountains, where their descendants now live on the Cherokee reservation straddling the North Carolina border.

East of Vonore and Red Clay lies Cherokee National Forest, the state's second most popular destination after the Smokies, which extend from the Little Tennessee south to the Georgia border. The park is bisected by the Hiwassee and Ocoee rivers, tributaries of the Tennessee known respectively for their trout-fishing and kayaking. Emmett Adams wrote "When You and I Were Young, Maggie" while living at the former mining community of Maggie's Mill near the town of Reliance. Beautiful spring-fed Chilhowee Lake is east of Benton, where WBIM broadcasts the colorful Baptist preacher Jasper Woody from daylight to dark. A few miles south lies the grave of Nancy Ward, an early Cherokee leader.

In Dayton, to the west of the Tennessee, the famous Scopes trial took place in July 1925. At stake was the right to teach evolution in Tennessee's schools. The teacher, John Thomas Scopes, was convicted but only paid a small fee, and his lawyer, Clarence Darrow, claimed victory. Prosecuting attorney William Jennings Bryan expired a few days after the trial, a broken man. Visiting from Baltimore, the journalist H.L. Mencken wrote that "the effort to repeal natural selection by law made the State ridiculous throughout the world, and its civilized minority has suffered severely from the ensuing ill fame." It wasn't until the '60s that the state finally permitted Darwin in its classrooms, and a bill has recently been introduced that would revert to a creationism-only curriculum.

Fiddler Curly Fox, famous for show pieces like "Black Mountain Rag," grew up to the south in Graysville, while Hargus "Pig" Robbins, who played keyboards on George Jones' "White Lightnin'" and many other sessions, was born in Spring City. Every summer, Pikeville sponsors three Ninemile bluegrass festivals; it's the hometown of Homer Davenport, whose three-finger banjo style preceded bluegrass by two decades.

Farther north, Crossville sits along the Cumberland Plateau, a 50-mile-wide level plain of grassland and forest rising 1,000 feet from the surrounding countryside. Stock up on fireworks, bandanas, and decanters at the Hank Williams Jr. Country Store. So what if *The New York Times* don't appreciate him!

TENNESSEE'S FOURTH-LARGEST CITY, CHATTANOOGA (pop. 154,000) means "Rock-Rising-to-a-Point" in Creek dialect. The word is thought to describe Lookout Mountain. "The name might sound outlandish and strange to some ears," the city's postmaster noted in 1838,

Arnim Leroy "Curly" Fox with his wife, **Texas Ruby** were both fiddlers on the Opry. A native of Graysville, north of Chattanooga, Fox was a great showman, while Ruby's vocals influenced Patsy Cline and Loretta Lynn. In the '60s, Ruby died in a trailer fire while Curly was performing. Les Leverett.

"but if our city was a success, it would become familiar and pleasant, and there would not be another name like it in the world."

A century later, Chattanooga did indeed become a household name following the 1941 release of Glenn Miller's "Chattanooga Choo Choo," written by Mack Gordon and Harry Warren and featured in the movie *Sun Valley Serenade*. Miller's record became the first certified million-seller. As for the actual "Choo Choo," there is no such train. Rather, the name referred to Southern Railways' 1909 terminal station, which now houses the Chattanooga Choo Choo Holiday Inn. Red Foley topped the charts with "Chattanoogie Shoe Shine Boy" in 1950.

The Tennessee River writhes through the city and dips south into Georgia, reentering the state to the west at its border with Alabama and Mississippi. Learn more about the river's unique ecosystem and watch the river otters frolic at the Tennessee Aquarium, which opened in 1992; it's the world's largest fresh-water fishpond. Next to the Aquarium is Ross' Landing Park, where some Cherokees began their forced trip west by riverboat. Paddlewheel around Moccasin Bend on the Southern Belle ($6.50) and hear Charlie Faircloth recounting local lore.

Stroll along the Riverwalk to the 1891 Walnut Street Bridge. Once plied by mule-driven streetcars, the bridge is now reserved for pedestrians. On the north side, browse at Books by the Bridge (201-G Frazier Ave.) Downtown, the Radisson Read House, a 1926 beaux art edifice made of brick and terra-cotta, is one of the state's nicest hotels. Jefferson Davis came close to being shot by the hotel owner's brother after delivering a fiery speech defending secession at the Crutchfield House, the Read's predecessor. Among the Read House's past occupants were Winston Churchill, Tallulah Bankhead, and Al Capone.

Chattanooga's river-powered foundries and smelters made it a strategic point during the Civil War. The bloody Battle of Chickamauga (34,000 casualties in two days), waged nearby, "sealed the fate of the Confederacy," in the words of Gen. D.H. Hill.

Although not as associated with music as Nashville or Memphis, Chattanooga has had an interesting and diverse musical past, and the present offerings are bountiful as well. Old-time fans will want to visit the Mountain Opry, a wholly amateur venue established by local barber J.J. Hillis in 1979 "on a wing and a prayer." The jam sessions, which take place Friday nights atop Signal Mountain in the town of Walden (off highway 127), hark back to the days of gas station pickin' sessions and, in the words of one enthusiast, "are about as downhome as they come."

Chattanooga's WDOD was one of the earliest stations to broadcast country music. Nonagenarian Bob Douglas, who lives nearby on Walden Ridge, still fiddles as he did with the Louvin Brothers on those early programs.

Music venues include the Tivoli Theater, Memorial Auditorium, and the University of Tennessee at Chattanooga arena (or roundhouse) for bigger concerts. Bands also play at Market Street Performance Hall, and at the Sand Bar a mile outside town. The city's Nightfall series features free headliner concerts downtown on Friday nights. In late April, the Bessie Smith Traditional Jazz Festival takes place, followed by the Riverbend Festival in June, and the National Folk Festival in October.

More than 20 years ago, **Norman Blake** and his wife **Nancy** rejected Nashville's commercialism and moved south to Georgia, where they have focused on various kinds of traditional acoustic music. Norman grew up in Chattanooga, while Nancy is a Missourian. His 1929 Gibson is "like me," he jokes, "just as cantankerous as they come." Courtesy Scott O'Malley & Associates.

Try to track down Boots Roots, a street musician who plays country blues, or the Dismembered Tennesseans, who have been making string-band music for 40 years — long before they became executives. For traditional black gospel, seek out the Faith Temple Songbirds.

Multi-instrumentalist Norman Blake, best known for his flatpicking acoustic guitar, also comes from Chattanooga. Over the years, he has been recruited by an impressive roster of artists, including Johnny Cash, Bob Dylan, Joan Baez, John Hartford, and Steve Earle. Now in his fifties, Blake considers himself an old-time country musician. Early in his career, he worked "on the edges of the rockabilly pond," recording at Sun with the Dixie Drifters.

After spending the late 1960s and early '70s in Nashville, he eventually grew tired of country's "crass commercialism" and moved to northern Georgia, where he whiles away his spare time listening to old 78s of Charley Patton and Gid Tanner. For the past 20 years, he has collaborated with his wife Nancy, who plays cello, mandolin, and fiddle. Their last four consecutive albums, the most recent being *Hobo's Last Ride* (Shanachie), have all received Grammy nominations.

ELISABETH "BESSIE" SMITH, THE AFRICAN-AMERICAN CONTRALTO who blended blues and jazz, is the first person who comes to mind when music fans think of Chattanooga. Born in

1898, she grew up in Blue Goose Hollow, on West Ninth Street at the foot of Cameron Hill. Tennessee's most famous blues artist made her professional debut at Chattanooga's Ivory Theatre, for which she earned $8, and promptly bought a pair of roller skates.

Smith, who preferred moonshine to top-shelf, had good reason to sing the blues. Over her entire career, Columbia paid her a flat fee of $125 for most record sides, and $200 tops; she received no royalties. She died from injuries sustained in a 1937 car accident in Mississippi, and some believe that her life could have been saved if she had received prompt treatment. Although thousands filed past the bier at her funeral in Philadelphia, Smith's grave remained unmarked until 1970, when Janis Joplin donated a headstone.

In addition to being a great singer, Smith was also a prolific writer. As perhaps the final indignity, many of Smith's compositions are credited to others, among them pianist Clarence Williams and Perry Bradford, who either pirated her songs or bought them on the cheap. In "Thinking Blues," she plays the part of a despondent yet defiant spurned lover, warning her man that "you've got to reap what you sow." And in "Devil's Gonna Git You," she curses the "dirty two-timer" who has cheated on her, declaring that she wants "nothin' that's been used/or that's second-hand."

As Albert Murray wrote in *Stomping the Blues,* "Old Pharoah in the spirituals may often stand for Ole Marster as well as the ruler of a sinful and oppressive nation; and Egyptland is often the U.S. South as well as the mundane world. But the man who imprisons the woman body-and-soul in Bessie Smith's lyrics is neither sheriff nor warden. He is the slow and easy but sometimes heartless lover."

CHATTANOOGA IS LOCATED IN THE HEART OF APPALACHIA yet its inner city is 40 percent black, making the city something of an anomaly. The African-American museum (730 M.L. King Boulevard) features exhibits on Bessie Smith and other native musicians, including Valaida Snow, the "Queen of the Trumpets," who survived three years in a concentration camp during WWII; Ellington's legendary bassist Jimmy Blanton; classical pianist Roland Hayes, and the Rev. Cleavant Derricks, who composed "Just a Little Talk with Jesus" and hundreds of other gospel songs. From the 1940s to the 1970s, "Big Nine" (East Ninth Street) was a mecca for jazz and R&B musicians. Edwin Horne, grandfather of Lena, co-owned the People's Drug Store at Ninth and B. Chattanooga-born saxophonists include Yusef Lateef and Bennie Wallace; the latter, who wrote the scores for *Bull Durham* and *White Men Can't Jump,* is not an African-American.

The Chattanooga Regional History Museum (400 Chestnut) is first-rate, while the Mary Walker (3031 Wilcox Boulevard) chronicles the achievements of black inventors. Baseball buffs will want to visit Chattanooga's vintage Engel Stadium, named after Joseph William Engel, the Lookouts' former pitcher, scout, and PR stuntman who once traded shortstop Johnny Jones to the Charlotte Hornets for a turkey. Satchel Paige, Harmon Killebrew, and a young Willie Mays once played for the farm clubs here. The team song used to be an old Appalachian ditty called "(Cut Down) The Old Pine Tree" — to make bats, perhaps.

The city also happens to be a cookie monster's paradise. Moon Pies (marshmallow cookie sandwiches) were invented here 80 years ago (in the 1950s, country duo Lonzo and Oscar eulogized the marshmallow sandwiches in song). L'il Debbie Snack Cakes, sort of the Southern Twinkies, take shape in nearby Collegedale. The Krystal Corporation, renowned for its square hamburgers, is headquartered here as well. For good barbecue, take Broad Street from downtown to Hot Sauce Charlie's, at 3625 Tennessee Avenue in the Saint Elmo district.

To the south in Georgia, the still-operating Rock City was once famous far and wide for its signs painted on hundreds of barns along the highway. The gardens were the brainchild of Chattanooga businessman Garnett Carter's wife, Freida. He also built the country's first miniature golf course (now defunct), naming it after Tom Thumb.

Lazy Jasper, the Morgan County seat, lies south. The town was laid out on land donated in 1820 by Betsy Pack, born Elizabeth Lowery, the daughter of Cherokee chief John Lowery. Detour on 27N through the long Sequatchie Valley to Powell Crossroads, but watch out for free-ranging chickens along the highway; this long rift valley (formed between two parallel faults) has turned out some great fiddlers, notably Jess Young, a former coal miner who recorded "The Old Hen Cackled" in 1925, rejected an offer to join the Opry, and died of TB. Confederate Railroad, which won the Country Music Association's coveted new group of the year award a few years back, started out in the Whitwell area.

Nashville

The strutting peacock of Middle Tennessee, Nashville is also the 40-county region's political and economic anchor. The original settlement, Fort Nashborough, dates to Revolutionary days; the name was changed because it sounded too British. In his 1834 *Tennessee Gazetteer,* Eastin Morris described Nashville as "altogether one of the most romantic, healthy and flourishing little cities in the Valley of the Mississippi." He noted its undulating and rocky site, beautiful cedar groves and evergreen hills — "the richest variety of landscape scenery" — and the Cumberland River, which "seems to wander where it should."

Seventy years later, O. Henry showed considerably less enthusiasm towards the city. In a short story entitled "The Municipal Resort," he bemoaned its steep hills, a reckless and unintelligible hackney driver, and relentless drizzle which he deemed "not so fragrant as a moth-ball nor as thick as pea-soup." Modern-day mystery writer Steve Womack finds contemporary Nashville in the wee hours to be "a strange compound of insomniac music types, graveyard-shift workers, and people looking for love or trouble and not caring very much which one they find first."

Indeed, the state's capital and second-largest city (pop. 506,000) after Memphis has many different faces, depending on who is attempting to describe it. Once known as the "Athens of the South" for its many colleges and universities, Nashville is now more commonly called "Music City U.S.A." (Local deejay David Cobb coined the term in 1950.) Banks and industry may drive the local economy, but it's Nashville's musical past and present that draw most of the tourists, numbering some 10 million annually. Music aficionados flock here to hear live music, explore the legacy of the *Grand Ole Opry,* and visit the well-appointed Country Music Hall of Fame and Museum.

Nashville is also sometimes called "the Third Coast" because it ranks with New York and Los Angeles as a major recording center — a remarkable achievement considering its relatively small size. The local music industry comprises a veritable labyrinth of song publishers and licensing rights organizations, attorneys and accountants, arrangers and costume designers, video producers and disc masterers, voice-over specialists and record label printers, and the ubiquitous marketing reps and PR flacks. Nashville even has its own Music Yellow Pages. For the most part, the industry prefers to remain anonymous,

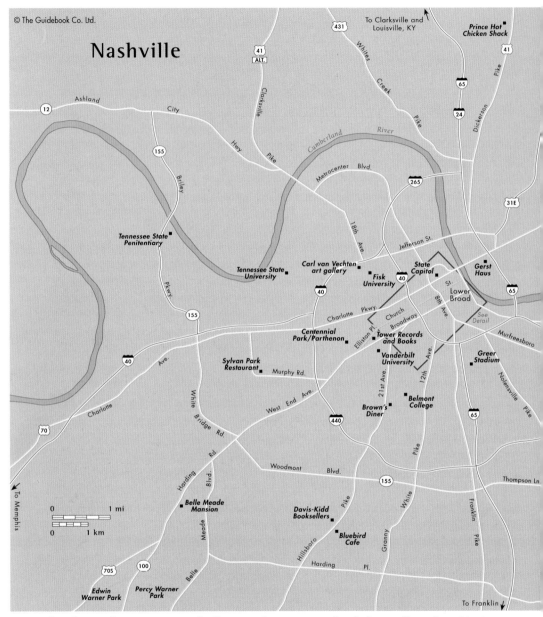

© The Guidebook Co. Ltd.

Nashville

but the "civilian" visiting Nashville can at least view its façade by strolling along Music Row, which extends from the Hall of Fame south to Belmont College. (For a good map of the Row, consult Sherry Bond's *The Songwriter's & Musician's Guide To Nashville.*)

The music itself, however, is very accessible, mostly at small clubs as well as at several larger venues. For the most up-to-date listings, pick up the free weekly *Nashville Scene*, published Wednesdays and available in street boxes and stores around town. For getting

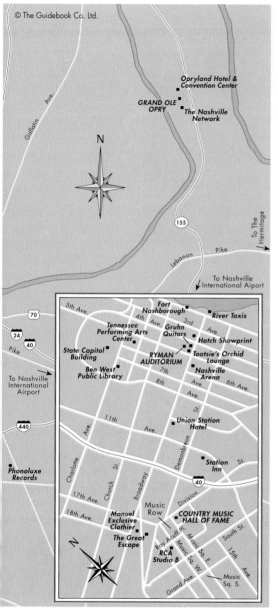

© The Guidebook Co. Ltd.

your bearings, Gousha's $6 *Fastmap* is a good investment. Nashville has a pretty decent bus system, but since the city is spread out (Opryland is nine miles northeast of downtown) and there are many worthwhile places to visit, renting a car makes sense and is relatively cheap. Keep your eyes peeled for spontaneous developments — such as a George Jones concert following a minor-league baseball game (the Nashville Sounds) at Greer Stadium, or Johnny Cash, backed by the Nashville Symphony, reciting the Gettysburg Address at an Italian Street Fair.

Traditionally, Nashville has been synonymous with country music, and country continues to be its cash cow, with the industry employing some 25,000 people. However — not to take away from Vince and Reba and Garth and Lorrie and Tanya — today's Nashville music scene consists of much more than just country. Some of the world's best musicians now live here, including hometown boy John Jackson (who plays guitar for Bob Dylan), and a host of transplants: Steve Winwood, Al Kooper, Janis Ian, and Duane Eddy; and Steppenwolf's John Kay, NRBQ's Al Anderson, Fleetwood Mac's Bob Welch, and the Eagles' Bernie Leadon. Even pop's Neil Diamond has "kicked the tires" here of late. National acts such as Los Lobos are managed out of Nashville, and gospel biggies like the Winans, Take 6, and Amy Grant have made it their base. Songwriters' nights blanket the town like gas stations.

Even in past decades, Nashville's musical output has been surprisingly diverse, with early labels like Bullet, Dot, Excello, and Nashboro turning out pop, R&B, and country. Elvis recorded "It's Now or Never" and some 250 other sides, *après* Sun, at RCA's Studio B, while James Brown cut "Hot Pants" and "Sex Machine" here. Deejay John R. at WLAC, a rhythm-and-blues powerhouse from the mid-1940s to the '70s, maintained that he didn't just play hits, he *made* them (including Otis Redding's first single, "These Arms of Mine").

Soul singers Joe Tex and Ruth Brown passed through town, as did gospel's Clara Ward and Mahalia Jackson.

In his early days, Jimi Hendrix jammed at the New Era club on Jefferson Street after hurting his leg parachuting at Fort Campbell in Clarksville, Tennessee. People called him "Marbles" then because, being from Seattle, they thought he talked funny. Bob Dylan visited twice in the '60s, yielding *Blonde On Blonde* and *Nashville Skyline*. Duane Allman and his brother Greg were born here, although their band coalesced considerably later in Macon, Georgia. In the early '80s, the late Lenny Breau graced Music City with his exquisite jazz-derived guitar; he, in turn, was influenced by session man Hank Garland.

Of course, Nashville has been at least a temporary way station for virtually every major country artist, its garishness epitomized by Webb Pierce's guitar-shaped swimming pool and, today, by huge billboards touting the latest stars. Thumb through the Country Music Foundation's 592-page tome on the genre's "pickers, slickers, cheatin' hearts & superstars." One of these is Nashville native Muriel Deason aka Kitty Wells, whose stage name is based on a song dating to 1861. Dubbed the Queen of Country Music, she sang such classic tearjerkers as "Icicles Hanging from Your Heart" and "Will Your Lawyer Talk to God." In all, she racked up 23 number-one country records, including the first ever by a female artist ("It Wasn't God Who Made Honky Tonk Angels," 1952).

Other native Nashvillians include the singers Rita Coolidge, Carlene Carter (daughter, in turn, of singers June Carter and Carl Smith), and Pearl Butler (whose musical partner Carl came from Knoxville); pianist/crooner Cecil Gant (his "Owl Stew" described a whorehouse on Fourth Avenue South); trumpeter Doc Cheatham, who accompanied Billie Holiday; songwriters Gene Allison ("You Can Make It if You Try") and Warner Mack; gospel host Bobby Jones, and BMI head Frances Preston (who started out there as a receptionist).

In order to maximize your visit to Music City, local promoter Daniel Petraitis recommends approaching Nashville's music with as much of an open mind as you can muster. "If you try and pigeonhole it and put it in a cage, you wind up missing a lot of great stuff," he said, citing Steve Earle and Maura O'Connell as examples. Having grown up on the Jersey shore where he was weaned on Springsteen, Petraitis admits that it took him a while to empathize with songs such as, say, Mark Chesnutt's "Bubba Shot the Jukebox."

KRISTI ROSE AND THE HANDSOME STRANGERS

Saturday September 7th
12th & Porter

with The Charlie White-Jerry Boonstra Band

Kristi Rose picking corn on a hot summer day.

INCREASINGLY, NASHVILLE'S DIVERSITY reflects the national trend toward synthesizing different genres of music into new hybrids. A good example is singer Kristi Rose, who periodically stages her legendary Thrillbilly Lovefests at various venues around town. Flanked by a bevy of backwoods beauties perched atop haystacks and swigging longnecks, the diva sings a rave-up, yodeling version of "Glory Hallelujah!" as well as her own originals.

Rose also sings "eclectic theatrical country" with a combo at the Gas Lite and a more rock-tinged set with her Handsome Strangers at Wolfy's. Raised on a farm straddling the Illinois-Kentucky border, she spent a dozen years in New York playing punkabilly before relocating to Nashville in the early '90s. Her influences range from Jeanne Pruett and the Farmer Boys, to Patti Smith and Jason and the Scorchers.

Thrillbilly diva **Kristi Rose** periodically conducts one of her Lovefests around town, personally manning the kissing booth and framing the stage with "backwoods beauties" atop haybales. It's about as far as you can get from the country music industry's Fan Fair, held in June at the state fairgrounds. Photo by Baxter Buck. Poster by Kevin Bradley of Voo Doo Rocket, Inc.

She likes Nashville's boomtown atmosphere but has little interest in pounding the beat on Music Row, its commercial music center. "I mean, the idea of passing around a tape that would show that I could sing, and looking for songs, and [that] somebody was going to make me into the next *whomever,* is not something that I could ever see working for me."

Indeed, her songs may not be treacly enough by Music Row standards. In one, she sings "I don't want you, I don't need you, I don't love you . . . right now . . . come back tomorrow." *The New York Times* designated her long black coif as Nashville's "next big hair," and she doesn't mind being grouped with present and past winners Lyle Lovett and Loretta Lynn. She's also a big fan of pin-up girl Bettie Page, a Nashville native.

Kristi's husband Fats Kaplin, who grew up in New York, has handled fiddle and accordion for the Tractors, an Oklahoma shuffle band with a California horn section whose debut album sold more than two million copies. Fats now works with the Manhattan Transfer. He has also worked with a group of other Nashville-based musicians who have set up their own indie label called Dead Reckoning, which means piloting a boat without mechanical aid. Its artists include the singer-songwriters Kevin Welch and Kieran Kane, slide guitarist Mike Henderson, fiddler Tammy Rogers, and Nashville's own Harry Stinson, who has drummed for everyone from Etta James to George Jones, in addition to singing backup and producing.

Other small labels such as Almo Sounds, Winter Harvest, Veritas, and Magnatone, as well as Warner's American Recordings and Arista/Nashville, also produce this type of roots music, known alternately as insurgent country, alternative, and Americana.

Decidedly less campy than Kristi Rose, Muriel Anderson said she "commutes" to Nashville from her hometown of Elmhurst, Illinois. The former fingerpicking champion started out playing folk and bluegrass and switched to classical guitar — mainly because she could study it in college. Now her music synthesizes these and other styles. "I was trying to decide what type of music I was going to play," she told me between sets at the Sutler, "and finally came to the decision that I had to play what I loved to play — and I love a lot of different styles of music."

Along the same esoteric lines, the Nashville Mandolin Ensemble — a big band made up solely of string instruments — appears around town sporadically, with a repertoire ranging from classical Spanish music and Charles Mingus to the "Star Trek" theme (which the group retitled "Where No Mandolin Has Gone Before").

Anything goes in Music City.

THE *GRAND OLE OPRY,* WHICH BEGAN AS A RADIO SHOW in the '20s, is the cornerstone of Nashville's music industry. One of its early stars, Roy Acuff, has observed that had it not been for the Opry, "Nashville would have been just like any other capital city — pretty dead." Indeed, the Opry is the main reason that people associate Nashville with music in much the same way that they equate Vegas with gambling.

After 1932, when WSM increased its signal to 50,000 watts, the Opry could be heard all the way from Texas to Canada, which in turn attracted talented musicians from throughout the South. Encouraged by the program's great success, by the mid-1940s recording studios began setting up shop here, and today the six largest record companies have branch offices in Nashville.

The Opry began in October 1925 when local businessman Edwin Craig opened a 1,000-watt radio station in order to advertise National Life, his family's insurance company. The station's call letters, WSM, stood for "We Shield Millions." Some early guests on the *WSM Barn Dance*, as it was first known, included Sumner County's Dr. Humphrey Bate and His Possum Hunters, and an 83-year-old fiddler from Smith County named Uncle Jimmy Thompson, whose niece Eva accompanied him on piano.

In 1927, the program's stage manager, George D. "Judge" Hay, spontaneously created the famous name.

> One Saturday night, the barn dance program was scheduled to follow a network program, the 'Music Appreciation Hour,' featuring a concert orchestra directed by Dr. Walter Damrosch in a program of classical music. Announcing the final number on the program, Dr. Damrosch had said, 'Most artists agree there is no place in the classics for realism. However, I am going to break one of my rules and present a composition by a young composer whose latest number depicts the onrush of a locomotive,' and he directed the great orchestra through the number and then closed the program with the customary sign-off.
>
> 'Judge' Hay, waiting in the studio to announce the Barn Dance which was to follow and listening to the network program on the monitor, had heard Dr. Damrosch's comments. As he got the signal from the operator in the control room that he was on the air, Hay spoke into the mike:
>
> 'For the last hour, we have been listening to music taken largely from grand opera and the classics, and heard Dr. Damrosch tell us there is no place for realism in that kind of music. In respectful contrast to Dr. Damrosch's presentation, for the next three hours we are going to present nothing but realism. We now present our own *Grand Ole Opry!*'
>
> ~ Powell Stamper, *The National Life Story*

Hay then handed the mike to harmonica wizard DeFord Bailey, a Davidson County native, who played his "Pan American Blues" without accompaniment. One of the Opry's few African-American performers, Bailey was dismissed in 1941, allegedly for refusing to learn new tunes, and spent the rest of his life as a bootblack. (See Morton and Wolfe's excellent biography of him.)

In its early years, the Opry had few real competitors. Even in the early 1960s, there were still only 115 country music stations nationwide (compared to more than 2,000

In 1925, Nashville businessman **Edwin Craig** opened radio station WSM to promote his family's insurance company. The station's *Barn Dance* — soon renamed the *Grand Ole Opry* — became National Life's crown jewel. Among the program's earliest performers were 77-year-old fiddler Uncle Jimmy Thompson (accompanied by his niece Eva on piano), Dr. Humphrey Bate and his Possum Hunters, and singer Obed "Dad" Pickard. They all came from Tennessee. Les Leverett.

today). At its inception, the Opry was transmitted from a bare-bones studio on the fifth floor of the National Life building. Before long, the company built a 500-seat studio to accommodate an audience, and subsequently the program moved to several other venues around town before settling in at the downtown Ryman Auditorium in 1941, where it remained for the next 30 years.

The Opry's final move occurred in 1974, after a new Grand Ole Opry House was built at the Opryland U.S.A. theme park (see p. 203). The show is still broadcast on WSM-AM (650) as it has been since the 1920s, only the owner is no longer National Life. Oklahoma-based Gaylord Entertainment now manages the Ryman and the Opry, as well as WSM, Opryland, cable stations TNN and CMT, the Wildhorse Saloon dance hall on Second Avenue, the showboat *General Jackson,* and even a fleet of passenger ferries plying the Cumberland River between Opryland and downtown. Indeed, Nashvillians must sometimes feel as though there's little that Gaylord *doesn't* own (except the new Ma Bell skyscraper, or the new 20,000-seat civic arena).

THE RYMAN, NEWLY RENOVATED AND OPEN FOR SPECIAL CONCERTS, was built in the 1890s by a reformed riverboat captain who had seen the light. Thomas G. Ryman called it the Union Gospel Tabernacle. A horse show held there in 1901 attracted an elaborately dressed audience in which the ladies took extra pains, a local newspaper reported, "to dress the hair becomingly in most cases, and the pretty and appropriate airgretts and pompons now so much worn gave the finishing touches to many exquisite toilettes."

Well before Roy Acuff and Minnie Pearl came on the scene, the Ryman was one of the South's premier venues, attracting everyone from Caruso and Isadora Duncan to the Ziegfield Follies. Former stage manager Lula Naff's memorabilia collection is housed in the public library's Nashville Room (Ben West branch, 225 Polk).

Solo harmonica player **DeFord Bailey** (1899-1982), who grew up east of Nashville, was the *Grand Ole Opry's* first African-American performer and one of only a few in the program's 70-year history. He liked to imitate the sounds of birds, coon dogs, and trains. Management dismissed him in 1941 for refusing to learn new tunes. For the rest of his life he worked as a bootblack. Les Leverett.

Tour the Ryman, or better yet, take in a concert there. Bluegrass concerts are held on summer Tuesday nights. The building is now air-conditioned, so you won't swelter like in the old days, and the old wooden church pews have been cushioned. The setting is said to have inspired Garrison Keillor's *Prairie Home Companion* radio show.

Even the great Merle Haggard, who doesn't particularly like Nashville, feels "humbled" at the Ryman. "When a performer stands in front of that mike," Haggard once wrote, "he's standing right where Hank Williams stood, where Lefty's been, where Elvis performed and some fool told him to go back to driving a truck. You know, when you're standing there, you're on the sacred ground where all the grand old masters of country music have played."

HIGH SCHOOL AUD.
HOHENWALD, TENNESSEE   8 P. M.
FRIDAY MARCH 24 1945
IN PERSON   **GRAND OLE OPRY**   **STAR**

ROD BRASFIELD.

Copyright 1969   Heritage Poster Co. - 815 16th Ave., So. - Nashville, Tenn.

Opry comedian **Rod Brasfield** (1910-1958), a Mississippian, based his Uncle Cyd character in Hohenwald, southwest of Nashville. He often teamed up with Sarah Ophelia Colley, better known as Minnie Pearl. Red Foley was Rod and Minnie's straight man. Hatch Showprint.

Novelist Lee Smith described the Ryman audience as "worshipful" in *Devil's Dream*. The steady stream of fans who approach its footlights to "pause and snap" reminded her of a communion service. Jack Hurst's picture book covers the Opry from the '20s to the '70s.

"The Mother Church of Country Music" hosted its last Opry on March 15, 1974, after which the show moved to Opryland.

SOME CYNICS COMPLAIN THAT OPRYLAND does not adequately convey the "downhome" spirit of country music, that it is too homogenized and touristy. This is like boycotting malls due to their sameness, and thereby missing out on their variety and convenience. The fact of the matter is, the same company that runs Opryland also manages the Fiesta Texas amusement park.

Like Dollywood, Opryland *used to* offer an endless barrage of food stalls and rides in a theme park that could just as well be set in Kansas as in Tennessee. Diamond Rio, Billy Dean, and Sweethearts of the Rodeo got their first leg up at the park's outdoor theaters. However, the theme park closed for good in 1997. Gaylord Entertainment plans to open new retail and entertainment businesses in its place by the year 2000.

Music buffs will want to go to the Opry, which is held on weekend nights (one show Friday, two on Saturday, and additional ones during peak season). On the outside, the Opry House looks like a Methodist Church; the inside is bigger (4,400 seats) and less intimate than the Ryman and lacks its creaky charm. (Touring the old Ryman, Bob Hope once quipped, "Do they keep bats in here?") Opry figureheads Roy Acuff and Minnie Pearl have both passed away, and it's unlikely that we will ever see the likes of Hank and Patsy and Ernest Tubb again.

Still, if you can swallow its premeditated kitsch, the Opry offers a wide range of music under one roof, from old-timer Lewis Crook (who joined in 1929) to upstart Alison Krauss. Ads for local products like Martha White Flour and Goo Goo Clusters (both early sponsors) are interspersed throughout, giving the show an old-fashioned ambience. Even the most jaded tend to come away with a smile.

Next door to the Opry House, the Grand Ole Opry Museum covers the show's golden era. Thoughout the year you can attend a live taping at one of TNN's three studios, and your mug might end up in some 60 million households. If you need a breather, take a ride on the *General Jackson*. Gaylord's Opryland Music Group also happens to own the rights to 40,000 songs, including Hank Williams' crown jewels.

Even if you're not staying there, you're welcome to wander through the infinite Opryland Hotel, which even sports its own rainforest where you can cool your heels after visiting the park. A couple of the bars feature live music. The hotel's nearly 3,000 rooms make it the largest convention complex in the United States, and you never know who will be doing business there: I once met some emu ranchers in town for their annual meeting!

Over the holidays, the hotel is festooned with some 1.4 million lights.

Across Briley Parkway from Opryland, Ernest Tubb's Midnight Jamboree gets underway following Saturday's Opry; both shows are broadcast over WSM. The Jamboree features Opry warhorses and new talent alike, and won't cost you a nickel.

———

WHILE THE FOLKS AT THE CHAMBER OF COMMERCE prefer to call it "The District," the traditional name of "Lower Broad" (short for Broadway) is perhaps a more apt description of the downtown area near the Ryman where Opry performers and fans once congregated for drinks and debauchery. By the early 1970s, a proliferation of pawnshops, massage parlors, and debris left in the Opry's wake on Monday mornings, began to grate on the city's collective nerves, ultimately forcing the Opry's move to Opryland. For the next two decades, the Ryman lay fallow and Lower Broad became a virtual ghost town. Tootsie's Orchid Lounge remained open but had lost its reason for being.

Over the past five years, however, Lower Broad has resurrected some of its former glory, hopping with clubs like Wolfie's and Robert's Western Wear. The Ernest Tubb Record Store is an institution and a good place to find traditional country; vinyl freaks should visit Lawrence Brothers (409 Broadway), a couple of doors down. Other good record stores are Phonoluxe (2609 Nolensville), Great Escape (1925 Broadway) and Tower (2400 West End).

A must-see is Hatch Showprint, near Tootsie's at 316 Broadway. Run by the Country Music Foundation, Hatch makes show posters the old-fashioned way from its old linoleum and wood-cut blocks. The posters make great souvenirs, and you can tour the premises. Hatch opened its doors around the corner in 1879 (which my grandmother would have described as "old old"). Where else can you buy a poster of the Lollypop & Sparky traveling minstrel show, or a life-sized Bill Monroe three-sheet? After leaving Hatch, poke around Gruhn Guitars, a few doors up Broadway. It's the largest antique fretted instrument dealer in the world. If you must, wait in line at the Hard Rock Cafe for a drink (where you can pay obeisance to Buddy Holly's tan wool sweater with a snag on the right sleeve) or stop in at the Wildhorse Saloon (owned by Gaylord, but then, what isn't?) for a line dance.

A pint-sized replica of Fort Nashborough stands on a bluff where Broadway dead-ends at the Cumberland River. Here, settlers signed the Cumberland Compact, Middle Tennessee's first (non-Indian) governing document, and Rachel Donelson, who later married Andrew Jackson, sicced dogs on hostile Indians. In the summer, concerts are held in nearby Riverfront Park.

———

HUNDREDS OF THOUSANDS OF TOURISTS file through the doors of the Country Music Hall of Fame and Museum every year. It's a wonder that the number hasn't quadrupled, given the genre's surge in popularity over the past decade. Aside from plaques showing some 70-plus Hall of Famers, the museum's permanent collection delineates country's various sub-genres, such as bluegrass, Cajun, Western swing, rockabilly, and honky-tonk. There's also an overview of the Opry's illustrious 70-year history and an exhibit on songwriters.

You can see Patsy Cline's Confederate flag cigarette lighter, discovered at the site of her fatal plane crash near Camden, Tennessee, and some 3,000 other artifacts. Special exhibits pay tribute to seminal figures like Johnny Cash, who lives in nearby Hendersonville but grew up in the Arkansas Delta.

"There's actually a surprisingly small number of Tennessee-born and bred musicians, singers, and writers in Nashville," notes the museum's Bill Ivey. "It's mostly a kind of mecca that people come to from other places." Gibson Guitars, which is headquartered in Nashville, sponsored a recent exhibit on Hank Williams.

The museum is run by the Country Music Foundation, a not-for-profit group set up in the early 1960s by the for-profit Country Music Association for the express purpose of raising money to build a museum. The CMF's library and music center, located in the museum's basement, is open Monday through Thursday by appointment only; books can be paged but browsing the stacks is not permitted. The foundation also publishes *The Journal of Country Music* three times a year, operates its own small record label, and administers Hatch Showprint and RCA's Studio B (see below).

Covering the Country Beat

When I used to cover the police the only time you'd read about country music was when Hank Williams got drunk and set himself on fire in bed or when Hank Snow got arrested comin' over the bridge 105 miles an hour. But Mr. Craig was still going to that *Grand Ole Opry* many Saturday nights and mixing and mingling with those people. Everybody who came downtown hated it on Monday morning; they'd see all this debris around Fifth and Broad where the crowds had gathered to go into the old Opry House. But once the record companies started establishing here and the economy began to build many people reluctantly began to say, "Well, we'd better see who in the industry is worthy to run for the chamber of commerce," or, "Is there anybody in there we want to talk to about being active on some civic endeavor?"

~ John Seigenthaler

JUST DOWN THE HILL FROM THE MUSEUM, you will find yourself in the thick of Music Row — not the industry's, but the tourist's. Here stand an aggregation of "museums" dedicated to country acts like Barbara Mandrell, Hank Williams Jr., and Alabama. Since the area only extends for a block or two, serious country buffs need not devote an inordinate amount of time here. Those of a cynical bent will have a field day perusing the schlock shops (don't miss the rhinestone suits on display at the George Jones Gift Shop). You can pile on at Shoney's, a locally-based restaurant developed by sax player Ray Danner (he bought the franchise from a man named Shoenfeld). While exploring the Row, it's good to repeat Shoney's upbeat mantra: "When you smile you are beautiful."

ALSO WITHIN WALKING DISTANCE OF THE MUSEUM, RCA's historic Studio B (on Roy Acuff Place) falls within the boundaries of the real, working Music Row, a mere block from the barber shop where the late producer Owen Bradley — credited with building the town's first studio — used to get his hair cut. Over a 20-year span beginning in 1957, the folks at Studio B turned out an amazing 47,000 songs, including such classics as "Only the Lonely," "He'll Have To Go," and "It's Now or Never." Exhibits trace the history of recorded music from cylinders (1870s) to CDs. Recently, the bare-bones studio has been revamped, and visitors can watch a recording session in progress.

The world's six largest record companies keep shop on or near Music Row. All but one (Warner Bros.) are foreign-owned, which seems ironic when you consider country music's quintessentially American roots. Sony and Matsushita have gobbled up Columbia and MCA, and Germany's BMG, Britain's EMI, and the multinational Phillips-Siemen control RCA, Capitol, and Polygram, respectively. Understandably, record sessions — held at some 100 studios around town — are closed to the public. Music Row also boasts an impressive roster of musical acronyms, viz., AFM, ASCAP, BMI, CCA, CMA, GMA, NEA, NARAS, NSAI, SESAC, SGA, and TSA.

For the most part, the Row consists of a hodgepodge of rather anonymous-looking "low rises," many of them converted houses. "Music Row is difficult to find," writes Sherry Bond, "and even when you are standing in the middle of it, you probably won't recognize it!"

With a population density of fewer than 1,000 people per square mile, Nashville makes New York (23,000) and even L.A. (6,500) seem like veritable termite mounds — which is one reason why musicians like doing business here. Drummer Dale Armstrong, for instance, said he can leave equipment in the back of his truck and not have to worry as much about getting robbed. "It's a good place to raise kids," he added.

On the other hand, it's not hard to find songwriters. "This is a song town above all else," an engineer named Marshall Morgan told me. "That's what propels Nashville." The Songwriters Guild of America alone has more than a thousand members, roughly a quarter of the estimated total. According to one joke, in order to find a songwriter in Nashville, all you have to do is scream "Waiter!" Writers either work alone or collaborate with partners, at music publishing houses or at home. Some earn salaries, others negotiate for royalties. The rewards are considerable: Getting your song on a country superstar's record can net hundreds of thousands of dollars and up.

On the other hand, blessed are aspiring songwriters who expect nothing, for they might not get egg in their faces. "Don't go to Nashville if you have any intention of doing something with your music because they will flat kill you," counsels Shad O'Shea in *Just for the Record*. "You will come back so dejected that you'll never attempt to write a song again. And your wallet will be a lot lighter."

Explore Music Row on foot to get the full effect. The district is located just south of downtown, near the Country Music Hall of Fame. The main thoroughfares are 16th and

17th Avenues (called Music Square East and West within the Row) between Division and Blakemore. People who work on the Row can be extremely helpful and friendly. However, since they're busy at work, one shouldn't expect too much.

NASHVILLE IS BLESSED WITH A WIDE ARRAY OF MUSICAL VENUES. Its small clubs, in particular, offer an astonishing range of high-quality, eclectic, and affordable live music. Arguably the most famous of these is Amy Kurland's Bluebird Cafe, where songwriters play their own music. Kurland, who opened the club in 1982, is considered the Gertrude Stein of Nashville music. Kathy Mattea and dozens of other tunesmiths have earned their spurs at the Bluebird, which served as a backdrop for River Phoenix and Sandra Bullock in *The Thing Called Love*. Kurland grades the performers and once gave Garth Brooks an A-, back when he was holding down a day job at Boot Country (for the record, her only straight A went to David Wilcox).

Show up well in advance of show time as capacity is limited to 110, and lines are long. The Bluebird is open seven days a week; writers nights are held on Sunday, open mike on Monday. Be forewarned that this is a *serious* listening room, and audience members who talk during performances will be shushed. Besides the Bluebird, other clubs catering to songwriters include Douglas Corner, the Commodore Lounge, the Broken Spoke Saloon, Courtyard Cafe, and Joe's Village Inn.

During the industry's NAMM week, I happened to stop by the Station Inn, where Jorma Kaukonen (Hot Tuna, Jefferson Airplane) shared the stage with four other performers. This "guitar pull" was part of the club's Top Guitarists Showcase. I was surprised to find one of my teenage favorites playing in Nashville, and even more surprised to hear him outdueled by some of the other guitarists (Phil Keaggy's feedback version of "John the Revelator" practically incited a riot). Located a few blocks from the old Union Station, the Station Inn specializes in bluegrass.

The same week, I went to hear a band called Bonepony in the parking lot of Jamaica, an eatery on Broadway, and ended up chatting with harmonica executive Cham-Ber Huang — and with Charlie McCoy, the session harmonica player. At the trade show, I caught a live performance by Naked to the World (a California acoustic band), watched banjo innovator Earl Scruggs sign autographs, and heard Merle Haggard's guitarist Clint Strong play bebop. In short, you never know what to expect in Nashville, other than a generally high level of talent. Try to catch Kentucky-born soul singer Jonelle Mosser, who has been known to stand on furniture while belting it out until the wee hours.

If the Bluebird and the Station Inn represent songwriters and blugrassers (for the latter, also try the Bell Cove in Hendersonville), then the Sutler epitomizes the abstruse world of mixed-genre clubs. On any given night here, tucked into a nondescript strip south of downtown, you might hear barrelhouse or Delta blues, hillbilly bop, crooners, fingerpickers, jazz samba, and "symphonic hoedowns" by the Goose Creek Symphony, in addition to the town's ubiquitous singer/songwriters.

I once went to the Sutler hoping to catch a local act called the Wooten Brothers, who are originally from Virginia. Specifically, I wanted to hear Victor Wooten, considered one of the world's best electric bassists, but Victor was on the road with Béla Fleck, so his older brother Regi, normally the band's guitarist, sat in on bass. Regi, who taught Vic, proved to be a virtuoso in his own right on his "second instrument," playing lightning-fast runs and slapping his way through "Brick House." Other clubs that feature a melange of genres include the Ace of Clubs, Blue Sky Court, Diamond 'N the Rough, the Exit/In, and 12th & Porter.

A hot club as of this writing — meaning it's probably *passé* by now — is Robert's Western Wear on Broadway, where a neo-hillbilly band named BR5-49 held court for a year or two, playing for tips. Once Arista signed and recorded the group, its days at Robert's were numbered. Still, this bare-bones venue is worthwhile purely from a sociological viewpoint, where Vanderbilt PhD's cavort with Lower Broad floozies.

In addition to its clubs, Nashville also offers a number of other live music venues, such as the downtown Tennessee Performing Arts Center (TPAC) and the Starwood Amphitheater south of town. During the academic year, Vanderbilt's Sarratt Center also hosts concerts. In the summertime, top national acts perform on the banks of the Cumberland as part of the city's "Dancing in the District" series. During the Summer Lights Festival held in June, half a dozen stages are set up between the capitol and the Davidson County courthouse. The range of artists who play Nashville is strikingly diverse and not at all limited to country music, which some Nashvillians regard as a kind of besequined albatross.

———————

FISK UNIVERSITY IS A PLEASANT PLACE TO STROLL, and its first-rate library contains the effects of such black authors and leaders as Charles Waddell Chestnutt, Aaron Douglas, Marcus Garvey, Charles S. Johnson, and James C. Napier. Established in 1866 during the post-Civil War Reconstruction era, the predominantly black college owes its existence to the valiant efforts of the Jubilee Singers. This spirituals group toured America and Europe in the 1860s to raise money for the fledgling school's building fund. After hearing them in Switzerland, Mark Twain wrote, "I think in the Jubilees and their songs America has produced the perfectest flower of the ages; and I wish it were a foreign product, so that she would worship it and lavish money on it and go properly crazy over it."

Prominent African-American leaders have lectured at Jubilee Hall — the Hall that the Singers built — and inside hangs a portrait of the original group executed by Queen Victoria's court painter. Past faculty members have included the writer W.E.B. DuBois; James Weldon Johnson, who wrote "Lift Ev'ry Voice," known as the Negro national anthem (his brother J. Rosamond had a big hit with "Under the Bamboo Tree"), and painter Aaron Douglas, under whose leadership the school amassed its impressive Harlem Renaissance collection (including art by William H. Johnson, Alma Thomas, and David Driskell). All are housed in the school's Carl van Vechten art gallery, named for the art dealer who convinced

On Oct. 6, 1871, the **Fisk Jubilee Singers** left Nashville on a fundraising tour that rescued Fisk University, formed five years previously, from financial ruin. The group's 11 singers and pianist only planned to be away for a few weeks, but ended up on the road for seven years. Since they performed mostly before white audiences — including a weeping Queen Victoria — the songs were, in their words, "purged . . . of all ungainly africanism." From the tour's proceeds, Fisk built Jubilee Hall (above) on the site of an old slave pen. Courtesy of the Center of Popular Music, Middle Tennessee State University.

Georgia O'Keefe to donate her late husband Alfred Steiglitz's Impressionist paintings to Fisk. Located at 18th Avenue North and Jackson Street, the gallery is open Tuesday through Friday and weekend afternoons. Don't leave town without seeing it.

Missouri native Jimmie Lunceford studied at Fisk before forming his first band, the Chickasaw Syncopators, in Memphis in 1927. Later he moved to New York's Cotton Club, where his precision orchestra, built around its ensemble and section work (complete with white tuxedos and tap-dancing saxophonists), included such great instrumentalists as Trummy Young and Sy Oliver (though they weren't given much opportunity to solo).

Meharry Medical College once trained some 40 percent of the nation's black physicians. Its former president, Dr. David Satcher, is Surgeon General.

Tennessee State University opened its doors in 1909 when the state legislature mandated a teacher training institution for Tennessee's 473,000 "colored people." Duke Ellington's great bassist Jimmy Blanton, who joined the band in the late '30s and died a few years later from tuberculosis, earned his degree at TSU. "He played melodies that belonged to the bass and always had a foundation quality," Ellington wrote in *Music Is My Mistress*. "Rhythmically, he supported and drove at the same time." At nearby Hadley Park — one of the first devoted to African-Americans — Frederick Douglass addressed former slaves in 1873.

Musicians will tell you that one of Music City's greatest assets — albeit low-profile — is the Nashville Community Music School on Edgehill. Founded in 1984 by the late jazz bassist W.O. Smith, this school offers 50-cent lessons to poor youths. Some of Nashville's finest musicians offer their teaching services *pro bono*. Smith played bebop on New York's 52nd Street (that's him on Coleman Hawkins' famous version of "Body and Soul") before settling down as a TSU music professor for 40 years, until his death in 1991. His autobiography, called *Side Man*, is an interesting read. If you're feeling generous, the school is a good cause. A $125 donation will send a child to summer music camp for a week, and $510 will underwrite lessons for four children for a whole school year.

Vanderbilt University must be counted as the jewel in Nashville's educational crown and one of the best schools in the South. Like Fisk, it was built during Reconstruction. A local Methodist Episcopal bishop, Holland N. McTyeire, founded the school in 1873, with a little help from his friend, Commodore Cornelius Vanderbilt. Their wives were cousins from Mobile, and Mrs. Vanderbilt managed to prevail upon her husband, a New York shipping and railway magnate, to donate a cool million as seed money — which laid a lot of track back then. The Blair School of Music is considered top-notch in its field (mostly classical). Kirkland Hall, with its conspicuous bell tower, houses the college's administrative offices and revolving historical exhibits. The well-stocked Heard library (1.7 million volumes) is open to Vandy students; for a fee, outsiders can obtain an annual user's card. Check the Sarratt Student Center for music, film, and dance happenings.

Belmont College's alumnae include actress Mary Martin and comedienne Minnie Pearl, and more recently, country star Trisha Yearwood and gospel's Steven Curtis Chapman. Established in 1890, Belmont was once a tony finishing school for girls. Rules were strict in Victorian times: one young lady who waved at a passing buggy was banished to her room for 24 hours. The pink Italianate mansion overlooking the campus is "Belle Monte," the former residence of Adelicia Acklen, who in the mid-19th century was reputed to be the richest woman in the country.

Rather befitting its status as "the Athens of the South," Nashville is home to the only existing full-scale replica of Greece's Parthenon, constructed in 1897 for the Tennessee Centennial Exposition, which was opened by President McKinley. A collection of 18th and 19th-century American paintings is housed inside, as well as a 42-foot statue of the goddess Athena made by local artist Alan LeQuire. In 1916, women's suffragist Anne Dallas Dudley lobbied for the 19th Amendment by marching from the Parthenon to the Hermitage Hotel downtown, where both sides had set up camp. Tennessee cast the deciding yea vote. The surrounding park is a nice place to while away an afternoon reading, paddleboating, or playing a game of pickup volleyball. Train fans can climb aboard an 1851 steam locomotive.

Nearby, visit the salon of couturier Manuel Cuevas — Manuel for short — whom singer Ray Price once deemed "the best damn tailor in the world." The Mexico native has made clothes for (to name a few) Elvis, The Man in Black, and Gram Parsons, and also allegedly helped his mentor, Nudie of Hollywood, stitch Hank Williams' famous suit with the music notes. Manuel's clientele consists mostly of country stars and rockers; ordinary folks are welcome to browse the racks too, although his rhinestone-studded threads don't come cheap.

EVEN WITHOUT ITS RICH MUSICAL OFFERINGS, Nashville's history is fascinatingly eclectic. The place seems to grow and attract all manner of iconoclastic characters, such as William Walker, who managed to install himself as the president of Nicaragua in 1856, only to get himself executed in Honduras four years later. Nashville has also been the home to more than a few entrepreneurial businesses-turned-giants, such as Shoney's and Hospital Corporation of America. (These two could be viewed as complementary.)

This local color is at least partially defined by the region's pioneering roots: "the great leap westward," as Theodore Roosevelt put it. In 1779, two westering parties led by James Robertson and John Donelson — Andrew Jackson's future father-in-law — migrated overland and by flatboats. They settled along the Cumberland River's French Lick and built Fort Nashborough.

(Incidentally, it was Teddy Roosevelt who coined the phrase "good to the last drop" while drinking coffee at the Maxwell House Hotel, built downtown on Fourth and Church streets and destroyed by fire on Christmas day, 1961. Other guests included Caruso, Buffalo Bill, and Tom Thumb. A rather soulless, high-rise reincarnation of the Maxwell House has been erected on MetroCenter Boulevard north of town.)

Heading west, Union Station (Romanesque) was once a depot for the Louisville & Nashville railroad and now serves as a luxury hotel. Nearby the 1877 Customs House (Victorian Gothic) and 1934 U.S. Post Office (Art Deco) are worth perusing. The copper statue of Mercury which fell from the roof of Union Station in 1952, presaged the L&N's relocation to Louisville five years later.

Across the street, the National Baptist Publishing Board turns out some 14 million books and periodicals a year (Thomas Nelson prints a zillion Bibles in Nashville as well) and its gift shop carries a wide range of literature for the spiritually inclined. As you head west, after crossing a bridge over the tracks, *The Tennessean*, the state's largest daily, is on the right side. Vanderbilt's ivy towers are a few blocks farther on the left. Just before Tower Records/Books/Videos, a right turn leads to Elliston Place, where you can browse through Elder's antiquarian bookstore and Mosko's newsstand.

Scarf down a cheeseburger at Rotier's or a "meat-and-three" — your choice of one entrée and three side dishes — at the Elliston Place Soda Shop. For soul food, try the Swett's location on Clifton Avenue. Brown's Diner fixes Waylon's favorite burger as well as — burp — frito chili pie and cold Bud on tap, and you may bump into John Prine or the Everly Brothers. For the ultimate dessert, continue west on Broadway — now called West End Avenue — and turn right on Murphy Road, which winds downhill to Sylvan Park Restaurant. Here, Charlesetta Hughes has been making pies early every morning for more than 30 years. Go for the chocolate, crowned with four fingers of meringue. The coconut cream at Belle Meade Cafeteria on West End also gets raves. Or if you're on the run, grab a Goo Goo Cluster, made locally by the Standard Candy Company and identified as being "in the food group farthest from spinach."

In north Nashville, Prince Hot Chicken Shack on Ewing Lane dips, batters, fries, and then re-dips its spicy chicken. It comes in extra hot (lethal), hot (survivable), and mild (lightweight). Half a bird costs five bucks and change, and you might run into sexy country star Lorrie Morgan, who has been known to patronize the joint (her father George sang "Candy Kisses" and "Room Full of Roses"). Nearby on Nolensville Pike, Phonoluxe offers a diverse selection of CDs and records; afterwards you can inhale a flan next door at the La Hacienda tortilleria. (Used discophiles should also try the Great Escape on Broadway.) When the spirit moves you, drop by Temple Baptist's 2,400-seat sanctuary on Sunday mornings at 10 and hear the church's Praise Choir.

Since the early 1960s, music industry folks have been conducting their power breakfasts at the Pancake Pantry, located in a section of town known as Hillsboro Village. In nearby Green Hills, you can gorge yourself intellectually at Davis-Kidd Booksellers, with umpteen square feet of books, including a whole section on Nashville and other Tennesseana; songwriters convene Friday night at its Second Story Cafe. Bookstar on West End is also a good source for books.

Downtown at Eighth and Union, the Ben West public library features a special Nashville Room upstairs. The Tennessee State Museum provides a solid historical and cultural overview; nearby, a Civil War museum is housed in the basement of the War Memorial Building. For digging up old genealogical and military records, visit the Tennessee State Library and Archives. Across the street, the 1859 state capitol — the highest point in the city — is worth a self-guided tour. President James K. Polk's tomb marks the entrance, and the remains of architect William Strickland are embedded within the building's walls of fossilized limestone, quarried by slaves and prisoners.

While on the subject of paths of glory leading but to the grave, you might consider strolling through one of Nashville's decorated bone yards. Established by a former slave, Greenwood Cemetery on Elm Hill Pike is the final resting place of Cornelia Shepard (one of the original Fisk singers), DeFord Bailey — the Opry's first black performer — and civil rights leader Rev. Kelly Miller Smith. Nearby at Mt. Ararat lie the remains of Dr. Robert Fulton Boyd, a Meharry graduate who ran for mayor in 1893, and primitive sculptor Will Edmondson, whose 1937 show at the Museum of Modern Art was the first by a black artist (his work is displayed at Cheekwood, see below). Mt. Olivet boasts Lady Acklen's Gothic vault and the grave of Tom Ryman, who built the Ryman (he lived in a house on Second Avenue South until his death in 1904). At the Nashville City Cemetery, you'll find the graves of Gen. James Robertson, the city's founding father, and Capt. William Driver, who named the flag "Old Glory."

You are tired and weary; you've seen some great music, eaten your fill of that heavy Southern food, and zeroed in on a few good books. Head out to the affluent Belle Meade neighborhood and plunk yourself down under a big tree at the state's largest municipal park (actually two adjoining parks, named after brothers Percy and Edwin Warner). Foot and horseback trails cut through its 2,600 acres of hilly forest and open green expanses. Belle Meade Mansion, once a thoroughbred farm, and the Cheekwood botanical gardens and fine arts center are both located within striking distance. Farther west, canoe along the windy Harpeth River or visit the Narrows of the Harpeth State Historic Site, where slaves chiselled a 100-yard tunnel through solid stone as a detour between the two sides of a four-mile hairpin bend. Fifteen miles west of town on highway 100, the Loveless Cafe serves up fried chicken, biscuits, red-eye gravy, and homemade peach and blackberry preserves; expect a line on weekends.

Andrew Jackson,
the seventh U.S. President

East of Nashville, President Andrew Jackson once monitored the Trail of Tears from his window at the Hermitage. "Old Hickory" was a staunch supporter of the Removal Act of 1835, authorizing federal troops to forcibly escort Native Americans west to Oklahoma; thousands died of starvation and exposure. Indians call this tragedy "nunna-da-ul-tsun-yi," meaning "the place where they cried."

Five miles south of town, Traveller's Rest was the home of Jackson's campaign manager, John Overton, who also had a hand in founding Memphis. The Colonial Dames of America manage the site as a working farm typical of the early 19th century. Radnor Lake once supplied water for the L&N's steam engines. The railroad company turned it into a wildlife sanctuary in 1923, and half a century later, the area became the state's first official natural area, a popular retreat for hikers and bikers.

The town of Franklin — former home of early Opry stars Sam and Kirk McGee — is the site of the former (and short-lived) Lost State of Franklin, formed by a group of settlers who decided to set up their own laws.

This footnote in history occurred prior to Tennessee's statehood, when North Carolina was deciding whether to protect its holdings west of the Appalachian Mountains. Downtown Franklin is laced with historic buildings, including the 1823 Gothic-style Masonic Lodge, Tennessee's earliest surviving three-story structure, and the immaculately restored Carter House (1830), which survived the Battle of Franklin in 1864. Uncle Bud's and Dotson's are known for their catfish, and you might bump into the likes of Eddie Rabbitt, Jimmy Buffett, and Wynonna, among the many stars who live in the vicinity.

George "Possum" Jones and his wife, Nancy, live in Brentwood, between Franklin and Nashville. A few years back, the Beaumont, Texas, native made a dramatic comeback with his rendition of Bobby Braddock and Curly Putnam's "He Stopped Loving Her Today," which some country connoisseurs deem the greatest tearjerking song of all time, although my choice would be his cover of "If Drinkin' Don't Kill Me (Her Memory Will)." George, who was previously married to the late Tammy "D-I-V-O-R-C-E" Wynette — also a long-time Nashville-area resident — has developed his own line of Country Gold Pet Food.

Barbara Mandrell and the Cashes hang their hats in Hendersonville, along the shores of Old Hickory Lake. Any number of cheesy tour bus operators will be happy to show you (the outside of) their digs.

Middle Tennessee

Middle Tennessee has been called "the dimple of the universe," a land of rolling green hills, pastures, and farms. Those who are able to tear themselves away from Nashville's neon lights will discover a beautiful countryside, much of which has remained almost unchanged since Revolutionary War days.

An hour southeast of Nashville on Interstate 24, Murfreesboro briefly served as the capital of Tennessee from 1818 until 1826, when it was supplanted by Nashville, where the government has remained ever since. Actually, Murfreesboro was a good choice seeing as the state's geographical center lies a mile northeast of town. It's the state's sixth largest city, with a population of 54,000.

Middle Tennessee State University's Center of Popular Music specializes in Southern music. Among its holdings are tens of thousands of records and pieces of sheet music, as well as songbooks, videos, books, periodicals, photographs, and clippings.

In July, the town's Uncle Dave Macon Days pays homage to the old-timer who grew up near McMinnville. Even if you're not a fan of his clawhammer banjo, you have to admire Uncle Dave's chutzpah: he complained that Earl Scruggs "ain't a bit funny" and predicted Bing Crosby would never get anywhere until he learned how to sing louder.

The festival, held at Cannonsburgh Pioneer Village and considered one of the South's most authentic, is spearheaded by MTSU professor Charles K. Wolfe, an authority on early country music. His *Tennessee Strings* is a must-read. Gospel's Tipton Family and country's Hank Flamingo come from this area, and old-line Nashville songwriter John D. Loudermilk, a North Carolina native, lives here.

Northwest of town, Stones River National Battlefield commemorates the Civil War battle that cost 23,000 lives. Reenactments are staged periodically, and the well-stocked book shop alone is worthwhile.

Rutherford and seven other counties surrounding Nashville comprise the state's fastest-growing area. Murfreesboro itself boasts a large contingent of antique dealers and malls. Between Nashville and Murfreesboro, Smyrna, once home to the late Texas-born songwriter Townes van Zandt, supports a $2 billion Nissan plant — the country's largest such facility under one roof. (An equally massive Saturn factory sits to the west in Spring Hill.) Nearby, LaVergne's Ingram Industries is the world's largest book, record, and video distributor, with a quarter of a *billion* titles and 10,000 employees worldwide.

For a somewhat sleepier experience, kill some time in Loafers Corner, east of Smyrna. Heading south, country and gospel fans should visit the Louvin Brothers museum in Bell Buckle. Charlie and Ira, who came from Alabama with a guitar and mandolin on their knees, worked in a Memphis post office prior to singing their duets on the Opry. They popularized "Knoxville Girl," a murder ballad.

THE CENTURIES-OLD NATCHEZ TRACE BEGINS in Natchez, Mississippi, and ends in Nashville, at Cockrill Spring in Centennial Park, near the McDonald's on West End Avenue. After skirting the Vanderbilt stadium, it runs southwest out of town; traces of it, so to speak, can be found in the Warner parks. In succession, buffalo, Indians and settlers all used this ancient path. In the early 1800s, before the steamboat was invented, flatboaters plied their wares south and hoofed it back home on the Trace. So did Gen. Andrew Jackson after his victory at the Battle of New Orleans — and Aaron Burr after his humiliation. For more, read Jonathan Daniels' *The Devil's Backbone.*

From Vanderbilt, take 21st Avenue South to the little town of Bethlehem. Turn right onto Old Hillsboro Road (highway 46), and left onto the quiet, undeveloped Natchez Trace Parkway, which begins near Leipers Fork. Continuing southwest, it takes an hour to reach an exit leading to the grave of Meriwether Lewis, senior commander of the Lewis and Clark expedition and governor of the Louisiana Territory, whose "firmness and perserverance yielded to nothing but impossibilities" (Thomas Jefferson). Lewis' death here on the night of October 11, 1809, at age 35, is usually attributed to some sort of foul play, or possibly death by his own hand after having been wounded. Forensic scientists have not come up with anything conclusive, but based on the site's present state, my theory is wasps.

At some exits, you can park your car and walk along the old Trace, which predates Columbus. Fall Hollow, located a dozen miles north of Lewis' grave, is a nice place to take a dip.

SOUTHWEST OF THE TRACE, THE LATE MINNIE PEARL (Sarah Ophelia Colley) grew up in Colley-town, east Centerville, although the freight railroad station of Grinders Switch west of town became home in her comedy skits on the *Grand Ole Opry.* She made her Opry debut in 1940 and soon joined Roy Acuff's weekly radio show. In 1975, Minnie was voted into country's Hall of Fame, becoming its second female inductee (after Virginia's Patsy Cline).

Her stage persona was modeled after a "country girl comin' to town for a little tradin' and flirtin'." Yet ironically, unlike many early country artists, Minnie was college-educated and well-to-do. For many years, she and her longtime husband, Henry Cannon, lived in a five-bedroom house with a swimming pool and tennis courts on Nashville's tony Curtiswood Lane, next door to the governor's mansion.

Located near an old switch where trains were turned around, the community can be exceedingly difficult to find — most of the roads are unmarked — and when you do find it, Grinders Switch consists of little more than an abandoned depot, barn, old-fashioned farm implements, and *country*. It also happens to be the first place in the U.S. at cobalt was shipped by rail, after Thomas Edison visited in order to inspect a stran -looking rock that had been found at nearby Wolf Creek. (He also spent time in Memphis.)

> *Come with the love light gleaming*
> *In your dear eyes of blue*
> *Meet me in Dreamland, sweet dreamy Dreamland*
> *There let my dreams come true.*
> ~ Beth Slater Whitson, 1909

The section of Hickman County between Grinders Switch and Only — home of Tennessee's Only Baptist Church (apparently no pun intended) — is especially scenic, but you will need your DeLorme state atlas and lots of spare time to get lost.

Originally, Only was called Dreamer. The community was later renamed for early merchant Tom Sutton. Whenever anyone asked the price of any article in his general store, he would always reply, "Only five cents" or "Only ten cents" or "Only a dollar," whatever the price might be. Customers began calling it the "Only" store, the postmaster had the village's name changed, and the rest is history.

Minnie Pearl grew up in Colleytown, outside Centerville, but adopted the nearby railroad spur of **Grinders Switch** as her stage hometown. Perry Walker.

Just down the road is the community of Spot. On a business trip to Chicago, a local resident named Lewis Mathey was registering at a hotel when he dropped a splotch of ink on his address and the clerk asked him if he was from Spot. The name stuck — or blotted, as the case may be.

Other Hickman crossroads sport equally colorful names and corresponding histories. Little Lot, for instance, dates to 1814 when Hugh McCabe, who owned hundreds of acres, donated a very small tract for a schoolhouse and church. Martin Tidwell is one place formed from two surnames. Plunder's Creek honors the memory of a faithful hunting dog who disappeared there, while Pretty Creek once turned out a large proportion of comely women.

Other Hickman residents past and present include the songwriters Beth Slater Whitson ("Let Me Call You Sweetheart") and Ronnie Scaife ("The Whiskey Ain't Workin'"), and fiddling greats Paul Warren and Howard "Howdy" Forrester, and Dickie Wells, who plunged his trombone in the Basie band.

———

TO THE SOUTH, HOHENWALD MEANS "HIGH FOREST" IN GERMAN. Settled by Swiss immigrants, the small town is where Minnie's sidekick Rod Brasfield (a Mississippi native) once honed his act, which later brought down the Opry house:

"I-came-down-here-today-on-na-train," he would say, "yes-sir-came-down-on-na-train. An'-I-had-me-a-berth-on-na-train. A-berth-by-Ned. One-of-them-shelf-like-things-that-hangs-there-on-the-wall-of-the-train-one-on-top-of-the-o-ther-one-'cept-they-ain't-shelfs-they're-beds-by-Ned.

"An'-it-come-time-to-go-to-sleep-an'-I-climbed-up-to-my-berth-an'-by-Ned-they-was-two-women-in-my-berth.

"An'-I-said-well-by-Ned-one-of-y'uns-is-a-gon-na-have-to-leave."

Musicians have been known to flock to Hohenwald for the express purpose of picking through the used clothes at its many self-described "junk stores." For first dibs on the really *quality* junk, make the rounds bright and early on Wednesday and especially on Saturday mornings, which is when junk dealers cut the bales. Begin your shopping odyssey at Lawson's.

Heading south and west, you'll pass Lawrenceburg, where gospel songbook publisher James D. Vaughan once based his operations; Vaughan wrote "If I Could Hear My Mother Pray Again." The great singer-songwriter Melba Montgomery, who warbled some down-to-earth duets with George Jones in the early '60s, is a native of Iron City, just north of the Alabama line. Her biggest hit was "No Charge," released in 1974. Country singer Mark Collie comes from Waynesboro.

Farther south, the Alabama Music Hall of Fame is located in Tuscumbia, Alabama, near the old Muscle Shoals Sound Studios, whose rhythm section backed everyone from Aretha Franklin ("Respect") and Wilson Pickett ("Mustang Sally") to Willie Nelson ("Bloody Mary Morning") and Bob Seger ("Old Time Rock and Roll").

DUE SOUTH OF NASHVILLE IN GILES COUNTY, the town of Pulaski, a few miles west of Interstate 65, has the dubious distinction of being the birthplace of the Ku Klux Klan, which was founded in 1866 by six Confederate soldiers disenchanted with the war's outcome. General Nathan Bedford Forrest was elected Grand Wizard and membership soon grew to half a million, but the then-relatively benign group was forced to disband in the early 1870s. The parading, cross-burning, and lynching Klan didn't emerge until 1915, when a Georgia secret society adopted the name. In the years following World War II, it surfaced again, predominantly as an anti-civil rights force in the South.

Ironically, the single-story white brick building (209 W. Madison) where the group first met, is now occupied by the state public defender's office, and the bronze historical plaque has been turned around, silencing its message. Hate groups periodically converge on Pulaski, during which time many of the local shopowners lock their stores.

Pulaski is also the town where Sam Davis, a 21-year-old Confederate scout, was hanged in 1863 for refusing to divulge the name of a spy. "If I had a thousand lives," he said, "I would lose them all before I would betray my friends or the confidence of my informer." He rode on a wagon up a hill to the hanging site, where a small museum chronicles his story. The Hunter-Smith furniture store on the town square offers informal tours of his basement cell, complete with mannequin. Across the street, Sam's statue guards the Giles County Courthouse, where I saw an old man patiently whittling.

Due north, the town of Columbia, which calls itself the mule capital of the world, also maintains the home of President James K. Polk, the country's first dark horse candidate, who won the 1844 election despite failing to carry his own state. During his tenure, California and much of the Southwest — some half a million square miles — were added to the United States. Historians consider Polk a "near-great" president, and they say that only he and George Washington actually made good on all their campaign promises.

Every summer, the Frog Bottom festival gets underway in Marshall County, between Pulaski and Columbia.

To visit Hank Williams' Boyhood Home and Museum, head south on Interstate 65 to Georgiana, Alabama.

IN LATE AUGUST, MIDDLE TENNESSEE'S FAIREST damsels descend on Shelbyville for the Celebration, a fortnight-long equestrian extravaganza dating to the 1940s. Dressed in all their finery, the ladies ride sidesaddle while sipping iced tea and spilling nary a drop. What they're celebrating is the preeminence of the Tennessee Walking Horse, considered the Cadillac of its species. Born with its basic gait — picking the feet up and throwing them out — the walker is specially trained with shoes and six-ounce ankle chains. For the full atmosphere, try to attend the first Saturday night.

Incidentally, Jimmy Driftwood's "Tennessee Stud" is *not* a walker.

HEADING SOUTHWEST TO LYNCHBURG (pop. 361), the smell of sour mash hits you right between the eyes. Jack Daniel's Distillery brews Tennessee whiskey (celebrated in song by David Allen Coe) by mixing spring water with corn, rye, and barley malt, slowly dripping the concoction over and through maple charcoal, and then letting it set in barrels for four years. This charcoal "leaching" process is what makes it *Tennessee* whiskey, as opposed to Kentucky's bourbon, which is decanted straight into the barrel.

The nation's first registered distillery (1866) is named after the "Little Guy from Tennessee," Jasper Newton Daniel, who stood 5'2" and wore a big hat and coat to compensate for his short stature. He courted young girls but never married. In 1911, six years after kicking a safe, Daniel came down with gangrene and died. He left the business to his nephew Lem Motlow, who ran it until 1947.

You can watch the the 2,300-gallon tanks bubble and froth as birds chirp in the nearby rafters, and tour one of its 45 barrelhouses, each containing a million gallons of aging inventory. Every year, the company sells some 4.5 million cases of its No. 7 brand. Preaching abstemiousness, though certainly not abstinence, the company rewards employees with one free pint a month. "That's what we call a good Friday," the company's Roger Brashears told me with a wink.

Solo fiddler Uncle Bunt Stephens came from Moore County. In 1926, after winning a fiddle contest sponsored by Henry Ford, he requested an all-cash prize instead of cash and a new Lincoln.

Just up the road in Tullahoma, the George Dickel Distillery makes an equally formidable, though less famous, version of Tennessee whiskey. I haven't toured the facility but approve of the end product.

Highway 16 leads to Winchester, the birthplace of the late pop singer Frances Rose (Dinah) Shore, nicknamed "The Nashville Nightingale," who moved to Music City at age six. She racked up 80 chart hits, including "The Gypsy," as well as ten Emmy awards.

IN THE '50S, MONTEAGLE'S HIGHLANDER FOLK SCHOOL — founded by Tennessean Miles Horton in 1932 — led the charge for integration by training Southern labor organizers and activists such as Martin Luther King, Rosa Parks, Septima Clark, Bernice Reagon, and Julius Lester. New "freedom songs" were adapted from old spirituals, the most famous being "We Shall Overcome," popularized by Pete Seeger. The school's Guy Carawan went so far as to call Civil Rights "the singing movement." Busted in 1959 for selling beer and violating segregation laws, Highlander moved to New Market, near Knoxville, where it is now based.

Just down the road in Sewanee, the University of the South boasts what is probably the world's largest campus, some 10,000 acres, including a 200-acre stand of old-growth forest in Thumping Dick Cove (I kid you not) that has been designated a national natural landmark. Built in 1857, the campus or "Domain," whose history is depicted in the narthex of All Saints' Chapel, was the brainchild of Episcopal bishop Leonidas Polk. Its sandstone buildings make quite an impression. The university is perhaps best known for *The Sewanee Review,* dating back to 1892, making it the nation's oldest continuously published literary journal.

The town's Allen Brothers (Lee and Austin) were very popular in the 1920s, particularly for their rendition of "Salty Dog Blues." Otherwise, Grundy County would appear to have little to offer musically, but hiking is good along the Fiery Gizzard trail near Tracy City and throughout the Savage Gulf natural area to the north; the latter encompasses a narrow gorge with limestone cliffs. The demonic-sounding names come from the old blast furnaces used for testing coke.

Due north are the old stomping grounds of Uncle Dave Macon and singer Dottie West, from the communities of Smartt Station and Frog Pond, respectively. West bridged the gap between country and disco with hits like "A Lesson in Leavin'" and "Sometimes When We Touch." She hoped "to be 'doing it' when I'm 83," but a fatal car accident voided that possibility. Her daughter Shelly had a hit with "Jose Cuervo."

A SHORT JOG NORTHEAST ON HIGHWAY 70 LEADS to the town of Sparta, the longtime abode and final resting place of guitarist Lester Raymond Flatt who, along with Earl Scruggs,

revolutionized the band sound that we now call bluegrass. Born in 1914 at Duncan's Chapel on the Putnam/Overton country line, Flatt moved to Sparta at an early age. As a member of the Blue Grass Boys, a seminal mid-1940s band led by Bill Monroe, Flatt served as the indispensable (if underrated) "second man," supplying steady rhythm for Monroe's fast mandolin breaks and Earl Scruggs' innovative three-finger rolls.

His vocal delivery is said to have influenced Hank Williams — then a rising star — and he was a prolific songwriter to boot ("We'll Meet Again Sweetheart," "Bouquet in Heaven"). Flatt & Scruggs soon broke away from Monroe and formed their own band, the Foggy Mountain Boys, which performed everywhere, from the Opry to Carnegie Hall, before disbanding in 1969.

Lester Raymond Flatt wrote the book on bluegrass guitar. Watercolor by Claire Wasserman.

Flatt died a decade later and is buried in Sparta's Oaklawn Memorial Cemetery. Every June, a bluegrass festival (complete with cornbread bake-off and hog-calling contest) is held in Flatt's honor at the Foggy Mountain Music Park, where you will inevitably hear someone playing his "G-run" on the bass strings of a Martin guitar. Incidentally, don't refer to Flatt as the Baron of Bluegrass. He disliked this nickname, and anyone in the know is likely to give you the cold shoulder.

On Saturday nights, try John Henry Demps' Midway Music Barn, located five miles south of Sparta; better yet, attend the annual Benny Martin festival, honoring the local fiddler. In the vicinity, Fall Creek Falls State Park sponsors its Mountaineer Folk Festival in September, and the Old-Time Fiddlers' Jamboree in Smithville attracts tens of thousands over the Fourth of July weekend. Fiddler Frazier Moss, who has performed for three presidents, is a longtime resident of Cookeville. While in town, stop by the L&M music shop for a rundown on the local scene.

PERCHED ATOP THE CUMBERLAND PLATEAU, Jamestown is where Samuel Clemens, aka Mark Twain, was actually conceived (he was born in Missouri). The town supports a Mark Twain Avenue and a Mark Twain Park featuring the spring where the Clemenses fetched their water. He is thought to have used Jamestown (Obedstown) as a setting for parts of *The Gilded Age,* including the following passage on local hair styles: "Few of the men wore whiskers; none wore moustaches; some had a thick jungle of hair under the chin and hiding the throat — the only pattern recognized there as being the correct thing in whiskers; but no part of any individual's face had seen a razor for a week."

This is also the hometown of unaccompanied balladeer Johnny Ray Hicks, whose singing ancestors arrived here in 1817; some of Hicks' melodies and modes can be traced to Gregorian chants. Rumor has it that Artimus Pyle, drummer for party band Lynyrd Skynyrd, also lives in the area. Wild boar hunters can choose from several area lodges, such as Crooked Creek and Clarkrange. To the east, the Big South Fork National River and Recreation Area — BSFNRRA for short — is about as far away from civilization as you can get and offers 106,000 acres of good rafting, hiking, and fishing.

To the west, Secretary of State Cordell Hull came from Byrdstown, and World War II hero Sgt. Alvin C. York grew up in Pall Mall. Nearby Pickett State Park sponsors an old-timers festival on Labor Day weekend. To the west, sleepy Hilham conducts its annual "rolley hole" (marbles) tournament in September; Standing Stone State Park and Dale Hollow Lake lie to the north. Clarksville natives include runner Wilma Rudolph (who won three gold medals at the 1960 Olympics in Rome) and actor Frank Sutton Spencer — better known as Sergeant Carter on *Gomer Pyle, USMC.*

ALBERT GORE AND HIS SON AL, our vice president, are natives of Carthage, to the west. You can buy bait and tackle from the Gore Store — good for the country. The harmonica player DeFord Bailey also came from Smith County, as did the Opry's very first performer, Uncle Jimmy Thompson, who once won an eight-day fiddling contest in Dallas, or so he claimed.

To the south, check for special music and folklife events at Edgar Evins State Park, situated on Center Hill Lake. Proceeding west, Cedars of Lebanon Park features the country's largest stand of juniper (red cedar). Several years ago, the city of Lebanon set the world's square-dancing record as some 2,758 people did do-si-dos to "Wind the Clock Down."

MANY OF COUNTRY MUSIC'S PATRIARCHS AND MATRIARCHS live within striking distance of Music City, such as "Grandpa" and Ramona Jones of Ridgetop, north of Nashville. He became an old man in his early twenties after adding the persona to his stage act; she is an old-time fiddler and recording artist in her own right. The Adams Bell Witch Opry is also in this area, a few miles south of Kentucky.

Henry Ellis (Redd) Stewart, who wrote "Tennessee Waltz" with Pee Wee King, was born in Ashland City, northwest of Nashville. Over the years, more than 500 artists have recorded the song, including the 1950 hit by Patti Page, of "(How Much is) That Doggie in the Window?" fame. The gist of the waltz is, don't introduce an old friend to your darlin'. The early country singer Obed "Dad" Pickard also came from Ashland City.

Farther west, some 70 miles from Nashville, singer Loretta Lynn gives several annual concerts at her Hurricane Mills ranch, where scenes from *Coal Miner's Daughter* were filmed. Humphreys County is also the birthplace of Fiddlin' Arthur Smith, dubbed the King of the Fiddlers by Roy Acuff (who is the King of Country). Smith used to participate in ten-hour marathon jam sessions with his 12 siblings and picked up his long-bow style with its complex noting from local fiddlers.

Until his death a few years ago, former Public Enemy No. 1 Thomas H. Robinson lived to the south, in Pegram. Convicted of abducting a Louisville socialite in 1934, the Nashville native was scheduled to die, but Harry Truman commuted his sentence, and Robinson was released in 1970. (George "Machine Gun" Kelly was educated, and nabbed, in Memphis.) Alan O'Bryant, who fronts the Nashville Bluegrass Band, also lives in Pegram.

Highway 70 leads you back to Nashville. On the way, McEwen pokes up a barbecue at its St. Patrick's Irish Picnic & Homecoming in late July. The tradition dates to 1854, when local parishioners held a chicken supper to raise money for a church bell. The rest of the year, try the buffet at Dickson's East Hills Restaurant.

> Country music is feelin' and *heart*, not a bunch of stuff some asshole says the public wants just because he's made "an extensive study of the market."
> ~ Merle Haggard, *Sing Me Back Home* (1981)

On Valentine's Day 1928, **Mississippi John Hurt** (left, with hat) recorded for Okeh in Memphis. After the Depression he worked as a tenant farmer for the next 35 years. Towards the end of his life, the Delta blues guitarist and singer became famous ("Candy Man Blues," "My Creole Belle") after being rediscovered in his hometown of Avalon, Mississippi. Compared to Hurt, the other two musicians in this painting were "born to blush unseen." The main figure, Burl C. "Jaybird" Coleman, played guitar and harmonica with the Rabbit Foot Minstrels and Birmingham Jug Band in the '20s and '30s. Slide guitarist "Bo Weevil" Jackson (dressed in blue) sang in a high-pitched voice, worked for tips in Birmingham, and recorded in Chicago, twice, in 1926; his real name and origin remain a mystery. Mixed media by Florence Zinman.

Memphis

Compared to Nashville and East Tennessee, Memphis is a relatively recent arrival, a backwater town that didn't really come into its own until the close of the 19th century. Way back in 1542, natives allegedly snacked on explorer Hernando de Soto along the banks of the Mississippi, near the present-day city. Joliet and Marquette also passed through but didn't stay for long. As late as the 1810 Census, the fertile area now known as West Tennessee — everything between the Tennessee and Mississippi rivers, including Memphis to the southwest — was identified as "Indian Lands."

With a litle help from John Overton and Andrew Jackson, General James Winchester is generally credited with laying out Memphis and naming it on May 1, 1819, apparently inspired by the ancient Egyptian capital located on the Nile. This comparison was for many years "a subject of ridicule to those who saw but a few straggling houses perched upon the bluffs," according to James Phelan's 1888 state history.

Back then, West Tennessee was still considered frontier. Memphis grew slowly and the living conditions were primitive. In his early guidebook designed to attract settlers to Tennessee, Eastin Morris spent a dozen pages on Nashville but only a paragraph on Memphis, dismissing it as "a post town in Shelby County." (He accurately predicted, however, that it "must undoubtedly become the emporium of one of the finest agricultural districts in the western country.")

While visiting during a downpour in the late 1830s, Frances Trollope found the place "nearly inaccessible" due to its location on a high bluff overlooking the river: "Unfortunately a new road had been recently marked out, which beguiled us into its almost bottomless mud, from the firmer footing of the unbroken cliff. Shoes and gloves were lost in the mire, for we were glad to avail ourselves of all our limbs; and we reached the grand hotel in a most deplorable state." The Memphians' manner of "getting along" amused Trollope. "This phrase is eternally in use among them," she wrote, "and seems to mean existing with as few of the comforts of life as possible."

After suffering through the Civil War, Reconstruction, and several bouts with tuberculosis and yellow fever, Memphis experienced its first heady growth around the turn of the century when its population surpassed 100,000. Today it's the state's largest city, with a million people in the greater metropolitan area and 626,000 inner-city residents. To some Memphians it still seems like a small town, although it seems only fair to say that Nashvillians make the same claim.

BOTH PHYSICALLY AND PSYCHICALLY, MEMPHIS is defined by the Mississippi River which runs along the state's western flank, from Reelfoot Lake south to Memphis. One could even make a case that the river's sloughs, swamps, and levees give the West Tennessee Delta region its special jungle-like character, much more so than the region's arbitrary political

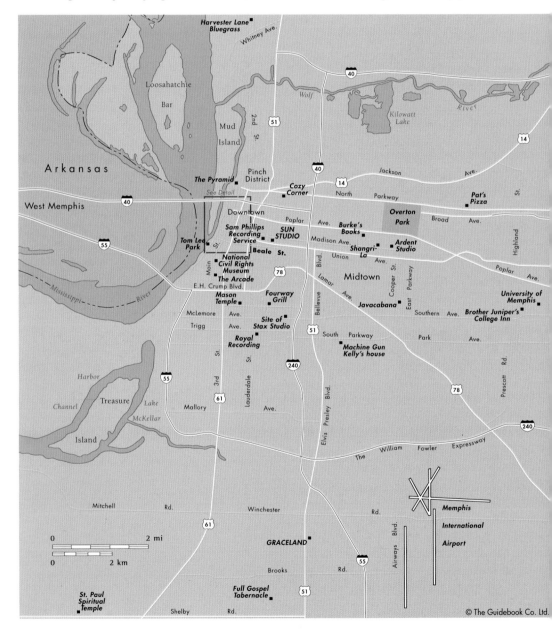

boundaries with Arkansas, Mississippi, and Missouri. Mississippi means "big river" in the Algonquin language. Sailing along the Louisiana coast, the Spanish explorer Pineda christened it Espiritu Santo — Holy Spirit. This century, Hammerstein eulogized its mysteries in "Ol' Man River" ("He jes' keeps rollin' along"); in Kerouac's hands, it became "the big mudhole rank clawpole old frogular pawed-soul titanic Mississippi."

The Mississippi drains water (and a huge quantity of mud) from an area covering 31 states and comprising roughly 40 percent of the North American land mass. Even more startling is the river's course, which is every bit as unpredictable as a country blues guitar solo. A "meander belt" map published by the Mississippi River Commission tracing its various bends and turns over the past two millennia, looks like a loosely braided piece of twine, with each strand following its own uniquely stubborn direction.

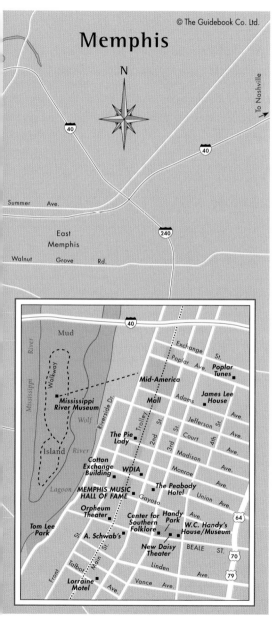

As Twain pointed out in 1873, "Nearly the whole of that one thousand three hundred miles of old Mississippi River which La Salle floated down in his canoes, two hundred years ago, is good solid dry land now. The river lies to the right of it, in places, and to the left of it in other places."

WEST TENNESSEE'S AFRICAN-AMERICAN population has long been proportionately larger than its counterparts in Middle and East Tennessee, a statistic which has fundamentally affected the music. Blacks make up some 40 percent of this grand division and they outnumber whites in Fayette and Haywood counties. By contrast, 31 of East Tennessee's 33 counties have black populations of less than five percent, while Nashville is one-quarter black.

Race relations in West Tennessee — and throughout the state — must necessarily be viewed in the context of the Civil War. Many still refer to this conflagration as the War Between the States, meaning that the

South did not rebel, as it were, against emancipation, that it was just an honest difference of opinion.

Thirty years after the war, John Trotwood Moore expressed hope that a monument could be erected in Tennessee. "On its top is going to be a negro — not the mythical slave with chains on him and terror in his face, which fool artists, who never saw a negro slave, and fool poets, who never heard one laugh, are wont to depict — but the jolly, contented, rollicking rascal that we knew and loved; the member of our household and sharer of our joys and sorrows. On its top, I say, there is going to be that kind of a negro, as he was, and he is going to be represented in the act of picking cotton, with a laugh, while he refuses with scorn a gun with which to fight his master for his own freedom. When that is done, it will be the crowning monument of the age."

A quaint conviction, and rather politically incorrect by today's standards, Moore's view contrasts sharply with the famous "mountaintop" speech that Rev. King delivered in Memphis the day before he was assassinated. King told a group of striking sanitation workers that he "remembered when Negroes were just going around scratching where they didn't itch, and laughing when they were not tickled. But that day is all over. We mean business now, and we are determined to gain our rightful place in God's world."

Nearly 30 years after King's death, blacks and whites continue to live in separate worlds, both literally and figuratively. Nevertheless, things *have* changed. For example, Memphis elected its first black mayor, former schools superintendent Willie Herenton, in 1991.

Even in the old days, relations between the two races, which in West Tennessee have shared the same planter culture for many years, were characterized by a certain "social affability" (in the words of one Memphian) that differs subtly from what exists in the rest of the state. Putting racial considerations aside, the pace of life in the Delta is slower, and its people gentler and more accessible.

———

IT IS THIS GREATER BLACK PRESENCE that gives Memphis music its special character. The cross-pollination of black and white, in particular, led to "the Memphis sound." As the MGs' drummer Al Jackson, Jr., once said, "The straighter you play it the better. You try to stay out of the way because you are selling the tune itself and not the drummer." Adds trumpeter/producer Willie Mitchell, "The time isn't like a metronome; it's kind of like shuckin' you, puttin' you on. Even Memphis jazz players play real fast but just a little bit behind the beat, relaxed, lazy-like. It feels good."

Memphis and the surrounding West Tennessee Delta have supplied an arsenal of talent that includes such luminaries as Tina Turner, Bobby Bland, Fred McDowell, and Alberta Hunter, as well as lesser-knowns greats like Joe Hill Louis, O.V. Wright, Phineas Newborn Jr., Little Laura Dukes, James Carr, Noah Lewis, Willie Mabon, Queen C. Anderson, Memphis Slim, and Peetie Wheatstraw, aka "the Devil's Son-in-Law."

Take my advice folks and see Beale Street first.
~ W.C. Handy, "Beale Street Blues"

SOME 60 YEARS AGO, THE LEGENDARY ROBERT LEROY JOHNSON arrived in Memphis after rambling through the Delta. Unslinging an archtop guitar from his back at what is now Handy Park on Beale Street, Johnson proceeded to work through the changes of "Cross Road Blues," in which he sells his soul to the devil in exchange for greater musical prowess; he died from poison a few years later. Today, a sculpture of bandleader William Christopher Handy, cornet in hands, overlooks the scene, where street musicians conduct informal jam sessions.

Back in 1884, one Virgilio Maffei opened the long-defunct Pee Wee's saloon at 317 Beale, where Handy later wrote "Mister Crump," believed to be the first transcribed blues. The composer found "The Stem" to be a fertile proving ground, and he drew inspiration for his music from a statue of St. John the Baptist pointing to heaven which once stood on the eastern tower of the Beale Street Baptist Church at 379 Beale. A few doors down, at 352, Handy's former house has been turned into a museum.

As for Maffei, legend has it that he stood only four and a half feet tall but once arm-wrestled Jack Johnson into submission and would swim back and forth across the Mississippi for a light aerobic workout. Ol' Man River can also be dangerous: folksinger Jeff Buckley recently drowned near the same spot.

In the early days, jug bander Gus Cannon entertained Beale Streeters with his Jug Stompers, pioneering a type of music that has been largely relegated to history, having been eclipsed by pop, rap, and twang. The Mississippi native once claimed "no education 'cept Mother Wit," but that's all the composer of "Walk Right In" and "Baby Let Your Mind Roll On" really needed. Cannon was one of the first bluesman to use the banjo — even played it with a slide. He lived to 105.

Howlin' Wolf and B.B. King started their careers on Beale, as did a teenaged Elvis Presley, who soaked up the then-mostly black atmosphere and bought his threads at Lansky's department store. Until recently the old Lansky's building housed the Center for Southern Folklore and has now been reincarnated as Elvis Presley's Memphis, a Graceland-sponsored nightclub. Meanwhile, the King's former outfitter, Bernard Lansky, now manages the Peabody Hotel's upscale clothing boutique. Times change and we change with them.

The Center for Southern Folklore, located at 209 Beale — former site of pianist Joyce Cobb's club — is an excellent place to peruse vintage photos of Beale in its heyday, buy CDs of Memphis music, and hear live music, from jazz and gospel to punk rock. In late July, it sponsors a terrific four-day festival featuring an eclectic mix of music from throughout the mid-South, ranging from country guitarist Roy Harper to Othar Turner's Fife & Drum Band.

The son of slaves, jug band pioneer **Gus Cannon** (1874-1979) led one of Beale Street's most popular bands. Cannon played blues on the banjo, sometimes using a bottleneck slide. His first banjo was fashioned from a bread pan, broom stick, and raccoon-skin head. Colin Escott/ Showtime Archive.

A. Schwab's dry goods store has changed little since the 1950s. The founder's grandson Abe keeps the books and takes special orders for black cat-bone ("depending on availability," he jokes). The bone, and dozens of other exotic substances (get-away root, devils shrub, dragon blood, and African mojo bean) are located on the left as you enter the store. Many of these are used for various hoodoo ceremonies of African origin, and books explaining how can be found upstairs. Hoodoo is still practiced by many Memphians, so be respectful and don't make wisecracks — at least not within earshot. The store also sells a wide array of shades, brims, and threads, and its two floors of inventory include everything from spats, garters, and top hats, to Masonic supplies, lye soap, and harmonicas, not to mention 44 kinds of suspenders and bric-à-brac thick as hail. Indeed, if you can't find it at A. Schwab's, their motto goes, then you are better off without it! Down the street, the 1,000-seat New Daisy Theater (1920) is a good example of early movie theater design. It is now a concert hall, and some regard the New Daisy as the best live-music venue in town.

Historically, the Beale Street neighborhood has been populated and managed by African-Americans. Until the barriers began to erode in the 1950s and '60s, Beale was virtually segregated from white Memphis. For example, the Palace Theater held a special "midnight ramble" on Fridays for whites; all other shows were black-only. White musicians attended black jam sessions, but when the police arrived, they had to slip out the back door.

In a radio interview, B.B. King reminisced that when he first arrived on the scene in the late '40s, Beale Street was "a city within itself":

> All the people that had jobs, they'd go to work in the mornings dressed beautifully — as we used the word, 'sharp.' They go to work sharp, change clothes on the job, shower in the evening and come back, about 4:30 or 5 o'clock. And everybody's hangin' on Beale Street, you know, sharp, and got their guitars, the guys that played music and whatever. So I had a chance to learn a lot. And it was fascinating to me. And you could come down there and stay from, oh, they would start to gathering, people that had early jobs, went to work early, would get off around 3, 3:30. So from 3:30 till 10, 11, at night, man! Beale Street was jumpin'! Some of them just played, just for what you call . . . just for playin'. Other words, they didn't do it for a living. But some of them were so good. And you'd find saxophone, trumpet players, keyboard players — all of this in the park . . . You'd also find guys gambling, you'd find guys drinkin', you'd find guys doing a little bit of everything that people do.

This was when the Civil Rights era really began, according to King, who started his career as a deejay at WDIA, the black-owned and operated radio station. Competing station WHBQ employed a white deejay named Dewey Phillips who, on his *Red Hot & Blue* program, encouraged his listeners to visit the House of the Blues record store on Beale. One of these listeners was Elvis Presley who, like B.B. King, had migrated north from Mississippi.

In the late 1960s and early '70s, the powers-that-be decided to raze the slums surrounding Beale Street. "The idea was to clear property that was in blighted condition to make room for progress — usually a concrete parking lot," according to saxman Edward "Prince Gabe" Kirby, who dubbed these efforts "urban removal." In the '80s, Beale Street was reopened as a tourist attraction. The contemporary version — a five-minute walk from downtown — appears as an oasis of shlock shops, bars, and neon, rimmed by acres of weed-choked empty blocks.

"In refurbishing the streets, the city went too far, removing the soul of the place with its layers of decay," writes Mark Winegardner. "What remains might be historically accurate, much as a movie set would be, but is nevertheless too antiseptic to ever again pose as the place B.B. King once called 'college for blues men.'" (The rundown neighborhood a few blocks south will give you a rough idea of what Beale *used* to look like.)

That's not to say that you can't still have a good time on Beale despite Handy's admonition that "business never closes till somebody gets killed." Today, it's one of Memphis' safest neighborhoods. The street, which runs for three or four blocks, is blocked off and well-patrolled, enabling tourists to amble freely from club to club. Gibson plans to build a guitar factory near Beale, and sources say that the surrounding entertainment complex (clubs, shops, and permanent music exhibit) will double the district's size.

Regrettably, Memphis seems to have more talented musicians than venues where they can play, so it is not unusual to run into an occasional out-of-funds bluesman. One midnight, while sitting in the Blues City Cafe, a companion (possibly the singer James Govan) suggested that I meet guitarist Fred Sanders, who was sitting outside in his car. We took a ride but ran out of gas, and by the time I pushed us to the nearest station, we had been joined by a drug runner and a prostitute. In return for buying him $10 worth of gas, Fred treated me to an early-morning tour of a scary-looking section of town.

Sometimes these artists are vindicated, however, and the gap between talent and recognition closes. A few years back, I heard a rumor that James Cotton was grilling steaks in a Beale Street bar and playing his harmonica on breaks. Recently, he won a Grammy for his CD titled *Deep in the Blues*. Other musicians are "born to blush unseen," such as the Memphis-born singer Johnny Ace, whose "Pledging My Love" became a big hit in 1955, months after he killed himself playing Russian roulette in Houston.

———————

BEFORE VISITING GRACELAND, stop at the Memphis Music Hall of Fame, located downtown just a few blocks from Beale, right around the corner from the Peabody Hotel. The place is crammed to the last square inch with information on rhythm and blues, rockabilly, and soul music. You can admire Isaac Hayes' canary-yellow suit and platform shoes (the Covington, Tennessee, native won an Academy award for his soundtrack to *Shaft*) and bone up on the history of WDIA ("The Goodwill Station"), which in 1948 became the first Southern radio station to adopt an all-black programming format. Displays tell the histories of the Stax, Hi, and Goldwax record labels and flesh out the careers of various Tennessee-born bards like songwriters Lloyd Arnold McCollough and Dickey Lee and the ever-cagey Alex Chilton of Box Tops and Big Star fame, whom *The New Yorker* once described as either "the most overrated or the most underrated artist in the history of rock and roll." The Replacements even named a song after him.

Unfortunately the Beale Street Blues Museum covering early Memphis music has closed. Hopefully John Montague, who owns both collections, will find a way to combine them under one roof.

MANY MEMPHIANS EXPRESS A KIND OF BEMUSED BAFFLEMENT at Elvis Presley's staying power some 20 years after his death in 1977. Located south of downtown on Highway 51, Graceland continues to draw 700,000 visitors a year. Even though the Georgia Colonial mansion where Elvis lived for his entire adult life has earned a spot on the National Register, most people don't really come to see the house but to experience the King of Rock 'n' Roll viscerally.

Although Chuck Berry and Bo Diddley are often credited with inventing rock — a kind of musical mutt — it was Elvis who popularized the form and made it a household word. As Buddy Holly said, "Elvis Presley made it possible for all of us to follow." In John Lennon's words, "If there hadn't been an Elvis, there wouldn't have been a Beatles."

A House Fit for an American King

Near Memphis International Airport, I-55 intersects with Elvis Presley Boulevard. Graceland is clearly marked, both on roadsigns and our sorry map, which indicates "Graceland" with a red square, and no further explanation. No "Home of Elvis Presley." None necessary, apparently. Throughout the trip I looked on the map for other famous homes that were deemed similarly self-explanatory. Even Monticello was appendaged by "Home of T. Jefferson," and only Mount Vernon spoke for itself. This, then, seems to be a distinction cartographers have reserved for an odd pair of American originals: the Father of Our Country and the King of Rock 'n' Roll.

. . . The front of the house is not gaudy, and the house itself is of the minimum size necessary to qualify as a "mansion." Its architecture is neither Antebellum Southern nor Hollywood glitz; in fact, with its gray stone walls, black shutters and four modest columns, Graceland could easily be mistaken for a dormitory at a Midwestern women's college. It could, except for the steel bars covering all the windows.

~ Mark Winegardner, *Elvis Presley Boulevard: From Sea to Shining Sea, Almost*

The best time to visit is August 15th — his death anniversary — when thousands attend a candlelit vigil held in the street in front. Some are *bona fide* mourners, like the Gates of Graceland Entourage in their matching red T-shirts, who openly weep and console each other as they file down from the grave. ("The idea," according to Graceland's official guidelines, "is to have a continuous single file flow.") The balance could be described as a combination of moderate fans, curiosity seekers, and those cynics who call the tribute "Death Week." Many are too young to have attended one of his concerts by the time he died; some hadn't even been *born.*

The rest of the year, simply ante up $16 and a bus will deliver you through the pearly gates and up the hill. Elvis Presley Enterprises, which administers the estate, has gone to well-orchestrated lengths to put a positive spin on the King's legacy. (They claim that Elvis did not, for instance, make the tear in the pool table felt.) His jumpsuits and gold records are displayed inside, and you can stroll the pretty grounds and visit the family grave where his dust reposes, despite what the tabloids say. The upstairs is off-limits, and please, no flashes: they fade the upholstery fabric. Indigent fans can visit his grave for free before tours; call for details.

Across the street, you can fritter away your hard-earned money at the Graceland Crossing souvenir complex. I invested 99 cents on a mini-mag promising to reveal the King's "most intimate secrets," and another $12.99 on a TCB jacket patch resembling a piece of pink shag carpet. "Taking Care of Business" was Elvis' official slogan; he gave TCB medallions to members of his Memphis Mafia and had it painted on his jet. You will run into everyone and his brother at the Crossing. I chanced upon Elvis' former beltmaker, who was being interviewed by a French TV reporter ("He liked them wide").

The most noteworthy Elvis-related sites in Memphis are Sun Records (see below); the Overton Park bandshell, whose wooden benches look the same as they did on July 30, 1954, the date of his first official pelvis gyration; then-segregated Humes High; Poplar Tunes, where he shopped for records; Libertyland Amusement Park (the Zippin' Pippin was his favorite ride), and Baptist Memorial's Trauma Room One, where he died. You can also visit Tupelo, Mississippi, where he spent his first 13 years, as well as Graceland Too in Holly Springs, which has been dubbed "the Taj Majal of Elvisology." On the other hand, ain't nothing like the real thing, and Graceland is it — in spite of its rabid commercialism.

Did I neglect to mention that Elvis and Elvis Presley are registered trademarks of Elvis Presley Enterprises?

SUN CALLS ITSELF THE BIRTHPLACE OF ROCK 'N' ROLL, mainly due to the fact that, in 1954, Elvis recorded his first single here ("That's All Right Mama," backed by "Blue Moon of Kentucky"). Before Elvis, studio owner Sam Phillips mostly recorded black blues and R&B artists like Howlin' Wolf, Walter Horton, Little Junior Parker, Eddie Snow, Harmonica Frank, Billy "the Kid" Emerson, and the Prisonaires — who resided at the state penitentiary in Nashville. Some rank Jackie Brenston's "Rocket 88" (1951), cut at Sun and

Back in the 1950s, **Sam Phillips** (right) made records and **Dewey Phillips** broke them; the two were not related. Sam, who remains active in the music industry, founded Sun Records; he grew up in W.C. Handy's hometown of Florence, Alabama. Dewey (1926-1968) hosted WHBQ's *Red Hot & Blue* and in July 1954 became the first deejay to play Elvis' first record ("That's Alright Mama"). The original wild man, Dewey came from Adamsville, a small town on the Tennessee River. Photo by Masel Priesman, courtesy of Colin Escott/Showtime.

released on Chess, as the first-ever rock 'n' roll record. Phillips also recorded B.B. King's monster hit, "Three O'Clock Blues."

After Elvis' success, Phillips shifted his focus to white artists, the most famous being Carl Perkins, Jerry Lee Lewis, Johnny Cash, and Roy Orbison. The label's legion of lesser lights included Billy Lee Riley, Charlie Rich, Carl Mann, Warren Smith, and Malcolm Yelvington; others, such as local favorites Johnny and Dorsey Burnette, never made Phillips' cut.

These cool cats forged a new, albeit short-lived genre called rockabilly that fused black R&B with white C&W. Characterized by a heavy backbeat, twangy lead guitar, and slapping string bass, with plenty of echo and enough yelps, gulps, and hiccups to rival a dog pound, it has been described as "a music of almost classical purity and definition." Rockabilly has influenced a host of subsequent performers, including the Stray Cats, Sleepy LaBeef, and Reverend Horton Heat; seek out James Eddie Campbell in Memphis and High Noon in Nashville.

Sun still records, but it is no longer considered a powerhouse in industry circles. Sam Phillips has flown the coop and, along with former session men Roland Janes and Stan Kesler, runs his own establishment nearby on Madison. In recent years, a glut of other studios (see below) have sprouted up that handle most of the work. This includes remixing demos by everyone from Travis Tritt to Primal Scream, who are looking for more of a rock sound, and hopefully a little of that old Memphis magic.

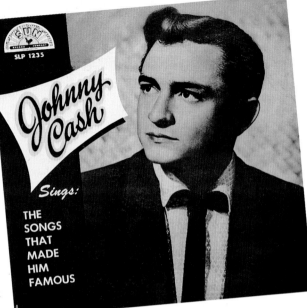

Arkansas native and longtime Hendersonville resident **Johnny Cash** cut his first record at Sun Records, a rockabilly number called "Hey Porter." In the '60s, the Man In Black sang on Bob Dylan's *Nashville Skyline* and married June Carter, of country music's fabled Carter Family. More recently his work (such as *Unchained*) has been categorized as "alternative."

Today's Sun Studio has been gentrified — they even have a little cafe downstairs — but you can't take anything away from this 20 x 35-feet shrine of American music. Here, armed with little more than two Ampex 350 four-tracks in what had been a radiator repair shop, Phillips captured The Million Dollar Quartet of Presley, Cash, Perkins, and Lewis for eternity. The tour costs $5; pompadours and pink pegged slacks not required.

THE GREAT STAX STUDIO, which once rivaled Motown in turning out soul hits, has not fared as well as Sun. The studio has been reduced, literally, to a parking lot on the corner of McLemore and College. Jim Stewart and Estelle Axton drew from the blighted neighborhood's great talent and released such classics as "Soul Man" (recorded by Sam & Dave), "Born Under a Bad Sign" (Albert King), and "I've Been Loving You Too Long" (Otis Redding). Fittingly, the Japanese P-Vine label has leased the rights to Stax and plans to reissue CDs of its 150 albums along with their original artwork. Nearby, at 998 Mississippi, try the fried chicken at the Fourway Grill, open seven days a week from 7 a.m. to 11 p.m. Souvenir bricks and photos of the studio in its heyday, along with LPs, can be had at Shangri-LA Records on Madison.

"Now looky here, I did not say I was a millionaire . . . " **Howlin' Wolf** (1910-1976), second from right, caught in the act of picking cotton. Born Chester Arthur Burnett, the Mississippi native found that he was unable to yodel like Jimmie Rodgers, "so I turned to growlin', then howlin' and it's done me fine." The Wolf, who would crawl onstage, cut his first sides in Memphis. Ernest Withers/Panopticon.

DEPENDING ON YOUR TIME CONSTRAINTS, you may want to check out other studios around town. They are not generally open to the public, but you can call ahead and try to arrange for a tour. The biggest one is Ardent (2000 Madison), which records rock, country, and blues. Easley Recording (2272 Deaderick), formerly owned by the Bar-Kays, has worked with the Panther Burns, Grifters, Impalas, and other contemporary Memphis bands. Willie Mitchell, who produced Al Green for the defunct Hi label, still runs Royal Recording (1320 Lauderdale), working with the likes of Ann Peebles and Otis Clay.

If all else fails, you can certainly visit the ghosts of studios past, such as Meteor, which cut everyone from Elmore James to Charlie Feathers, and Plastic Products, the rockabilly record presser, both formerly located on the 1700 block of Chelsea Avenue. At Chelsea and Thomas, what was American Studios is now rubble; here, soul songwriter Dan Penn ("Dark End

When they write the stories about Sun Records, they always mention Elvis Presley, Johnny Cash, Jerry Lee Lewis and so on but they never mention Junior Parker, Ike Turner, Howlin' Wolf or Little Milton — and that's a pity. We were the roots. The beginning of Sun Records.

~ Little Milton

of the Street") and engineer/producer Chips Moman cut Elvis' comeback album, not to mention the Box Tops, Dionne Warwick and Neil Diamond. Travis Wammack's "Scratchy" emerged from Sonic Studios at 1692 Madison, now an antiques store.

For arcane trivia about underground Memphis music (how Big Star got its name, where Tav Falco used to live, et cetera), pick up a copy of "Kreature Comforts: A Lowlife Guide to Memphis" ($2.50), published irregularly and possibly available at various bohemian outlets around town. While driving around town, tune your radio to WEVL 90 FM, offering everything from blues to techno. The nonprofit station spotlights local talent such as pianist Mose Vinson during its Blues on the Bluff series held in July.

———————

LIKE ANY LARGE CITY, MEMPHIS OFFERS ITS FAIR SHARE of cultural amenities, such as art museums, historic houses (including one built in the 1830s), ballet, symphony, botanical gardens, and the ubiquitous zoo. Every 10 minutes, a 50-cent trolley runs down Main Street from Beale Street north to the Pinch district, whose clubs feature live jazz on Sunday afternoons. On the way, it passes the ornate Orpheum Theater and the Holiday Inn Crowne Plaza — local entrepreneur Kemmons Wilson built the first one here on Summer Avenue in 1952, complete with air-conditioning and Muzak. This stretch of Main, known as the Mid America Mall, is closed to traffic. Try the country ham breakfast at the 1919-vintage Arcade Restaurant, where Elvis used to hang out with his buddies. A few blocks farther south is Earnestine & Hazel's, a live music club that used to be a bordello.

A few blocks from the trolley's south terminus, the National Civil Rights Museum has been added onto the former Lorraine Motel where Rev. King spent his last day. On April 4, 1968, he was gunned down while standing on the balcony outside Room 307, which has been turned into a rather macabre shrine chronicling that fateful day's events. The museum documents African-American history from slavery days to the present. Allow at least half a day to take it all in.

For something a little different, try the National Ornamental Metal Museum, situated south of downtown on a bluff overlooking the river and offering one of the finest views between Cairo and New Orleans. Note the pagoda's catfish windvane and a collection of zany barbecue contraptions. One of the museum's administrative buildings served as a

Civil War hospital. The Delta Axis Contemporary Arts Center offers a bracing alternative to the Dixon Gallery and the Brooks Museum, the city's more traditional art collections.

Southeast of town, the life and culture of Mississippi Valley Indians (A.D. 1000 to 1500) is the focus of the Chucalissa archaeological park and C.H. Nash Museum, run by the University of Memphis anthropology department. The Institute of Egyptian Art and Archaeology sponsors exhibits in the school's art gallery, located at 3750 Norriswood. The U of M has gone through five name changes since opening its doors in 1912. Just a few years ago, when it was called Memphis State, Anfernee Hardaway played ball here before graduating to the NBA. Eat breakfast at Brother Juniper's College Inn.

If you've got the money ($130-$1,345), spend at least one night in The Peabody Hotel, the city's most famous landmark. For a free yet equally upwardly mobile experience, non-guests are welcome to take the elevator to the roof and enjoy the view. Every morning at 11, after having fortified themselves with corn and millet, the hotel's English call ducks "march" from their rooftop palace to an elevator which transports them to the lobby fountain, where they splash around until bedtime. Sixty years ago, a historian theorized that this very fountain is where the Mississippi Delta begins, and the lobby is certainly an entertaining place to watch people as well as ducks. For a change of pace, walk upstairs to the mezzanine and peruse the hotel's memorabilia collection.

The city's second most famous landmark is a 32-story glass building called the Pyramid whose base is as big as six football fields. Used for concerts and other events, its surface can be BLINDING on a bright day. You can tour the innards for $3.75. The skyscraper-like nod to ancient Egypt has not been without its detractors, but it does jibe with the oft-stated thesis that Memphis, which people associate with Elvis and Reverend King, is indeed Death City, emanating a "Lenten feel." Boss Crump lobbied heavily for the nearby Memphis-Arkansas Bridge, which was completed in 1949. All lanes lead via Interstate 40 to the Southland Greyhound Park in West Memphis, Arkansas. The track is three times more popular than Graceland, although many of its patrons are repeat visitors.

Stack-o-Lee's in the bend,
Ain't doin' nothin' but killin' good men.

SOME BELIEVE THAT THE SONG "STAGOLEE," a hit for Lloyd Price in 1959, can somehow be traced to the James Lee House (circa 1869) at 239 Adams, which was formerly inhabited by the scion of a local steamboat dynasty. In one version, a bad-eyed roustabout named Jim Stack Lee kills a man for his Stetson and ends up in Hell, where he proceeds to relieve the Devil of his responsibilities. Not much is known about the real-life Lee.

Speaking of which, river history buffs can take an $8 sightseeing tour on one of the Memphis Queen Line's five boats (closed January and February; docks at the foot of Monroe). Available charters range from a 45-passenger paddlewheeler to the chandeliered *Memphis Showboat*, which accommodates 599.

The five-block-long River Walk diorama at Mud Island details the Mississippi's serpentine 900-mile course from the Great Lakes to the Gulf of Mexico, and it comes complete with bridges, levees, and tree-lined streets. Concerts reverberate through the 5,344-seat open-air amphitheater. In the vicinity, King Vidor filmed the baptism scene for his late-'20s *Hallelujah*, regarded as one of the first cinematic attempts to portray blacks realistically. (Movie buffs should also note that MGM's roaring Leo the Lion was born in Memphis.)

As you would expect in a city that is 43.5 percent black, there are a number of historical attractions of special interest to African-Americans, including Auction Square on North Main where slaves were sold; the Jacob Burkle Estate at 826 N. Second, once a stop on the Underground Railroad, and the Mason Temple at 930 Mason, where Rev. King proclaimed that he had "been to the mountaintop." Another King, B.B., started out as a deejay and "Pepticon Boy" at WDIA 1070 AM, which operates a small museum at 112 Union. The nation's first black-owned radio station fostered the careers of Bobby Bland, the Spirit of Memphis, and many others.

South of town, the St. Paul Spiritual Temple is an elaborate folk art complex that has been described as an "acid Jungian dreamscape." Only members of this maverick black Masonic sect are allowed inside, and even photographing the outside is prohibited. "Voodoo Village" (as some Memphians call it) is located on Mary Angela Road off Shelby, due east of Coro Lake.

W.C. Handy once entertained the owners of the Mallory-Neely House, located along "Millionaire's Row" in midtown Memphis, which is east, not north, of downtown. The band was asked to play in a back room where they could be heard but not seen. Also in midtown, the Pink Palace museum (with planetarium and IMAX theater) is devoted to the cultural and natural history of the Mid-South. Piggly Wiggly supermarket mogul Clarence Saunders built the palace and promptly deeded it to the city, without ever having lived there.

After you have had enough culture, rent a car or bike and proceed 15 miles north to Meeman-Shelby State Park (tel. 876-5215). Memphians have shortened its name to Shelby Forest, which is something of a misnomer since a fair share of it is swampland. There are several trails, including one which is eight miles long and doesn't loop, and an Olympic-sized pool. Or you can rent a canoe from the Wilburns in Moscow, Tennessee (tel. 877-3766) and paddle the Wolf River. Experienced canoeists might prefer to try the Ghost River stretch near LaGrange, which passes through a remote cypress forest (call the Wolf River Conservancy, tel. 320-2889). Back in Memphis, the less adventurous can take a dip at any of the city's 16 pools, all for free (tel. 325-5759 for locations).

The more daring can venture an hour south to the garish casinos of Tunica, Mississippi, and pass time at the slots while hearing big-name country acts such as Merle Haggard, whom I heard at the Sam's Town Hotel and Gambling Hall just a week before his induction into the country hall of fame. By the way, gambling isn't allowed in Memphis. Pile on the Blue & White Diner in Tunica, or try Kathryn's on Moon Lake in Lula.

Farther south in Clarksdale, Tennessee's musical debt to Mississippi quickly becomes apparent as you browse through the Delta Blues Museum, which also encompasses other forms of music. Scanning the museum's list of Mississippi-born artists, it seems like *everyone* came from the Hospitality State: blues greats Charley Patton and Elmore James, the tearjerking Tammy Wynette, and seminal jazz saxophonist Lester Young, to list just a few. Bessie Smith died at the Sunflower Hotel here after getting into a car wreck north of town on Highway 61, a road which is itself legendary in blues lore. For further exploration, pick up the "Delta Blues Map Kit" ($7.50) at the Stackhouse/Delta Record Mart, 232 Sunflower Ave. The Sunflower River Blues Festival gets underway in August.

Parchman Penitentiary's ominous death row, surrounded by an enormous asphalt lot and miles of barbed wire, inspired John Grisham to write *The Chamber.* A number of prominent bluesmen such as Bukka White and Son House served time at The Farm, so named because its prisoners once picked cotton in the surrounding fields. Now the best place to hear the real deal is farther downstream in Helena, Arkansas, at the King Biscuit Blues Festival, held in October.

Visit the Nesbitt, Mississippi, home of Jerry Lee Lewis. If you're lucky, you may get to see "the Killer" in action on his Jet Ski. Tours are available in the summertime, and they've got chicken in the barn.

Relatively obscure yet influential, **Rubin "Rube" Lacey** of Pelahatchie, Mississippi, passed through Memphis in 1927 and played guitar and mandolin on some blues records for the Columbia label. Five years later, he became a Baptist minister and traveled from state to state, eventually settling in California, where he cut an album of religious songs. He died in Bakersfield in 1972. Mixed media by Florence Zinman.

West Tennessee

Aside from boasting the state's largest city, West Tennessee is the site of the biggest earthquake in North American history (the New Madrid) and the country's most notorious Civil War battle (Shiloh). This area has also reared such musical legends as Tina Turner, Sleepy John Estes, and Carl Perkins, who grew up in Nutbush, Brownsville, and Tiptonville, respectively. Rich in folklore, this area also provided the backdrop for the ballad of Casey Jones, the train engineer whose family was living in Jackson at the time of his crash. A blood feud between two rival clans in the northwestern corner inspired Mark Twain's *Adventures of Huckleberry Finn*. Davy Crockett once plied his flatboat along the Obion River, delivering goods to this primarily agricultural area fed by the Mississippi and Tennessee rivers and their tributaries. Less famous but equally compelling are the legends surrounding the 19th-century boxing matches of Skullbone, Tennessee.

> The Mississippi first seemed to recede from its banks, and its waters gathered up like a mountain, leaving for a moment many boats, which were on their way to New Orleans, on the bare sand, in which time the poor sailors made their escape from them.
>
> ~ Eliza Bryan, describing the shock of Feb. 7, 1812

FOR TWO YEARS BEGINNING IN 1811, even before Memphis existed, the New Madrid earthquake rocked the Tiptonville area where northwestern Tennessee meets Missouri and Kentucky. One of the 2,000-plus shocks measured 8.7 on the Richter scale (San Francisco's 1906 quake was only an 8.3). The Mississippi ran backwards for several hours, and "the earth was in continual agitation" for one ten-day stretch, according to an eyewitness. Fortunately, only a few people were injured due to the region's then-sparse population. The quake did, however, dramatically alter the terrain, creating Reelfoot Lake, which now consists of 25,000 acres of water and wetlands.

Heading down the river, steamboat inventor Nicholas Roosevelt passed the epicenter shortly after the big one struck and had to turn a deaf ear "to the cries of the terrified inhabitants of the doomed town" who feared his flame-spewing boat almost as much as the quake.

The naturalist Audubon happened to be canvassing the area at the time and noted an "awful commotion in nature." For some, it was a call to party. After a particularly strong temblor, one westward emigrant passing through Gibson County grabbed the nearest woman and, whistling a jig, proclaimed that "if we got to go down, we might as well go a-dancing."

Geologically speaking, the earthquake was caused by a horst-and-graben thrust — literally, up and down — unlike the more typical variety, which involves tectonic plate-shifting. Evidence still exists in the form of the Tiptonville Dome off highway 22 near the Lakeview Grocery. To learn more about "shakes country," pick up Knox and Stewart's *New Madrid Fault Finders Guide* at the Reelfoot Lake visitors center.

Native Americans see it differently. According to legend, a Chickasaw chief's son with deformed feet — Reelfoot — abducted a Choctaw princess named Laughing Eyes. In retaliation, the Great Spirit rocked the earth, drowning Reelfoot's village, and the lake formed where he had angrily stamped his feet.

Along the Greasy Island bayou of Reelfoot Lake, bald cypress trees shoot up their side roots (or "knees"), whose function is unknown. Fishermen navigate this murky obstacle course in "stumpjumpers" with forward-facing oars. The enormous lake was formed in 1812 by the New Madrid quake, the most powerful in North American history. Nineteen boats were swallowed up, and churchbells rang in Washington D.C. Photo by Perry Walker.

Reelfoot Lake is advertised as a fisherman's paradise (bass, crappie, bluegill, and bream), but you wouldn't want to put your toes overboard. Every creature but the Loch Ness Monster finds a home beneath its dark surface, from alligator gars, ditch eels, and the predaceous bowfin to giant fish that tip the scales at 200 pounds. Bald cypress trees grow along the shore, shooting up "knees" from their side roots and completing the spooky atmosphere.

Riding in a "stumpjumper" — rowboats with forward-facing oars specially designed to navigate the lake's thick vegetation, hidden snags, and shallow bottom — is the best way to explore the lake. The lake supports 300 bird species including the golden and bald eagles. At the waterfowl contest held in August, the winner of a duck and goose calling contest advances to the world championship in Stuttgart, Arkansas. Stay at Gooch's Resort — bring your own insect repellent — and eat at Boyette's (frog legs and quail in season) or the Lakeview Restaurant.

Yet another species evolving from this primordial muck and mire is rockabilly great Carl Lee Perkins, who grew up on the lake's edge and got his first break down the river at Sun Records. You can tour a replica of his boyhood home, a three-room shack with no electricity or indoor plumbing, which has been moved "inland" to Tiptonville, and visit with his Uncle Hubert, who runs a tire center and leads the local Church of Christ choir.

Although Perkins, who wrote "Blue Suede Shoes" and "Dixie Fried" (about a razor fight), lived in the big city of Jackson for many years, you can hear those Lake County roots in his bluesy guitar riffs, heavy drawl, and traditional values. As a boy, he learned rhythm by observing field hands snap their fingers while picking cotton. A black neighbor sold him his first guitar for a couple of dollars and a one-legged chicken named Peg. After a bout with throat cancer, he pledged to sing "What a Friend We Have in Jesus" at every concert; his band included his two sons on bass and drums, a Tiptonville pal on piano, and a sheriff's deputy on rhythm guitar.

NOW UNDERWATER, THE STEAMBOAT LANDING OF COMPROMISE, Kentucky, once stood somewhere northwest of Tiptonville. Mark Twain described it as a "wretched place" consisting of a woodyard, log store, a few dwellings, and possibly a schoolhouse, and the former riverboat pilot was intrigued by newspaper accounts of a blood feud that he had read about in the late 1850s. "In no part of the South," he wrote, "has the vendetta flourished more briskly, or held out longer between warring families, than in this particular region."

Twain embellished on the facts in *Life on the Mississippi* (1883) by establishing a church in Compromise where the Darnall and Watson clans sit in opposite pews, each loaded to the gills with firearms.

> Sundays you'd see the families drive up, all in their Sunday clothes — men, women, and children — and file up the aisle, and set down, quiet and orderly, one lot on the Tennessee side of the church and the other on the Kentucky side; and the men and boys would lean their guns up

against the wall, handy, and then all hands would join in with the prayer and praise; though they say the man next the aisle didn't kneel down, along with the rest of the family. I don't know; never was at that church in my life; but I remember that's what used to be said.

Soon after, in a short story published in *Century Magazine*, Twain described a similar feud, this time between the Grangerfords and Shepherdsons. This piece turned out to be the kernel around which he built "Huck Finn" (the feud appears in Chapter 18).

Today's Compromise lies submerged in brackish waters beyond where a dirt road dead-ends into the Mississippi. It remains a wretched place, redolent of fresh fish and swarming with insects. Take 22 north to the community of Bessie; instead of following the highway to the right, continue straight for eight miles.

Tiptonville's original business district is also under water, some 1.5 miles east of its present-day site. Nicknamed the "town on wheels," it was destroyed by Federal gunboats in the Civil War and then flooded by the Mississippi, after which levees were built.

The area in question is known as The Bend, where the Mississippi runs south into Tennessee, loops north into Kentucky — where it passes the former town (and quake epicenter) of New Madrid, Missouri — and then turns south again. The river circles around a piece of land that measures 19 miles around but only two at the base; the north end belongs to Kentucky, the base to Tennesssee. As a result, it's been described as "the only part of Kentucky where the sun rises and sets in Missouri" or "the only part of Kentucky you can get to only by going through Tennessee."

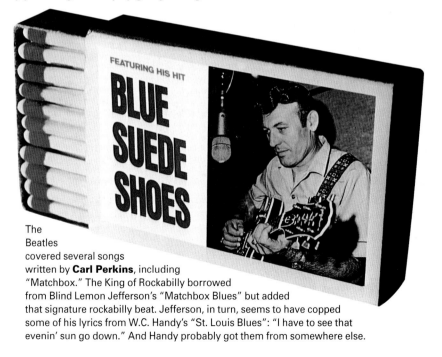

The Beatles covered several songs written by **Carl Perkins**, including "Matchbox." The King of Rockabilly borrowed from Blind Lemon Jefferson's "Matchbox Blues" but added that signature rockabilly beat. Jefferson, in turn, seems to have copped some of his lyrics from W.C. Handy's "St. Louis Blues": "I have to see that evenin' sun go down." And Handy probably got them from somewhere else.

BORDERING THE EASTERN EDGE OF REELFOOT LAKE, Obion County is well supplied with running water from the Obion River's many streams and creeks: the Cane, Clover, Cypress, Davidson, Deer, Dillard, Grassy, Grove, Harris, House, Indian, Lick, Mill, and Pawpaw. Fittingly, Obion means "many forks" in a Native American dialect. Known as the land of green pastures, this county harvests many pecks of corn, wheat, tobacco, soybeans, cotton, oats, and clover, as well as supplying wood to the furniture and lumber markets. The county seat of Union City is hometown to Rick Christian, who wrote "I Don't Need You" for Kenny Rogers, and singer Sherrill Parks ("Ring, Ring, Telephone, Ring").

In the county's southwestern corner, Kenton has gained fame for its population of white squirrels. Gypsies left a pair here in the 1850s who chased all the grey squirrels out of town. You can purchase white-squirrel souvenirs (postcards, bumper stickers, ceramics) at the pharmacy and special shirts from city hall. The best place to see them scampering around is on wooded streets such as those in the Maple Heights neighborhood. Pat Jordan tells me that Bruce Lane once adopted one of the squirrels as a pet — he named it Bubba — which worked out OK until a neighbor's cat caught it offguard.

Other Obion forks: Davy Crockett helped lay out the town of Troy in the 1820s, Dixie Gun Works on highway 51 is the world's leading purveyor of antique firearms, and West Tennessee's only covered bridge livens up Trimble, close to the Dyer County line.

To the east, Weakley County once owned bragging rights to the state's biggest tree, a 150-foot bald cypress which sprouted in the Dark Ages. A person could stand inside its hollow trunk and, holding a 14-foot pole horizontally, turn a complete circle without touching the inner walls. Some years ago, the tree was struck by lightning and the top section broke off. This loss apparently deflated the county's collective ego, and its residents set about rectifying the situation.

Area forester Rick Stutts put out the alarm, local resident Joe Atnip furnished a tip, and deer hunter Mark Allen tracked down the new champ just two miles west of the old one. It, too, is a cypress, with a circumference of 28 feet, six inches. To verify this yourself, bushwhack east from Etheridge's Levee Road (between Sharon and Greenfield), "just north of the main ditch but south of the old channel." It's roughly three quarters of a mile, and good luck!

Usually deserted, the Big Cypress Tree State Natural Area, located along the Obion's middle fork, has a few nice trails, all of which evaporate into swampland. Avoid the buggy late-afternoon hours. From highway 45E/43, head west on Kimery Store Road and follow signs. North on 45E, Eddlemon's truckstop makes a terrific catfish dinner. Weakley County is also home to Opry comedian and banjo champ Mike Snider (Gleason) and former governor Ned WcWherter (Palmersville); fiddler Mallard Stringer and my mother Betty both come from Greenfield.

In March, the Battle of the Monsters Truck Pull rocks the West Tennessee Agricultural Pavilion in Martin. During Dresden's Tennessee Iris Festival in April, which pays homage to the state flower, you might find yourself whistling "When It's Iris Time in Tennessee," one of the state's five official songs. (FYI, the state tree is the tulip poplar.)

Also in April, Henry County's industrious fishermen snag some nine thousand pounds of catfish from adjacent Kentucky Lake, the TVA's largest project, located along a wide stretch of the Tennessee River. Combined with 1,300 pounds of cornmeal, 240 gallons of vegetable oil, and 200 pounds of salt, it makes for what is billed The World's Biggest Fish Fry, held in Paris, which is not far from Milan (pronouned MY-len). This is no ordinary picnic but a weeklong celebration complete with professional rodeo, softball tourney, parade, and dignitaries luncheon.

Paris Landing State Park offers rooms overlooking Kentucky Lake, plus an 18-hole golf course and Olympic pool. Land Between the Lakes, a giant recreational area wedged between the lake and the Cumberland River to the east, is popular with hunters, hikers, and wildlife viewers.

————————

HERE THE TENNESSEE, WHOSE HEADWATERS ORIGINATE in East Tennessee, actually flows *north* toward the Ohio River and the Mississippi, which then turns south again. Following it south by car, however, takes you to Benton County, where Patsy Cline died at age 30 in a 1963 plane crash. The Winchester, Virginia, native was the Country Music Hall of Fame's first female inductee. Farther down river in Decatur County, I had a pleasant chat in Parsons with a waitress named Darla who invited me to her church, Iron Hill Pentecostal, for a singing. Parsons native Little David Wilkins' "Butter Beans" spoofed the well-known hymn, "Just a Closer Walk with Thee."

Sparsely populated Perry County straddled the river until 1845, when its western half was lopped off and turned into Decatur, making Perry the only West Tennessee county located wholly east of the Tennessee. On a map showing the three Grand Divisions, it looks as if someone had chomped a bite from Middle Tennessee's apple.

This area was once a hotbed for family groups like the Weems String Band ("Greenback Dollar," "Davy"), which used bagpipes and a catfish-skin banjo. The Perry County Music Makers ("I'm Sad and Blue") featured Nonnie Smith on zither; her brother Bulow played guitar.

Fiddling champ Charlie Sipes harks from Scotts Hill, just over the Henderson County line, and R&B saxophonist Sam "the Man" Taylor grew up in Lexington.

————————

PROCEEDING SOUTH, THE TENNESSEE BISECTS HARDIN COUNTY, splitting its southern border between Alabama and Mississippi. The 4,000-acre Shiloh National Military Park, located

50 miles south of I-40 on highway 22, commemorates the Civil War's bloodiest two-day battle, waged in 1862; the two sides suffered some 24,000 casualties. In "What I Saw at Shiloh," Ambrose Bierce reported that the underbrush often caught fire and "roasted the fallen men . . . . The contraction of muscles which had given them claws for hands had cursed each countenance with a hideous grin." (Ironically, the word "shiloh" means "peace" in Hebrew.) Although Gen. P. G. T. Beauregard's Confederate forces finally withdrew, Shiloh was considered a stalemate because Federal troops were too spent to pursue them.

To the northeast, Savannah claims to be "the Catfish Capitol [sic] of the World" and sponsors its National Catfish Derby Festival in August, including a competition for the world's best hushpuppies (corn fritters). While here on official business, Ulysses S. Grant once ensconced himself in the Cherry Mansion; two blocks away, the Tennessee River Museum covers everything from trilobites to steamboats. Due north in Adamsville (McNairy County), the Buford Pusser Home and Museum honors the real-life sheriff whose tough antics were depicted on the big screen in *Walking Tall*.

THE AREA BETWEEN MEMPHIS AND REELFOOT LAKE, paralleling the Mississippi flood plain and, to the east, the plateau slope of West Tennessee, is among the state's richest in terms of its musical heritage. It has even been postulated (by McKee and Chisenhall) that through the "golden triangle" of Brownsville, Ripley, and Jackson courses "a blues vein as rich perhaps as that of the Mississippi Delta." This may be a slight exaggeration, but the area can claim credit for producing not only Tina Turner, known as the Queen of Rock and Roll, but a plethora of blues and R&B greats as well, from Sleepy John Estes to Bobby Blue Bland.

Rock and soul diva **Tina Turner** (left) comes from Nutbush, a tiny hamlet in West Tennessee. She moved away at age 16 to join her mother in St. Louis, met Ike, and the rest is history. Her career has spanned such classics as "A Fool in Love" and "Private Dancer," plus a role in *Mad Max Beyond the Thunderdome*. This shot, taken at the Club Paradise in Memphis, dates to the early 1960s. Photo courtesy of Ernest Withers/Panopticon.

In the center is Haywood County, whose population, not coincidentally, is more than half black. And in the center of Haywood, along a stretch of highway 19, is little Nutbush, where Tina Turner (then Anna Mae Bullock) came into this world on November 26, 1939. She lived on the Poindexter farm, first sang at Spring Hill Baptist — Bootsie Whitelow's swing band also influenced her — and attended Brownsville's Carver High School. At age 16, she left to join her mother Zelma in St. Louis, which is where Ike Turner hooked up with her at the Club Manhattan. Today you're more likely to run into her in Hollywood or Paris (France, not Tennessee), or looming over Times Square.

Turner eulogized her hometown in the song and video, *Nutbush City Limits*. During the Tina Turner Celebration in August, you can tour Tina's birthplace, former homes, and church, Woodlawn Baptist, founded in 1866 by a former slave, Reverend Hardin Smith. The Nutbush Store's sweet potato pies and fried apple dumplings are outstanding. One summer, the store's proprietor, R.W. Turner, offered to let me live for free in an old, abandoned tarpaper shack on his tomato farm east of town (I didn't take him up on it). After we had a theological discussion, he gave me an article from *Guideposts* on the relative merits of philosophy and faith and made me promise to read it.

Lead rapper Speech, who sang "Tennessee" for Atlanta's Arrested Development, spent time on his grandmother's farm in Ripley. Back in 1953, the Ripley Cotton Choppers cut its one and only session for Sun and then "disappeared into the mists of time," in the words of Hawkins and Escott. In July, the town sponsors a tomato festival complete with gospel music.

JOHN ADAMS ESTES WAS BORN IN RIPLEY, but Sleepy John Estes, known for his distinctive manner of "crying the blues," spent most of his life in Brownsville. According to Big Bill Broonzy's autobiography, the singer/guitarist earned his nickname while working for the railroad. At age six, a baseball accident blinded him in one eye, so his job was to call the crew to line track.

> One day the boss kept on giving signs to us and we all just stood still and didn't move the track. So the boss got mad and walked up to us and said: 'What's the matter with you damn Negroes?' We couldn't say nothing so he looked at John Estes and said to him: 'What's wrong?' John Estes didn't say nothing, then the white man hitted him. John woke up, started to sing and we started to work, too. So after that we all called John Estes the sleeping track caller and that's how he got the name 'Sleepy John Estes.'

"Everything we was doing during the day was by John Estes' singing," Broonzy added. "If we wanted to go to the toilet during work time we would tell John Estes and he would sing it to the boss."

Estes, who composed "Someday Baby," "Rats in My Kitchen," and possibly "Milk Cow Blues" (some credit Kokomo Arnold), once lived behind a beer joint near the Twin Oaks Restaurant on highway 70 east near Brownsville, and his bust is displayed at the College Hill Theater. In "Goin' to Brownsville," he laments that "that woman I lovin' got great long curly hair/but her mother and father do not 'low me there." West of town, Sleepy John's grave lies unmarked in the Estes family plot at Durhamville Baptist Church, and if you drive along old state road 19 between Brownsville and Nutbush, you can still see Estes-style bungalows with porches — similar to the ones where Sleepy John liked to play.

He met his longtime bandmate Hammie Nixon, who played jugs and harmonica, at a local fish fry. Hammie was only 11, and Sleepy John, who was several years his senior, paid him a quarter out of his $2 salary. Thus began a relationship spanning many decades. In fact, Hammie, who sired 16 children, took Estes' daughter Virginia to be his last wife.

"Now I didn't see no whiskey, blues done made me sloppy drunk. . . ." **Sleepy John Estes** liked to practice on porches around Brownsville. This one along old State Road 19 is a country mile from the Estes plot in Durhamville. Perry Walker.

Up until his death last year at age 87, Estes's former mandolinist James "Yank" Rachell, also a Brownsvillian, remained musically active in Indianapolis, playing at the Slippery Noodle club and an occasional festival. As a young man, Yank traded a pig for his first mandolin — much to his mother's chagrin. Other musicians from the area include pianist Jab Jones and guitarists Son Bonds and Willie Newbern.

Songwriter Alex Harvey, who wrote "Delta Dawn" for Tanya Tucker when she was only 13, comes from Haywood County. So did author Alex Haley, who won the Pulitzer Prize for *Roots* in 1976 (tours of his boyhood home in nearby Henning are available) as well as flamboyant adventurer Richard Halliburton, whose *Royal Road to Romance* sold like hot-cakes in the 1920s. Abraham Lincoln buffs should perambulate the Felsenthal Collection at Brownsville's College Hill Center.

One day I ran into Brownsville's mayor, who said he remembered when a bell was sounded to remind blacks of their 10 p.m. curfew; today, the vice mayor is African-American. Every year the city, which touts itself as "a good place to live," hosts the Tennessee Peach Festival.

Three miles south, the Hatchie Scenic River's swampy forest and meandering sloughs have been preserved as an 11,000-acre national wildlife refuge for migrating and wintering waterfowl. Hunters and fishermen can use the area from mid-March to November. North of Brownsville, the West Tennessee Cotton Festival is held every August in Crockett Mills.

THE GREAT HARMONICA PLAYER NOAH LEWIS, who played with Sleepy John, Gus Cannon, and the Memphis Jug Band, hailed from Henning, west of Brownsville in Lauderdale County. "Lawd, he used to blow the hell out of that harp," Cannon once said. "He could play two harps at the same time, through his mouth and nose, same key, same melody. Y'know he could wrap his lips 'round the harp and his nose was like a fist." Tragically, Lewis died of complications from frostbite in 1961.

The grand prize for hapless endings, however, has to go to William George Tucker, also a Henning native. In the '30s, Tucker rambled through the Delta playing guitar in juke joints with Sonny Boy Williamson and Sunnyland Slim, among others. After a shooting incident, he was forced to assume a new name — John Henry Barbee — and cut a single record in Chicago, which did poorly. On tour in Europe in 1964, he became ill and returned to the States. Then he had a car accident, which landed him in jail — where he died of a heart attack.

Lauderdale's attractions include the 21,000-acre Chickasaw wildlife refuge, and Fort Pillow, built by Confederate troops.

Dyer County is not known for its output of musical legends, but for an interesting historical diversion, follow highway 51 north from Ripley. After crossing the Dyer line, you will be a few miles east of Key Corner, where Henry Rutherford began surveying the North Carolina land grants in 1783. The land wasn't actually divvied up until 1818, when the Chickasaw ceded it and settlers began arriving from Virginia and the Carolinas; the county was created in 1823. Rutherford planted his first stake on "a leaning sycamore tree on the east side of the Forked Deer River [then called the Okeena] with a gum pointer near the mouth of a spring branch." Gone are the sycamore and gum, but a tiny creek still flows into the river, and the spot has been duly marked.

To the south, the Tipton County seat of Covington spawned both the flashy singer/songwriter Isaac Hayes (now a New York deejay) and relatively obscure rockabilly legend Malcolm Yelvington. For its name if nothing else, drive southwest to the community of Peckerwood Point.

Until 1840, the Randolph depot, located due west of Covington, shipped more cotton than Memphis and there were a dozen saloons. Unfortunately, the railroad passed Randolph by, and plans for a canal between the Tennessee and Hatchie rivers fell through. In 1862, Federal troops torched the town, and it burned again in 1865. Needless to say, life in Randolph is considerably quieter these days.

Tales that are earnest, noble and gran'
Belong to the life of a railroad man.
— The original "Casey Jones"

THE REAL-LIFE STORY OF JOHN LUTHER "CASEY" JONES has become, in its various permutations, one of West Tennessee's most famous songs, described by Carl Sandburg (with a touch of poetic license) as "the greatest ballad ever written on the North American continent." The brave engineer received his training in Kayce, Kentucky — whence the nickname — but lived in a white clapboard house still standing in Jackson.

In the early morning hours of April 30, 1900, his old engine No. 382 traveling south from Memphis rear-ended a parked freight filled with shelled corn and hay on the outskirts of Vaughn, Mississippi, some 200 miles to the south. (For a number of years, a stand of wild corn from kernels scattered in the wreck marked the scene for railroaders.)

John Luther "Casey" Jones, brave engineer with a ramblin' mind.

Jones was running an hour and a half behind schedule when he spotted the train ahead. His pedal was to the metal and it was impossible to stop in time. Just before the collision, he valiantly ordered his brakeman, Sim T. Webb, to jump off.

The song's original composer was one Wallace Saunders, a "Negro wiper at the Illinois Central roundhouse" in Canton, Mississippi, who liked to hum a tune and improvise verses as he worked. His boss, Jim Tucker, persuaded him to write down the lyrics by offering a bottle of gin. Vaudevillians Seibert and Newton published the first copyrighted version in 1902.

Casey's house is now part of the sprawling Casey Jones Village, located a block south of busy Interstate 40 — and nowhere near a real, honest-to-God track. (Passenger train service today is limited to the Memphis-Dyersburg route.) Thursday nights, members of the Tennesse Plectral Society conduct a drop-in jam session at the Village's Old Country Store, playing songs that are at least 50 years old. The house contains his personal effects, photos, clippings, and all kinds of generic train memorabilia. Some versions of the song contained scurrilous lyrics, so his widow Janie spent the rest of her life defending his reputation, wearing black for 50 years.

The real Casey was born in 1863 and stood six feet four. He was known as a fast roller who kept his engine in prime condition, seldom stopped for water, and delivered "on the card." He handled his six-chime whistle with finesse, so that it sounded equal parts whippoorwill and Viking war cry.

In the crash, Casey was killed outright, an iron bolt driven through his neck. His arm was torn from its socket, the leather glove still on the hand of the severed arm and the hand clenched to the brake handle. A bale of hay rested on his chest. His funeral at Jackson's Mt. Calvary Cemetery cost nearly ten grand, which was a lot of dough back in 1900.

EQUALLY HEARTRENDING IS THE STORY OF SONNY BOY WILLIAMSON, who was reared near Jackson. I'm talking about so-called Sonny Boy I, whose given name was John Lee Curtis Williamson. Sonny Boy II, whose given name was Aleck Ford, which he subsequently changed to Rice Miller, came from Arkansas or Mississippi, depending on your musicological source. Both played harmonica and wrote famous songs.

Their lives overlapped, but Sonny Boy I, who was younger, became famous earlier in his career, which is how he became Number One. Sonny Boy II confused matters by labelling himself "the Original Sonny Boy" which, in a sense, was true, since he was older. If you can straighten it out, please notify the state tourism bureaus of Tennessee, Mississippi, and Arkansas.

Sonny Boy I, who wrote "Good Morning Little School Girl," "Elevator Woman," and "Love Me, Baby," is credited with adapting the harp, originally a novelty jug-band instrument, to electric blues. Crowned the King of the Harmonica, he influenced everyone from Howlin' Wolf to Eric Clapton. He played a C harp in G — known as the cross-harp style — which allowed him to bend notes more easily.

He also used a variety of special techniques such as fluttertonguing, and a speech impediment gave his singing "a tongue-tied and hectic quality" which spawned many imitators, according to David Evans. In fact, some players were so affected by Williamson's style that, following his death, they just up and quit.

In "T.B. Blues," Sonny Boy requested that his body be buried in Jackson. In 1948, when he was only 34 years old, he was murdered for pocket change in Chicago and his wish was granted. Located out in the boondocks southwest of Jackson at Blair's Chapel cemetery — actually several plots strung haphazardly along a stretch of hardscrabble road — Sonny Boy's tombstone requires a strenuous hike through kudzu-infested forest to a clearing at the top of a hill. Several rusty harmonicas rest on top.

Another local product, Big Maybelle, cut the first version of "Whole Lotta Shakin' Goin' On" (all 250 pounds of it) in the early '50s, before Jerry Lee got around to it. Plagued with drug problems, Mabel Louise Smith died in 1972 at age 48.

While in Jackson, stop at Suede's, a country-style restaurant opened by Carl Perkins, where you can examine several showcases of photos and mementoes while waiting for your catfish and tea. If you have any questions, ask the *maître d'*, Bart Swift, who is Perkins' son-in-law. The items on display include the four Beatles' Carl Perkins Fan Club membership cards, each one dutifully signed. Among the Fab Four's covers were Perkin's "Honey Don't," and "Matchbox," which he actually expropriated from Blind Lemon Jefferson.

"I'm a rompin', stompin', piano-playin' sonofabitch. A *mean* sonofabitch. But a great sonofabitch. A good person. Never hurt nobody unless they got in my way. I got a mean streak in me. Elvis did, too. He hid his. I don't hide mine. I gotta lay it open sometimes."

"Anything you would like to tell your fans?" the man from the country music magazine asked.

"Yeah. Kiss my ass. If they don't buy my records, they can bark my hole. And if they don't buy my albums, they can use my dick for a walkin' pole. God, that was awful. Erase that. Naw, I'll tell ya what I think of my fans. I think of them exactly the way they think of me."

~ From Nick Tosches' *Hellfire: The Jerry Lee Lewis Story*

Perkins, who passed away in early 1998, lived at the corner of Plantation Road and Country Club Lane in a large unostentatious white house with decorative black guitars framing the front door. This is where he led the simple life, enjoying his wife Val's biscuits, anticipating the day's *Jackson Sun*, and coming up with song ideas while riding around on his lawnmover. Every year he staged an annual benefit concert for the Carl Perkins Center for the Prevention of Child Abuse.

South of town, Perkins, Jerry Lee, and other cats once rocked the still-standing Pine Ridge Club, located on highway 18 near Medon. Fire gutted the insides but it's been rebuilt, and the single-story cinderblock structure remains intact. The New Pine Ridge sponsors live music on weekends.

Entrepreneur Isaac Tigrett, creator of the Hard Rock Cafe and, subsequently, the House of Blues franchise, is a Jackson native. Supporters describe Tigrett as a visionary who is helping to keep the blues alive, while critics have dissed his latest venture, calling it everything from a multimedia conglomerate to a "faux hillbilly club," and questioning why a branch hasn't opened in Memphis. Recently, the House of Blues started its own label, releasing records by local talent such as the Gales Brothers.

Singer Denise LaSalle ("Trapped by a Thing Called Love") runs a wig and clothing boutique and records for Malaco Records. A few blocks away, her husband, James E. Wolfe Jr., manages local radio station WFKX — which is kind of an abbreviation for 'Wolfe' kicks the airwaves — making him one of only a few hundred African-Americans to do so nationwide.

In the 1920s, music blared from Shannon Street's many speakeasies (including one invitingly called the Bucket o' Blood), located near downtown in the heart of black Jackson. Legitimate clubs opened after prohibition was repealed in 1933, and Sonny Boy left town four years later; he wrote "Shannon Street Blues" about his early days. The Shannon Street Blues Fest, featuring local performers, takes place in June.

Most of the block's old brick buildings have been torn down. Thankfully, the one containing Hayne's Fish Market survived the wrecking ball. Hayne's has been in business since 1928, when Herbert and Daisy emigrated south from Reelfoot Lake. Their descendants make a larruping-good plate of deep-fried buffalofish, which are related to carp and indigenous to the Mississippi Valley.

All over the Southeast, large hillocks testify to the former existence of a people called the Mound Builders, about whom we know very little. Saul's Mound, one of nine at the Pinson Mounds State Archaeological Area south of Jackson, is the second tallest in the United States. It stands 72 feet high and measures 330 feet in diameter. Dating to 1–500 A.D., it was probably used for ceremonies, not burial. After climbing 121 steps to the summit, you might be greeted by vicious biting flies. A manmade mound ("do not climb museum") houses an interpretive center.

Surveyor Joel Pinson discovered the mounds in 1820. As a later historian observed, "Voracious time has drawn them, with the days of other years, into her capacious stomach, where, dissolving into aliments of oblivion, they have left to be saved from annihilation only the faint glimmering chronicles of their former being."

THE 19TH CENTURY HERALDED THE RISE OF "FIST AND SKULL" boxing in the hamlet of Skullbone, north of Jackson in Gibson County. Gloves and head gear were disallowed, as were
punches below the collar, and the fights ended after one fighter had been knocked to the
ground. The pugilists came from the surrounding farm communities of Goosefoot, Frog
Jump, and Idlewild, and they went at it until both men "were give plumb out," as one
local bard put it, "just like two roosters fightin', and almost as bloody."

The pre-match manners, on the other hand, could be surprisingly urbane. For example, "Big Bill" Dowland once rode to Billy Mitchell's house in adjacent Weakley County
and hollered out, "Billy, wanna fight?" to which Mitchell replied, "Ain't had my dinner
yet. Have a seat on the front porch. I'll be with you in about 45 minutes." After Mitchell
finished eating, the two sat around talking until he had properly digested — and then
went at it hammer and tongs. Fittingly, Skullbonians fought for opposing sides in the War
Between the States.

This rural area was also home to Uncle Johnnie Williamson, whose family string band
furnished entertainment for picnics, barbecues, and concerts. He sang in black face, per-

formed magic, and danced
marionettes; lectured against
betting and boozing, and argued Scripture (even with
preachers), and served as a
makeshift doctor, undertaker,
and mediator. "He's the first
man I ever knew that lived nine
days in every week," said the
late Ben Hillsman of Trezevant.

In the '30s and '40s, thousands
trekked to the traveling Opry
show at Dowland Grove, a
clearing near the hamlet of
Skullbone; here, an unidentified
female accordionist entertains
the crowd.

In "downtown" Skullbone, coon hunters gather at twilight in front of Landon and Ruby Hampton's general store to discuss the upcoming evening's strategy and shoot the bull. This politically conservative neck of the woods is populated by "moss-back" Republicans whose ancestors consistently voted against Roosevelt by a margin of 2 to 1. (I noticed, however, that the coon hunts are integrated.)

Inside the store are atmospheric photos of the enormous crowds (as many as 20,000 people) who flocked to Dowland Grove, just up the hill, to see the traveling Opry perform in the 1930s and early '40s. These picnics took place after the crops had been harvested. Across the street, Annie Lou Stockard Dill is buried in the Pleasant View cemetery. Nicknamed the "Grand Ole Opry Sweethearts," she and her husband Bill ("Danny," from Huntingdon) once toured with Roy Acuff and Hank Williams; Bill wrote "Detroit City" with Mel Tillis.

Several hundred yards north is the single grave of Alford Mount (1802-1867), who chose to be buried in what was once his hog pen.

To the west, Bradford is known for its doodle soup — actually more of a gravy — made from chicken drippings, hot pepper, flour, and vinegar — preferably cooked over an open fire — and served with boiled chicken and biscuits. This concoction derives its name from the old doodle wagons, a kind of country store on wheels, that traveled the rural routes selling food and household commodities. Try the Kitchen Korner's variant. To the south, the singer T. G. Sheppard grew up in Humboldt.

Down the road in Crockett Country, don't-blink Gadsden is the hometown of Scotty Moore, who played guitar with Elvis for 14 years, during which he earned just $30,000 "but we got to be part of something pretty special," said Moore, who lives in Nashville and recently collaborated with two of his biggest fans: Keith Richards and Jeff Beck. To the east, rockabilly's Carl Mann, crooner of "Mona Lisa," came from the Carroll County seat of Huntingdon. Now saved, he only performs in church.

Proceeding south to Henderson County; the Reverend John A. Parker's grave in the Jones Cemetery is a nice quiet place to pause and reflect on the Civil War; take the Parker Crossroads exit from Interstate 40. Parker sympathized with the North until some Union troops defiled his property. His last wish was to be buried with his head facing south.

Landon and Ruby Hampton's general store is the self-proclaimed capital of the Kingdom of Skullbonia — by default.

He figured that this way, when Gabriel blew his trumpet, he could rise up and "kick the Yankees back north." All the other graves have an east-west orientation. When I visited Rev. Parker, his tombstone was decorated with a fresh Confederate flag.

Ellis Truett Jr., of the Lizard Lick community near Huron, maintains an impressive collection of antique musical instruments. They are the kind that "poor folks played," he says, including a locally made box dulcimer dating to the 1830s. Near Truett's log cabin is a one-room schoolhouse built by his grandfather.

To the Southwest, the singer Eddy Arnold, best known for "Bouquet of Roses," grew up and still holds court in Henderson, Chester County. "The Tennessee Plowboy" (*Time* called him "the Country Como") has racked up more number-one hits than any other country artist — almost three years, cumulatively! Elvis and Eddy shared the same manager, the slippery Col. Tom Parker. Swim and camp at the restorative Chickasaw State Park.

Whiteville, in northwestern Hardeman County, is the birthplace of Phineas Newborn, Jr., one of jazz piano's true individualists. It has been written that Phineas' prodigious two-handed style, influenced by Art Tatum and Bud Powell, reflects the whole history of jazz piano. Count Basie dubbed him "the Einstein of the Ivories." For proof, check out his rendition of "Stella by Starlight" on *Harlem Blues*, with Ray Brown and Elvin Jones.

Raised in Memphis from infancy, Phineas (pronounced FINN-ee-as or FINE-as) died there in 1989 at age 57. His brother, Calvin Newborne, [sic] still teaches guitar and plays around town with his band, the Owls. His on-stage theatrics (and those of Charlie "Ike" Burse) supposedly inspired Elvis. Estelle Axton, who mortgaged her house to open the Stax record label, is also a Hardeman Countian, having grown up in Middleton.

Slide guitarist Mississippi Fred McDowell, whose "You Got To Move" was covered by the Stones, grew up in Rossville, Fayette County, not far from the Shelby County line. Considered one of the great country bluesmen, McDowell reportedly felt at sea without his homemade inch-long slide, cut from the neck of a Gordon's Gin bottle. "Anything I say I can make them strings say," he told *Sing Out!* in 1969.

McDowell didn't become famous until the folk revival of the '60s, by which time he had moved to Como, Mississippi, to be near his sister. Had he stayed put in Rossville, perhaps his name would be *Tennessee* Fred. (Memphis Minnie, on the other hand, grew up in Algiers, Louisiana, and relocated to Tennessee — and I would bet even money that her second husband, Kansas Joe, comes from anywhere but.)

Somerville, the county seat, produced both obscure bluesman Homesick James ("Set a Date") Williamson, and famous gospel composer, Reverend W. Herbert Brewster, Jr., who wrote Mahalia Jackson's first million-seller, "Move On Up a Little Higher," and the Ward Singers' "Surely God Is Able"; he preached at East Trigg Baptist Church in Memphis. Country singer Bobbie Gentry, a Mississippi native, lived in Fayette for a spell. Her big hit was "Ode to Billie Joe," in which someone, for some reason, threw something off the Tallahatchie Bridge — wherever that is.

Though overshadowed by Memphis, the small towns of Shelby County have added many great musicians to the mix. Rosemark's Robert Calvin "Bobby Blue" Bland, a crony of

B.B. King's, is best known for "Turn Up Your Love Light" and his cover of T-Bone Walker's "Stormy Monday." He now lives in Germantown. Johnny Shines, who hoboed with Robert Johnson, played slide with Big Water Horton and Sunnyland Slim, and once busked for tips in Handy Park, came from the Frayser crossroads just north of the Wolf River.

From Raines hailed Joe Hill Louis, a.k.a. the Be-Bop Boy and His One Man Band, who played the wailing guitar on "Bear Cat" and died at age 36 from a tetanus infection. Harp and piano man Willie Mabon ("I'm Mad") came out of the north Memphis community of Hollywood, Tennessee.

Frank Stokes of Whitehaven, south of Memphis, is said to have possessed the finest blues voice that the city ever produced. He could set lyrics to virtually any subject — bluesman Joe Calicott said Stokes could write a song "about your foot." Listen to Stokes' wacky "Chicken You Can Roost Behind the Moon" and decide for yourself.

THE BIG CITY OF MEMPHIS itself has produced West Tennessee's greatest arsenal of talent over the years. Memphis-born Aretha Franklin has won more Grammys than anyone this side of East Tennessee's Chet Atkins. Memphis native Cora Walton, a.k.a. Koko Taylor, has picked up some 15 W.C. Handy awards. But it is the city's lesser-knowns who round out the story.

Viola McCoy sang and played kazoo with Fletcher Henderson's band (other early jazz artists included cornetist Johnny Dunn and drummer Jimmy Crawford), and singer Dee Dee Bridgewater carries on the jazz tradition today. Blues and R&B are well-represented by Memphis Willie B., who wrote his racy "Bad Girl Blues" about "women lovin' each other," and by Willie Nix, the tightest boogie drummer around, whose career was interrupted by a prison sentence. Across the river, West Memphis, Arkansas, produced both (Herman) Junior Parker and (Amos) Junior Wells.

In the country sector, Johnny Cash's Memphis-born daughter Rosanne (who is actually considered "new country") and songwriter Dickey Lee ("Patches," "Rocky," and "She Thinks I Still Care") toil in Nashville's lucrative vineyards. O'Landa Draper leads the Associates, a 40-member gospel choir, following in the footsteps of soloist T.C. "Queen Candace" Anderson, who electrified East Trigg Baptist a half-century ago; her handle comes from a passage in the Bible.

"I never heard such rock and roll as on your back roads, Tennessee," sings Shawn Colvin, and Memphis has spawned some great rockers. Bill Black, who slapped bass for the early Elvis, and drummer J.M. van Eaton, one of the Little Green Men heard on "Great Balls of Fire," both came from Memphis. Rockabilly guitar granny Cordell Jackson began recording here in 1947 — *before* Sam Phillips — making her America's first female engineer and producer. Then there's saxman Don Nix, who wrote the lyrically-challenged "Going Down" for his idol Freddie King (*Getting Ready*, 1971); it has since become a standard rock jam, covered by Joe Walsh, J.J. Cale, and Led Zeppelin.

Native Memphian William Bell sang one of Stax's first hits, "You Don't Miss Your Water" (1961), which he wrote while homesick on a trip to New York; in '67 he co-penned "Born Under a Bad Sign" with Booker T. for Albert King. A teenaged Carla Thomas cut "'Cause I Love You" with her dad Rufus, of Funky Chicken fame, and that's her with Otis Redding on "Tramp." Stax songwriter David Porter ("Something Is Wrong With My Baby") grew up on the same block of East Virginia Street as Maurice White, founder of Earth, Wind & Fire; the seventies soul group (originally called The Salty Peppers) racked up 11 gold albums.

Little Johnny Taylor comes from Memphis, started out with the Mighty Clouds of Joy, and now records for the Ichiban label. He is not to be confused with Johnnie Taylor, who harks from nearby Crawfordsville, Arkansas, and began his career with the Soul Stirrers; "the philosopher of Southern soul" is on the Malaco label. Little Johnny, who is related to Koko, charted with "Part Time Love" and Johnnie followed suit, first with "Who's Making Love" and then "Disco Lady." Soon thereafter, in 1977, Rick Dees and His Cast of Idiots answered the latter with yet another hit: "Disco Duck (Part 1)." In this particular division, however, my favorite is "Disco Strut," by Booker T. Laury, the Memphis barrelhouse pianist. As is typical of Memphis, where appearances can be deceiving, none of these songs is actually a disco song.

Useful Information

For additional tourist information, contact the Tennessee Department of Tourist Development at the following locations:

In the USA:
320 Sixth Ave. N., 5th Floor, Rachel Jackson Building, Nashville, TN 37243
Tel: 615-741-8299
Website: http:// www.state.tn.us/tourdev

In the UK:
Coach House Mews, R/O 99 Bancroft, Hitchin, Herts SG5 1NQ, England
Tel: 01462-440-784
E-Mail: Lofthse@gardencitynet.co.uk

East Tennessee (area code 423)

CONTACTS

Artsline (Chattanooga), 756-2787

Birthplace of Country Music Alliance, Box 216, Bristol, TN/VA, 37620

Bristol Historical Association, Box 204, Bristol, TN, 37621

Center for Appalachian Studies, East Tennessee State University, Johnson City, 929-5348; country and bluegrass program, 929-4270

Chattanooga Convention and Visitors Bureau, 2 Broad St., 800-322-3344

Knoxville County Tourist Commission, 800-727-8045

Northeast Tennessee Tourism Association, 800-468-6882

Overmountain Victory Trail Association, 753-3226

Pigeon Forge tourism department, 800-251-9100

Tennessee Overhill Heritage Program, 263-7232

VENUES

Beechwood Music Center, Fall Branch (near Kingsport), 348-7321

Bessie Smith Hall, 200 E. M. L. King Blvd, Chattanooga, 757-0020

Carter Fold, Maces Spring, Virginia, 703-386-9480

Down Home, 300 W. Main, Johnson City, 929-9822

Laurel Theater (Jubilee Community Arts), Knoxville, 522-5851

Memorial Auditorium, 399 McCallie, Chattanooga, 757-5156

Mountain Opry, Fairmount Road atop Signal Mountain, in Walden, Tenn. (Chattanooga area), 886-5897

Museum of Appalachia, Norris, 494-7680 or 494-0514

Neyland Stadium, University of Tennessee at Knoxville, 656-4444

Paramount Center for the Arts, 518 State St., Bristol, TN, 37620, 423-968-7456

Thompson Boling Arena, University of Tennessee at Knoxville, 656-4444

Tivoli Theater, 709 Broad, Chattanooga, 757-5156

University of Tennessee at Chattanooga arena, 4th at Mabel, 755-4706

Viking Hall, 1100 Edgemont, Bristol, 764-0188

PUBLICATIONS

The Loafer, Tri-Cities weekly (Wednesdays) with music listings

Knoxville News-Sentinel, music listings in Friday morning *detours!* section

The Chattanooga Free Press (afternoon) publishes a weekly events calendar (*The Chattanooga Times* is the morning paper).

For more on music of the Cumberland Plateau, see "The Cumberland Music Tour," published in 1988 by the Tennessee Arts Commission, 401 Charlotte Ave., Nashville, 37243; 615-741-1701.

RESTAURANTS

The Bonfire, 1020 Volunteer Parkway, Bristol, 968-5991; 24 hours

Buddy's Bar-B-Que, Knoxville (nine locations)

Cornbread's Coffee House, 109 E. Main, Jonesborough, 753-8187

Dumplin's, 701 Broad St., Chattanooga, 756-3522

Golden Girls Restaurant, Clinton (near Norris) — don't miss the Vols Room, decked out in orange and white

Hot Sauce Charlie's, 3625 Tennessee Ave., Chattanooga (St. Elmo's district), 265-2827

Pardner's BBQ, 5444 Hwy 11-E, Piney Flats (north of Johnson City), 538-5539

Pickle Barrel, 1012 Market St., Chattanooga, 266-1103

Sand Bar, 1011 Riverside Drive, Chattanooga, 622-4432

Shirley's Restaurant, Hampton (321 south of Elizabethton), 768-2092; all you can eat, open Fri.-Sun.

LODGING

Capri Motel, 3008 W. Market St., Johnson City, 926-2952

Charit Creek Lodge, Big South Fork, 429-5704

Chattanooga Choo-Choo Holiday Inn, 800-TRACK29 or 266-5000

General Morgan Inn & Conference Center, 111 North Main St., Greeneville, TN, 37743, 800-223-2679

Gordon-Lee Mansion B&B, (former Union hospital, in Georgia, three miles south of Chickamauga battlefield), 800-487-4728

Hale Springs Inn (1824), Rogersville, 272-5171

Hawley House, Jonesborough, 753-8869
Holiday Inn Select Downtown, 525 Henley, Knoxville, 522-2800
Martha Washington Inn, Abingdon, Virginia, 703-628-3161
Newbury House, Rugby, 628-2441
Radisson Read House, M.L. King at Broad Street, Chattanooga, 266-4121
Tannissee Lodging, Reliance, 338-2161; near Ocoee and Hiwassee rivers
Tennessee Ridge Inn, Gatlinburg, 800-737-7369
West Side Motel, 320 W. Broadway Ave., Maryville, 983-8161

ATTRACTIONS

Archives of Appalachia, ETSU, Johnson City, 929-4338
Bristol Motor Speedway, 764-1161
Big South Fork National River & Recreation Area, 879-4818
Chattanooga African-American Museum, E. Martin Luther King Blvd., 267-1076
Chickamauga/Chattanooga National Military Park, headquarters in Fort Oglethorpe,
    Georgia
Dollywood, 800-DOLLYWOOD
The East Tennessee Historical Society Museum, Clinch Ave, Knoxville; a new country
    music walking tour of downtown Knoxville begins at this museum
Great Smoky Mountains National Park, 423/436-1200
Historic Rugby, 628-2441
Lake Winnepesaukah Amusement Park, Rossville, Georgia, eight miles south of
    Chattanooga
Roan Mountain State Park, Roan Mountain, 772-3303
Scopes Trial Play, Dayton, Friday through Sunday at the Rhea County Courthouse,
    775-7206

EVENTS

African-American Cultural Festival, August, Chattanooga, 267-1076
Bessie Smith Traditional Jazz Festival, May, Chattanooga, 266-0944
Davy Crockett Birthday Party, August, Morristown, 586-6382
Dogwood Arts Festival, April, Knoxville, 637-4561 or 1-800-DOGWOOD
Dollywood Harvest Celebration, early October to November, Pigeon Forge,
    800-DOLLYWOOD
Dulcimer and Harp Festival, June, Cosby, 487-5543
Fall Color Cruise & Folk Festival, October, Chattanooga, 756-2787
Festival of British and Appalachian Culture, May, Rugby, 628-2340
Gatlinburg Fall Craftsmen's Fair, September, 436-7479
Grandfather Mountain Highland Games, July, Linville, N.C., 704-733-1333
Homecoming Bluegrass & Folk Music Festival, July, Dayton, 775-3555
Jim & Jesse's Bluegrass Festival, June, Elizabethton, 323-1876
Merle Watson Memorial Festival, April/May, Wilkesboro, N.C., 800-343-7857

Museum of Appalachia Fall Homecoming, October, Norris, 494-7680

National Storytelling Festival, October, Jonesborough, 753-2171

Old-Time Fiddlers Convention, August, Mountain City, 727-5800

Polk County Ramp [wild onion] Festival, April, Benton, 338-4504; a similar event is held in Cosby, Cocke County, in May

Rhododendron Festival, June, Roan Mountain, 725-2270

Riverbend Festival, June, Chattanooga, 754-8687

Smoky Mountain Fiddlers Convention, August, Loudon, 458-4352

Tennessee Valley Fair, September, Knoxville, 637-5840

Nashville (area code 615)

CONTACTS

Metro Historical Commission, 10th Ave. S., 862-7970

Nashville Chamber of Commerce, 161 4th Ave. N., 259-4755

Nashville Convention & Visitors Bureau, 161 4th Ave. N., 259-4700

Nashville Songwriters Association, 15 Music Square W., 256-3354

Tennessee Arts Commission, 401 Charlotte Ave., 741-1701

Tennessee Department of Tourist Development, 320 6th Ave. N., 741-2158

VENUES

Ace of Clubs, 114 2nd Ave. S., 254-2237

Bell Cove, 151 Sunset Drive (Hendersonville), 822-7074

Bluebird Cafe, 4104 Hillsboro Road, Nashville, 383-1461

Boardwalk Cafe, 4114 Nolensville Road, 832-5104

The Broken Spoke, 1412 Brick Church Pike, 262-7524

Club Mere Bulles, 152 2nd Ave. N., 256-2582

The Commodore (Holiday Inn Vanderbilt), 2613 West End Ave., 327-4707

Courtyard Cafe, 867 Bell Road, Antioch, 731-7228

Douglas Corner, 2106-A 8th Ave. S., 298-1688

Exit/In, 2208 Elliston Place, 321-4400

Gas Lite Lounge, 167 1/2 8th Ave. N., 254-1278

Grand Ole Opry, 889-6611 or 6600

Jamaica, 1901 Broadway, 321-5191

Joe's Village Inn, 4107 Hillsboro Road, 383-9115

Longhollow Jamboree, Goodlettsville, 824-4445

Nashville Arena, 150 2nd Ave. N., 880-2850

The Nashville Network (TNN), 2806 Opryland Dr., 883-7000 or 889-6840

Robert's Western Wear, 416 Broadway, Nashville, 256-7937

Ryman Auditorium, 116 5th Ave. N., 254-1445 or 889-6611

Sarratt Student Center at Vanderbilt, concert line, 322-2425

Starwood Amphitheater, 3839 Murfreesboro Road (south of Nashville), 737-4849

Station Inn, 402 12th Ave. S., Nashville, 255-3307

The Sutler, 2608 Franklin Road, Nashville, 297-9195

Temple Baptist Church, 3810 Kings Lane, 876-4084

Tennessee Performing Arts Center (TPAC), 505 Deaderick, 741-7975

3rd & Lindsley Bar & Grill, 816 3rd Ave. S., 259-9891

328 Performance Hall, 328 Fourth Ave. S., 259-3288

Ticketmaster, 737-4849; order tickets, 255-9600

12th & Porter, 114 12th Ave. N., 254-7236

Wolfy's, 425 Broadway, Nashville, 251-1621

PUBLICATIONS

Nashville Scene, free weekly published Wednesdays, 244-7989

The Tennessean (daily) see *Weekends* section on Fridays, 259-8000

For "Fiddle and Old-Time Music Contests In Tennessee" pamphlet, write the Tennessee
Arts Commission, 320 Sixth Ave. N., Nashville 37243

RESTAURANTS

Brown's Diner, 2102 Blair Blvd., 269-5509

Elliston Place Soda Shop, 2111 Elliston Place, 327-1090

Hap Townes Restaurant, 493 Humphreys, 242-7035

Jamaica, 1901 Broadway, 321-5191

Jimmy Kellys, 217 Louise Ave., 329-4349

The Loveless Restaurant, 8400 Highway 100 (eight miles west), 646-9700

Pancake Pantry, 1796 21st Ave. S., 383-9333

Prince Hot Chicken Shack, 123 Ewing Drive, 226-9442; open till 2 a.m., 4 a.m. on weekends

Rotier's Restaurant, 2413 Elliston Place, 327-9892

Sunset Grill, 2001 Belcourt Ave., 386-3663

Swett's, 2725 Clifton Ave., 329-4418

Sylvan Park Restaurant, 4502 Murphy Road, 292-9275

Tin Angel, 3201 West End, 298-3444

The Trace, 2000 Belcourt Ave., 298-2112

Uncle Bud's Catfish, 1214 Lakeview Dr., Franklin, 790-1234

LODGING

Clubhouse Inn and Conference Center, 920 Broadway, 244-0150

Hampton Inn, 1919 West End Ave., 329-1144

Hermitage Suite Hotel, 231 Sixth Ave. N., 800-251-1908

Loew's Vanderbilt Plaza, 2100 West End, 320-1700

The Opryland Hotel, 2800 Opryland Dr., 889-1000

Quality Inn Hall of Fame, 1407 Division, 242-1631

Shoney's Inn, I-40 & Demonbreun, 255-9977

Union Station Hotel, 1001 Broadway, 726-1001

ATTRACTIONS

Belle Meade Mansion, 5025 Harding Rd., 356-0501

Cheekwood (botanical garden and art museum), 1200 Forrest Park Dr., 353-2162

Country Music Hall of Fame & Museum, 4 Music Square East, 256-1639; books and
    records, 1 (800) 255-2357, 9 a.m.-5 p.m. (CST) seven days a week

Country Music Foundation's library and media center, same address as above, 256-1639

Hatch Showprint, 316 Broadway, 256-2805

The Hermitage (home of Andrew Jackson), 12 miles east off I-40, 889-2941

Nashville Room (Ben West Library), 225 Polk Ave., 862-5782

Radnor Lake State Natural Area, 1160 Otter Creek Rd., 373-3467

RCA Studio B, 26 Music Square West, 256-1639

Tootsie's Orchid Lounge, 422 Broadway, 726-0463

Wildhorse Saloon, 120 2nd Ave. N., 251-1000

STORES

Bookstar, 4301 Harding Rd., 292-7895

Davis-Kidd Booksellers, 4007 Hillsboro Rd., 385-2645

Elder's Bookstore, 2115 Elliston Place, 327-1867

The Great Escape, 1925 Broadway, Nashville, 327-0646 (also at 112 Second Ave. N. and
    111-B Gallatin Pike N.)

La Hacienda, 2615 Nolensville Pike, 256-6142

Mosko's (newsstand), 2204 Elliston Place, 327-3562

Phonoluxe Records, 2609 Nolensville Road, Nashville, 259-3500

Tower Records-Video-Books, 2400 West End Ave., 327-3722

EVENTS (INCLUDING MIDDLE TENNESSEE)

Antiques and Garden Show of Nashville, February, Nashville Convention Center,
    352-1282

Bell Witch Bluegrass Festival, August, Adams, 696-2589

Bending Chestnut Outdoor Concert (gospel), June, Franklin, 790-6836

Bluegrass and Old-Time Music Contest, August, Manchester, 596-2816

Cheekwood Jazz Festival, June, Nashville, 353-2163

Civil War Encampment, July, Stones River National Battlefield, Murfreesboro, 893-9501

Dancin' In the District, May-August, Nashville, 244-9533

Franklin Jazz Festival, August, 790-5541

Gospel Music Week, April, Nashville, 242-0303

Hillbilly Day, June, Lafayette, 666-2142

Historic Jonesborough Days, July, 753-5281

Hometown Memorial Bluegrass Festival, June, Sparta, 935-5012

International Country Music Fan Fair, June, Nashville, 889-7503

Irish Picnic and Homecoming, July, McEwen, 582-3986

Mule Day, April, Columbia, 381-9557

Old-Time Fiddlers Jamboree, July, Smithville, 597-8500
Tennessee Old-Time Fiddlers Championship, March, Clarksville, 648-0001
Tennessee State Fair, September, Nashville, 862-8980
Tennessee Walking Horse National Celebration, August, Shelbyville, 684-5915
Tin Pan South (songwriters festival), April, Nashville, 251-3472
Uncle Dave Macon Days, July, Murfreesboro, 893-6565
Wild Horse and Burro Days Celebration, August, Cross Plains, 654-2256
Williamson County Country Music Festival, August, College Grove, 368-7151

Middle Tennessee (area code 615, outside Nashville 931)
CONTACTS

Alabama Music Hall of Fame, Tuscumbia, Alabama; 800-239-AMHF
Center for Popular Music, Murfreesboro, 898-2449

ATTRACTIONS

Hank Williams Jr. Country Store, Crossville, 484-4914
International Bluegrass Music Association hall of honor, 207 E. Second St., Owensboro,
    Kentucky, 502-684-9025
Jack Daniel's Distillery, Lynchburg, 931-759-6180
Loretta Lynn's Ranch, Hurricane Mills, 296-7700
Natchez Trace Parkway, 601-842-1572
Nissan plant tours, Smyrna, 459-1444
Stones River National Battlefield, 893-9501

RESTAURANTS

Country Side Restaurant, Highway 50, Lynchburg, 759-4430
Miss Mary Bobo's Boarding House, Lynchburg, 759-7394
Pop's Happyland Restaurant & Truck Stop, 211 Dixie Lee Ave., Monteagle, 924-3180

LODGING

Cedar Lane B&B, Rt. 3, Lynchburg, 759-6891
Comfort Inn, 2325 Highway 46S, Dickson, 446-2423
Super 8 Motel, I-40, exit 287, Cookeville, 800-800-8000

Memphis (area code 901)
CONTACTS

Beale Street Blues Society, Box 3421, 38173; 527-4585
The Blues Foundation, 174 Beale, 527-BLUE
Chamber of Commerce, 22 N. Front, Suite 200, 575-3500
Memphis Convention & Visitors Bureau, 47 Union Ave., 543-5300 or 800-MEMPHIS
Tennessee Welcome Center, 119 Riverside Drive, 543-5333

VENUES

Automatic Slim's Tonga Club, 83 S. Second, 525-7948

Barrister's, 147 Jefferson, 526-5053

B.B. King's Blues Club, 147 Beale, 524-KING

Blues City Cafe, 138-40 Beale, 526-3637

Earnestine & Hazel's, 531 S. Main, 523-9754

Huey's, 1927 Madison, 726-4372; Sundays

King's Palace, 162 Beale, 521-1851

Mud Island Amphitheater, 125 N. Front, 576-7241

Neil's, 1835 Madison, 278-6345

New Daisy Theater, 330 Beale, 525-8981; Boxing on Beale first Tuesday of every month, World Class Jazz series

North End, 346 N. Main, 526-0319

Orpheum Theater, 89 Beale, 525-3000; Broadway shows, concerts, comedy, and film

Otherlands Coffee Bar, 641 S. Cooper, 278-4994

Overton Park bandshell, concerts April-June, 274-6046

Peabody: Mallard's, Plantation Roof, Skyway Room, 149 Union, 529-4000

The Pyramid, 1 Auction Ave., 521-9675

Rum Boogie Cafe, 182 Beale, 528-0150

Six-1-Six, 600 Marshall, 526-6552

PUBLICATIONS

Memphis Flyer. Free weekly paper with most comprehensive listings, published Wednesdays; 521-9000

Memphis Magazine. Monthly. Sold most everywhere for $3 (a subscription costs $15 per year @ Box 256, Memphis 38101)

Memphis Musician, six times annually

The Commercial Appeal, daily paper; see Friday's *Playbook* for listings

"Kreature Comforts/Lowlife Guide to Memphis," available at Shangri-LA (see "Stores")

"Walking Through Old Memphis," pamphlet on historical attractions; available through Memphis Heritage, Box 3143, Memphis 38103

RESTAURANTS

The Arcade, 540 S. Main, 526-5757

Arizona Restaurant, 394 N. Watkins, 272-9000

Automatic Slim's Tonga Club, 83 S. Second St., 525-7948

Bosco's Pizza Kitchen & Brewery, Germantown, 756-7310

Brother Juniper's College Inn, 3519 Walker, 324-0144

Buntyn, 4972 Park, 458-8776

CK's Coffee Shop, 24 hours, 12 locations

Cafe Ole, 959 S. Cooper, 274-1504

Cafe Samovar, 83 Union, 529-9607

Chez Philippe, 149 Union, 529-4188

Corky's, 5259 Poplar, 685-9771

Cozy Corner, 745 N. Pkwy., 527-9158

D'bo's, 3279 Kirby Pkwy. (East Memphis), 363-8700

Ellen's Soul Food, 601 S. Pkwy E., 942-4888

Four Way Grill, 998 Mississippi Blvd., 775-2351

Interstate Bar-B-Que, 2265 S. Third, 775-2304

Jim's Place East, 5560 Shelby Oaks, 388-7200

La Tourelle, 2146 Monroe, 726-5771

Le Chardonnay Wine Bar & Bistro, 2105 Overton Sq., 725-1375

Leach Family Restaurant, 694 Madison, 521-0867

Lulu Grille, 565 Erin (White Station Plaza), 763-3677

Maxwell's, 948 S. Cooper, 725-1009

Midway Cafe, 3378 Poplar, 458-6660

P & H Cafe, 1532 Madison, 726-0906; smoking encouraged

Rendezvous, 52 S. Second, 523-2746

Restaurant Raji, 712 Brookhaven Circle, 685-8723

Saigon Le, 51 N. Cleveland, 276-5326

Zinnie's, 1688 Madison, 726-5004

LODGING

Brownestone Hotel, 300 N. Second St., 525-2511

The Crowne Plaza, 250 N. Main, 527-7300 or 800-465-4329

Hampton Inn, 1180 Union, 276-1175 or 800-HAMPTON; seven other locations

La Quinta Inn, three locations, 800-531-5900

Lowenstein-Long House, 217 N. Waldran, 527-7174; $10 hostel

The Peabody Hotel, 149 Union, 529-4000 or 800-PEABODY

Radisson Hotel Memphis, 185 Union, 528-1800 or 800-333-3333

Red Roof Inn, 210 S. Pauline, 528-0650

Sleep Inn, Court Square, 800-627-5337

ATTRACTIONS

Center for Southern Folklore, 209 Beale, 525-3655

Chucalissa, 1987 Indian Village (off Mitchell), 785-3160

Delta Axis Contemporary Art Center, 639 Marshall, 522-9946

Delta Blues Museum, Clarksdale, Mississippi, 601-624-4461

Graceland, 3734 Elvis Presley Blvd., 332-3322

Home of Jerry Lee Lewis, Nesbit, Mississippi, 601-429-1290

Libertyland Amusement Park, 940 Early Maxwell Blvd., 274-1776

Memphis Queen Line, foot of Monroe Avenue, 527-5694

Memphis Music Hall of Fame, 97 S. Second, 525-4007
Mud Island, 125 N. Front, 576-7241
National Civil Rights Museum, 450 Mulberry, 521-9699
National Ornamental Metal Museum, 374 W. California, 774-6380
The Pink Palace Museum and Plantarium, 3050 Central, 320-6320
Sun Studio, 706 Union, 521-0664
Tom Lee Park, foot of Beale
W.C. Handy's House and Museum, 352 Beale, 527-3427, May-Sept.

STORES

A. Schwab Dry Goods, 163 Beale, 523-9782; browse the photos and 78s upstairs
All the Music, 3521 Walker Ave. (near U of Memphis), 454-9690
Audiomania, 1698 Madison, 278-1166; blues/jazz CDs/LPs
Blockbuster, 3484 Poplar, 327-8730 (two other locations; hear any CD with no obligation
     to buy)
Burke's Book Store, 1719 Poplar, 278-7484; new and used
Cat's, 1569 Union, 274-2287; six other locations
Shangri-LA, 1916 Madison, 274-1916; eclectic records, mags, posters &c.
Davis-Kidd Booksellers, 397 Perkins Extended, 683-9801
Memphis Drum Shop, 878 S. Cooper, 276-2328
Musitron, 2936 Poplar, 323-TRON
Old Negro League Sports Shop, 154 Beale, 527-5577

EVENTS (INCLUDING WEST TENNESSEE)

Beale Street Music Festival, May, 527-BLUE
Blues Ball, October, Memphis, 527-5683; local music industry's big gala
Chester County Barbecue Festival, July, Henderson, 989-5222
Conference On Freedom, September, National Civil Rights Museum, 521-9699
Cooper-Young Festival, September, Memphis, 527-5700
Crossroads Cross-Cultural Music Exposition, April, hundreds of bands, 576-8171
International Elvis Tribute Week, August, Memphis, 800-238-2000
Lauderdale County Tomato Festival, Ripley, 635-9541
Martin Luther King National Holiday, January, 521-9699
Memphis Blues Festival, August, 576-8171
Memphis In May International Festival, 525-4611
Memphis Music and Heritage Festival, July, Memphis, 525-3655
Mid-South Fair, September, Memphis, 140 years and running, 274-8800
National Catfish Derby, Savannah, 925-8094
Nat'l Field Trial Championship (bird dogs), February, Grand Junction, 878-1067
Native American Days, June, Memphis, 576-8171
Reelfoot Lake Eagle Watch Tours, December-March, Tiptonville, 253-7756

Tina Turner Celebration, Nutbush Heritage Productions, 772-4265 or 8157
W.C. Handy Awards, November, 527-BLUE
West Tennessee Cotton Festival, Crockett Mills, 696-5120
WLOK Stone Soul Picnic, September, 527-9565
World's Biggest Fish Fry, April, Paris, 642-3431

West Tennessee (area code 901)

MISCELLANEOUS

Alex Haley Home, Henning, 738-2240
Casey Jones Village, Jackson, 668-1223; old-time music on Thursdays at dusk
Felsenthal Lincoln Collection, Brownsville, 772-4883
Hatchie National Wildlife Refuge, Brownsville, 772-0501
Pinson Mounds State Archaeological Area, south of Jackson, 988-5614
Shiloh National Military Park, Shiloh 38376; 689-5696
Tennessee River Museum, 507 Main, Savannah; 800-552-3866

LODGING

Airways Motel, 576 Airways Blvd., Jackson, 424-3030; weekly rentals
Boyette's Motel, Tiptonville, 253-6523
Casey Jones Station Inn, 800-628-2812
Chickasaw State Park, west of Henderson, 989-5141; cabins and camping
Days Inn, 1919 Highway 45 Bypass, Jackson, 668-3444
Gooch's Resort, Tiptonville, 253-8955; campground
Hampton Inn, south of Savannah, 689-3031
Pickwick Landing State Park, 800-250-8615

ATTRACTIONS

Danny's Restaurant, Highway 412, Parsons, 847-2429
Denise LaSalle's Chique Boutique & Wigs, Jackson; 423-1565
Haynes Fish Market, 216 N. Shannon, Jackson; 423-1724
Reelfoot Lake visitors center, 800-421-6683 or 253-7756
Suede's, 2263 N. Highland Ave., 664-1956

Discography

Single CDs unless otherwise noted; see end of section for sources.

Acuff, Charlie. *Left-Handed Fiddler* (cassette). Order directly: 942 Birch St., Alcoa, Tenn. 37701.

Acuff, Roy. *Columbia Historic Edition*. Columbia.

Anderson, Muriel. *Heartstrings*. CGD (Box 168, Elmhurst, IL).

Arnold, Eddie. *The Essential Eddie Arnold*. RCA.

Atkins, Chet, and Lenny Breau. *Standard Brands*. One Way/RCA.

BR5-49. *Live From Robert's*. Neo-hillbilly. Arista.

Ballard, Hank, and the Midnighters. *Sexy Ways*. R&B. Rhino.

Beale Street Messaround. Early Memphis jug banders Will Shade, Charlie "Ike" Burse, and others. Rounder (LP).

The Best of Excello Records. Blues, with Slim Harpo, Lazy Lester, etc.

The Best of Nashboro Records. 1950s and '60s gospel. AVI.

Big Star. *Third/Sister Lovers*. Rykodisc.

Blake, Norman. *Whiskey Before Breakfast*. Rounder.

Blake, Norman and Nancy. *Blind Dog* (Rounder) and *Hobo's Last Ride* (Shanachie).

Bland, Bobby. *Years of Tears*. Malaco.

Bless My Bones: Memphis Gospel Radio, the Fifties. Rounder (LP).

Blizard, Ralph, and the New Southern Ramblers. *Southern Ramble* (Rounder) and *Blizard Train* (June Appal). Old-time fiddle.

Blue Highway. *Wind To the West* and *It's a Long, Long Road*. Bluegrass. Rebel.

Blues Masters, Vol. 12: Memphis Blues. From the Beale Street Sheiks through Bobby Blue Bland. Rhino.

Bowman, Charlie. *Moonshiner and His Money*. Old-time fiddling. County.

Breau, Lennie, and Brad Terry, *The Living Room Tapes*. dos Records.

Bridgewater, Dee Dee. *Dear Ella*. Verve.

The Bristol Sessions. Country Music Foundation (two CDs). Jimmie Rodgers, The Carter Family, Ernest Stoneman, and other pioneers of early country music.

Brown, Alison. *Look Left*. Vanguard.

Campbell, Milton (Little Milton). *The Sun Masters*. R&B/blues. Rounder.

[Gus] Cannon's Jug Stompers. *The Complete Works: 1927-1930*. Yazoo.

The Carter Family. *Anchored in Love*. Rounder.

Chilton, Alex. *Clichés*. Ardent.

The Complete Stax/Volt Singles, 1959-1968. Atlantic (nine CDs). The best of Memphis soul, including Otis Redding, Booker T. & the MGs, Carla Thomas, and the Bar-Kays, with 64-page illustrated essay.

Crawford, Hank, with Jimmy McGriff. *Tight* and *On the Blue Side*. Milestone.

Cropper, Steve, with Pop Staples and Albert King. *Jammed Together*. Stax.

Davis, Miles. *Seven Steps To Heaven*. With Memphis-born saxophonist George Coleman.

Davis, Stephen Allen. *The Light Pink Album*. Core.

DeMent, Iris. *My Life* (Warner Brothers) and *Infamous Angel* (Philo).

Dickinson, Jim. *Delta Experimental Projects Compilation*. New Rose (France).

Douglas, Jerry, and Edgar Meyer, with guitarist Russ Barenburg. *Skip, Hop & Wobble*. New acoustic. Sugar Hill.

Down Around Bowmantown: Portrait of a Musical Community in Northeast Tennessee. Now & Then (ETSU's Center For Appalachian Studies).

Draper, O'Landa and the Associates Choir. *All the Bases*. Contemporary gospel. Word.

Earle, Steve. *Train A-Comin'* (Winter Harvest) and *Essential Steve Earle* (MCA).

Early Rural String Bands of Tennessee. County. Includes Charlie Bowman, Dudley Vance, and G.B. Grayson.

Estes, John. *The Legend of Sleepy John Estes*. Delmark.

Ellington, Duke. *Solos, Duets and Trios*. Features bassist Jimmy Blanton, a Chattanooga native. BMG.

Fairfield Four, The. *Standing In the Safety Zone*. Warner Bros.

———. *Standing On the Rock*. AVI.

Falco, Tav, and the Panther Burns. *Shadow Dancer*. Upstart/Rounder.

The Fieldstones. *Memphis Blues Today!* High Water (LP).

The '5' Royales. *Monkey Hips and Rice*. R&B. Rhino (2 CDs).

Flamingo, Hank. *Hank Flamingo*. Giant.

Flatt, Lester, with Earl Scruggs & the Foggy Mountain Boys. *The Complete Mercury Sessions* and *Don't Get Above Your Raisin'*. Rounder.

Fleck, Béla and the Flecktones. *UFO Tofu*. Warner Brothers.

Ford, Tennessee Ernie. *Sacred Memories*. Curb.

Frazier, Nathan, with Frank Patterson and John Lusk. *Black Stringband Music From the Library of Congress*. Rounder.

Frizzell, Lefty. *American Originals* (Columbia) or, for the diehard fan, *Life's Like Poetry* (Bear Family, 12 CDs).

Front Porch String Band. *Front Porch String Band*. Old-time/bluegrass by Claire Lynch's influential early-seventies band. Rebel.

The Gales Bros. *Left Hand Brand*. House of Blues.

Gibson, Don. *Country Spotlight*. Dominion.

Grayson, G.B., and Henry Whitter, *Early Classics, Vol. 1. Old-time from Mountain City*. Old Homestead.

Green, Al. *Your Heart's in Good Hands* (MCA) and *Al* (Beechwood).

Greene, Richard. *The Grass Is Greener*. Rebel.

Grier, David. *Lone Soldier*. Rounder.

Griffith, Nanci. *Storms* and *Little Love Affairs* (MCA), and *The Last of the True Believers* (Philo).

Harper, Roy. *Songs of Yesterday* (cassette). Old Homestead.

Harris, Emmylou. *Wrecking Ball* (Elektra); *At the Ryman* and *Pieces of the Sky* (Reprise).

Hartford, John. *Goin' Back To Dixie*. Old-time fiddle and banjo. Small Dog A-Barkin' (Box 443, Madison, TN).

Henderson, Mike, and the Bluebloods. *First Blood*. Dead Reckoning. Contemporary blues from Nashville.

The Hi Records Story, Cream/Hi Records. Memphis soul/R&B with Bill Black, O.V. Wright, Willie Mitchell, Ann Peebles, Al Green, Ace Cannon, and Otis Clay.

Hi Times: The Hi Records R&B Years. Capitol (three CDs with 64-page booklet).

Highwoods String Brand, The. *Feed Your Babies Onions*. Old-time, upstate New York-style. Rounder.

The Hillbillies. Early old-time string band. County 405.

Hodges Brothers/Hi Rhythm Section. *Perfect Gentlemen*. Velvet.

Howard, Harlan. *All Time Favorite Country Songwriter*. Koch.

Howlin' Wolf. *Cadillac Daddy: Memphis Recordings, 1952* (Rounder) and *Killing Floor* (Charly).

Jason and the Scorchers. *A Blazing Grace*. Mammoth.

Jennings, Waylon. *Collector's Series*. RCA.

Jeter, Rev. Claude. *Yesterday and Today*. Spirit Feel (cassette). Anthology of Swan Silvertones' influential lead singer.

Jones, Ramona. *Lady's Fancy*. Old-time fiddle. County.

Jones, George. *One Woman Man*. CBS.

Jones, George, with Tammy Wynette. *We Love To Sing About Jesus*. Song.

Kane, Kieran. *Dead Rekoning*. Dead Reckoning.

Keaggy, Phil. *Blue*. Word.

King, Albert. *I'll Play the Blues for You*. Stax.

King, B.B. and Bobby Blue Bland. *Together for the First Time . . . Live*. MCA.

Krauss, Alison. *Every Time You Say Goodbye* and *I Know Who Holds Tomorrow*. Rounder.

Laury, Booker T. *Nothin' But the Blues*. Memphis blues and barrelhouse piano. Rounder.

Lawson, Doyle, and Quicksilver. *My Heart Is Yours* and *Heaven's Joy Awaits* (a capella quartet) on Sugar Hill, and *Hallelujah in My Heart* on Brentwood.

Lewis, Furry. *Fourth and Beale*. Country bluesman captured at his most unorthodox. Lucky Seven/Rounder.

The Louvin Brothers. *Songs That Tell a Story*. Rounder.

Lunceford, Jimmie. *Rhythm Is Our Business*. His influential orchestra started out in Memphis. ASV.

Lynch, Claire. *Silver and Gold* and *Moonlighter* (Rounder), and *Friends for a Lifetime* (Brentwood).

Mabern, Harold. *Straight Street*. Memphis-born jazz pianist. Columbia.

Mabern, Harold, with Geoff Keezer. *For Phineas*. Sackville.

Macon, Uncle Dave, with Sam and Kirk McGee. *Go Long Mule*. County.

Martin, Benny. *Tennessee Jubilee*. Flying Fish.

McCoury, Del. *A Deeper Shade of Blue*. Rounder.

McDowell, Fred. *Amazing Grace* (Testament), and *Good Morning Little School Girl* (Arhoolie).

McDowell, Fred, with Furry Lewis and Robert Wilkins. *When I Lay My Burden Down*. Biograph.

McGhee, Brownie. *The Complete Brownie McGhee*. Columbia (2 CDs). Also, *The Folkways Years 1945-59* (Rounder).

Memphis Horns, The. *Wayne Jackson & Andrew Love with Special Guests*. Telarc. Also, *Flame Out* (Rounder).

Memphis Jug Bands. Yazoo (double-LP).

Meyer, Edgar. *Uncommon Ritual*. Sony Classical.

Meyer, Edgar, with Mark O'Connor and Yo-Yo Ma. *Appalachia Waltz*. Sony Classical.

Monroe, Bill. *16 Gems*. Columbia.

Montgomery, Melba, with George Jones. *Vintage Collections*. Capitol.

Mountain City Fiddlers' Convention (1925). County.

Mudboy & the Neutrons. *They Walk Among Us*. Koch.

Nashville Bluegrass Band. *Waitin' For the Hard Times To Go*. Sugar Hill.

Nashville Mandolin Ensemble. *Plectrasonics*. CMH.

New Dixie Entertainers, The. *Maybelle Rag* (cassette). Old-time string band from Harriman, Tenn. Order c/o Mike Bryant, 423-435-4193.

New Lost City Ramblers, The. *Twentieth Anniversary Concert*. Flying Fish, 1987. With the Highwood String Band.

Newborn, Phineas, Jr. *Harlem Blues* (Contemporary) and *Look Out — Phineas Is Back!* (Pablo).

O'Brien, Tim and Mollie. *Away Out on the Mountain*. Sugar Hill.

O'Connell, Maura. *Stories* (Hannibal) and *Just In Time* (Philo).

O'Connor, Mark. *Liberty!* (Sony Classical), and *Heroes* (Warner Brothers).

O'Day, Molly. *Molly O'Day and the Cumberland Mountain Folks*. Bear Family (two CDs).

Orbison, Roy. *The Sun Years, 1956-1958*. Bear Family.

Parton, Dolly. *Slow Dancing with the Moon* (Song) and *Treasures* (Rising Tide).

Perkins, Carl. *The Classic Carl Perkins* (5 CDs), *Country Boy's Dream/The Dollie Masters, Up Through the Years, 1954-1957* (Bear Family); *Honky Tonk Gal: Rare & Unissued Sun Masters* (Rounder), and *Blue Suede Shoes* (Classic).

Phillips, Dewey. *Red Hot & Blue*. Radio broadcasts by legendary Memphis DJ.

Pickett, Wilson. *A Man and a Half* (two CDs) and *The Best of Wilson Pickett*. Rhino.

Poole, Charlie, and the North Carolina Ramblers. *Old-time Songs Recorded from 1925 to 1930*. County.

Presley, Elvis. *The Million Dollar Quartet*. With Jerry Lee Lewis, Johnny Cash, and Carl Perkins.

Psychograss. *Like Minds*. Sugar Hill.

Rachel, James. *James "Yank" Rachel* (Wolf Records, Vienna), and *Early Mandolin Classics, Volume 1* (Rounder).

Randolph, Boots, Jr. *Yakety Sax!* (Song)

Redding, Otis. *Dictionary of Soul*. Atlantic.

Rich, Charlie. *The Sun Sessions*. Varèse.

The Roots 'n' Blues Retrospective, 1925-1950. Columbia (four CDs). Old-time and blues, including Dudley Vance, Charlie Bowman, Peetie Wheatstraw, Leroy Carr, Molly O'Day, and the Anglin Twins.

Sam & Dave. *Hold On, I'm Comin'*. Atlantic.

Selvidge, Sid. *Twice Told Tales*. Elektra.

Sledge, Percy. *It Tears Me Up*. Rhino.

Smith, Bessie. *Beale Street Mama*. Charly.

Smith, Connie. *Greatest Hits on Monument*. Sony.

Smith, Fiddlin' Arthur, with Sam and Kirk McGee. *Milk 'em in the Evening Blues*. Folkways Records. Also try County Sales.

Spirit of Memphis Quartet, Sunset Travelers, and others. *Bless My Bones — Memphis Gospel Radio, the Fifties*. Rounder (LP).

Springfield, Dusty. *Dusty in Memphis*. Rhino.

Stanley, Ralph & the Clinch Mountain Boys. *Born To Ride* and *Long Journey Home* (Rebel), and *Saturday Night & Sunday Morning* (Freeland Recording, two CDs).

Staples, Mavis, with Lucky Peterson. *Spirituals & Gospel*. Gitanes/Verve.

Step By Step: Leslie Riddle Meets the Carter Family: Blues, Country, and Sacred Songs. Rounder.

Stoneman, Ernest V. *Me & My Autoharp*. Old Homestead (cassette).

Strength In Numbers. *The Telluride Sessions*. New acoustic "superband." MCA.

Stuart, Marty. *Honky Tonkin's What I Do Best*, and *This One's Gonna Hurt You*. MCA.

Swan's Silvertone Singers. *Heavenly Light* (Specialty) and *Love Lifted Me/My Rock* (two CDs), Specialty/Fantasy; and *Gusto* (LP, available through Cindy Lou's Musical Mail Order, Box 8008, Nashville 37207).

Take Six. *Take Six.* Reprise.
The Tractors. *The Tractors.* Arista.
Travis, Merle. *Best of Merle Travis.* Rhino.

Various artists. *True Life Blues: the Songs of Bill Monroe.* Sugar Hill.

Wail Daddy! Nashville Jump Blues. Ace (Excello).
Ward, Clara. *The Very Greatest.* AVI.
Watson, Doc. *Riding the Midnight Train* and *Remembering Merle.* Sugar Hill.
Welch, Gillian. *Revival.* Almo Sounds.
Wells, Kitty. *CMH Hall of Fame Series.* MCA.
White Country Blues, 1926-1938: A Lighter Shade of Blue. Sony (2 CDs).
White, Roland. *Trying To Get To You.* Bluegrass.
The Whites. *Doing It By the Book.* Word.
Williams, Hank. *Health & Happiness Shows.* Polygram (2 CDs).
Williams, James. *At Maybeck Recital Hall.* Concord.
Williams, Lucinda. *Lucinda Williams.* Chameleon/Elektra.
Winans, BeBe and CeCe. *Different Lifestyles.*
Wiseman, Mac. *Classic Bluegrass* (Rebel) and *Grassroots to Bluegrass* (CMH).
Wooten, Victor. *A Show of Hands* and *What Did He Say?.* Compass.
Wright, O.V. *That's How Strong My Love Is.* Soul. Cream/Hi.

Sources
Arhoolie/Folklyric, 10341 San Pablo Ave., El Cerrito, CA 94530; 510-525-2129. Strong blues catalogue.
Bear Family Records, P.O. Box 1154, 2864 Vollersode, West Germany. Phone: (04794) 1399. High-quality CDs and box sets featuring often overlooked American musicians, especially strong in country. Expensive. It may be easier to order through your local record store.
CMH Records, P.O. Box 39439, Los Angeles, CA 90039.
Center for Appalachian Studies, P.O. Box 70566 ETSU, Johnson City, TN 37614; 615-929-5348. Old-time, bluegrass.
Charly Records Ltd., 156/166 Ilderton Road, London SE15 1NT. Phone: (071) 639-8603. Similar to Bear Family. Reissues of blues, rhythm and blues, rockabilly, rock, jazz, gospel, and soul artists.
Country Music Foundation, 4 Music Sq. E., Nashville, TN 37203; 800-255-2357, 9 AM-5 PM (CST) 7 days a week. Outside the U.S. or Canada, call 615-256-1639.
County Sales, P.O. Box 191, Floyd, VA 24091; 540-745-2001. Great catalogue of fiddle music, old-time, bluegrass, and gospel.
Folkways Records, 416 Hungerford Road, Suite 320, Rockville, MD 20850.
High Water Recording Company, c/o Dr. David Evans, Music Department, Memphis State University, Memphis, TN 38152. Blues, gospel, and jazz.
Homespun Tapes, Box 694, Woodstock, NY 12498; 800-338-2737. Music instruction videos.

Old Homestead Records, Box 100, Brighton, MI 48116; 810-227-1997. Extensive list of obscure early country, bluegrass, and gospel LPs.

Rhino Records, 2225 Colorado Ave., Santa Monica, CA 90404; 800-432-0020 (24 hours). Outside the U.S., 818-587-6085. Early rock and soul.

Rounder Records, 1 Camp St., Cambridge, MA 02140; 800-443-4727. Old-time, bluegrass, blues, R&B, soul, gospel, and jazz.

Shanachie, P.O. Box 284, Newton, NJ 07860. 800-497-1043. Early blues and old-time.

Stackhouse/Delta Record Mart, 232 Sunflower Ave., Clarksdale, MS 38614; 601-627-2209. Blues.

Sugar Hill Records, P.O. Box 55300, Durham, NC 27717; 800-996-4455. Bluegrass.

Also see "Tennessee Folk Music Recordings: A Recommended List," published by the Tennessee Arts Commission, 320 Sixth Ave. N., Ste. 100, Nashville 37243.

Bibliography

Albertson, Chris. *Bessie.* Stein and Day, 1985.

Allen, Bob, ed. *Blackwell Guide to Recorded Country Music.* 1994.

All Shook Up: Mississippi Roots of American Popular Music. Mississippi Department of Archives and History, 1995.

Bane, Michael. *White Boy Singin' the Blues.* Penguin, 1982.

Bastin, Bruce. *Red River Blues: The Blues Tradition in the Southeast.* University of Illinois Press, 1986.

Bird, Christiane. *The Jazz and Blues Lover's Guide to the U.S.* Addison Wesley.

Blackwell, Lois S. *The Wings of the Dove: The Story of Gospel Music in America.* Donning Co., Norfolk, Virginia, 1978.

Boles, John B. *The Great Revival, 1787-1805.* University Press of Kentucky, 1972.

Booth, Stanley. *Rythm Oil: A Journey Through the Music of the American South.* Pantheon, 1991.

Bowman, Rob. *Soulsville, U.S.A.: The Story of Stax Records.* Schirmer Books, 1997.

Bruce, Dickson D., Jr. *And They All Sang Hallelujah.* University of Tennessee Press, 1974.

Bufwack, Mary A. with Robert K. Oermann. *Finding Her Voice: The Saga of Women in Country Music.* Crown, 1993.

Burton, Thomas G., ed. *Tom Ashley, Sam McGee, Bukka White: Tennessee Traditional Singers.* UT Press, 1981.

Cantor, Louis. *Wheelin' on Beale: How WDIA–Memphis Became the Nation's First All-Black Radio Station.* Pharos, 1992.

Cauthen, Joyce H. *With Fiddle and Well-rosined Bow: Old-Time Fiddling in Alabama.* University of Alabama Press, 1989.

Charters, Samuel. *Sweet As the Showers of Rain: The Bluesmen, Volume II.* Oak Publications, 1977.

Cohn, Lawrence. *Nothin' but the Blues: The Music and the Musicians.* Abbeville Press, 1993.

Corlew, Robert E. *Tennessee: A Short History.* UT Press, 1981.

Country Music Foundation. *Country: The Music and the Musicians.* Country Music Foundation, 1988.

Cusic, Don. *The Sound of Light: A History of Gospel Music.* Bowling Green State University Popular Press, 1990.

Davidson, Donald. *The Tennessee: Frontier to Secession.* Rinehart & Co., 1946.

Delmore, Alton. *Truth Is Stranger Than Fiction.* Country Music Foundation, 1977.

Ellington, Duke. *Music Is My Mistress.* Doubleday, 1973.

Epstein, Dena J. *Sinful Tunes and Spirituals: Black Folk Music to the Civil War.* University of Illinois Press, 1977.

Escott, Colin. *Good Rockin' Tonight: Sun Records and the Birth of Rock 'n' Roll.* St. Martin's Press, 1991.

———. *Hank Williams.* Little, Brown, 1995.

Faragher, Scott. *Music City Babylon: Inside the World of Country Music.* Carol Publishing Group, 1992.

Ferris, William. *Blues from the Delta.* Da Capo, 1984.

Geller, Larry. *If I Can Dream.* Simon and Schuster, 1989.

Gordon, Robert. *It Came from Memphis.* Faber and Faber, 1995.

Guralnick, Peter. *Last Train to Memphis: The Rise of Elvis Presley.* Little, Brown, 1994.

———. *Sweet Soul Music: Rhythm and Blues and the Southern Dream of Freedom.* Harper & Row, 1986.

Handy, W.C. *Father of the Blues: An Autobiography.* Collier Books, 1941.

Harris, Sheldon. *Blues Who's Who.* Da Capo, 1979.

Harrison, Daphne Duval. *Black Pearls: Blues Queens of the 1920s.* Rutgers University Press, 1988.

Heilbut, Tony. *The Gospel Sound: Good News and Bad Times.* Simon and Schuster, 1971.

Kirby, Edward "Prince Gabe." *From Africa to Beale Street.* Lubin Press, 1983.

Lornell, Kip. *"Happy in the Service of the Lord": Afro-American Gospel Quartets in Memphis.* University of Illinois Press, 1988.

Malone, Bill C. *Singing Cowboys and Musical Mountaineers: Southern Culture and the Roots of Country Music.* University of Georgia Press, 1993.

———. *Country Music, U.S.A.* University of Texas Press, 1985.

———. *Stars of Country Music: Uncle Dave Macon to Johnny Rodriguez.* Malone and Judith McCullough, eds. University of Illinois Press, 1975.

Marcus, Greil. *Dead Elvis: A Chronicle of a Cultural Obsession.* Doubleday, 1991.

———. *Mystery Train: Images of America in Rock 'n' Roll Music.* E.P. Dutton & Co., 1976.

Marsh, Dave. *Elvis.* Thunder's Mouth Press. 1996.

McCloud, Barry. *Definitive Country.* Perigee/Berkeley, 1995.

McDonald, Patrick. *A Collection of Highland Vocal Airs.* Norwood Editions, Norwood, Penn., 1973 (orig. 1784).

McKee, Margaret, and Fred Chisenhall. *Beale Black & Blue: Life and Music on Black America's Main Street.* Louisiana State University Press, 1981.

McNeil, W.K. *Southern Mountain Folksongs: Traditional Songs from the Appalachians and the Ozarks.* August House Publishers, Little Rock, 1993.

McNutt, Randy. *We Wanna Boogie: An Illustrated History of the American Rockabilly Movement.* Hamilton Hobby, 1989.

McWhiney, Grady. *Cracker Culture: Celtic Ways in the Old South.* University of Alabama Press, 1989.

Morton, David C., with Charles K. Wolfe. *DeFord Bailey: a Black Star in Early Country Music.* UT Press, 1991. See also Wolfe, Charles K.

Naipaul, V.S. *A Turn in the South.* Alfred A. Knopf, 1989.

Nathan, Hans. *Dan Emmett and the Rise of Early Negro Minstrelsy.* University of Oklahoma Press, 1962.

Neal, James H. *Music Research in Tennessee: a Guide to Special Collections.* Middle Tennessee State, 1989.

Oermann, Robert K., with Douglas B. Green. *The Listener's Guide to Country Music.* Quatro Marketing Ltd., 1983. See also Bufwack, Mary K.

O'Dair, Barbara, ed. *Trouble Girls: the Rolling Stone Book of Women In Rock.* Rolling Stone Press (Random House), 1997.

O'Shea, Shad. *Just for the Record.* Positive Feedback Communications Press, Cincinnati, 1986.

Palmer, Robert. *Deep Blues.* Penguin, 1982.

Parton, Dolly. *Dolly: My Life and Other Unfinished Business.* HarperCollins, 1994.

Pike, Gustavus D. *The Jubilee Singers, and Their Campaign for Twenty Thousand Dollars.* Lee and Shepard, Boston, 1873.

The Rolling Stone Illustrated History of Rock & Roll. Anthony DeCurtis and James Henke, eds. Random House, 1992.

Rooney, James. *Bossmen: Bill Monroe & Muddy Waters.* Da Capo, 1991.

Rosenberg, Neil V. *Bluegrass: a History.* University of Illinois Press, 1985.

Sawyer, Charles. *The Arrival of B.B. King.* Doubleday, 1980.

Seay, Davin. *Stairway to Heaven: the Spiritual Roots of Rock 'n' Roll from the King and Little Richard to Prince and Amy Grant.* Ballantine, 1986.

Sharp, Cecil J. and Olive Dame Campbell. *English Folk Songs from the Southern Appalachians.* Putnam's, 1917.

Shaw, Arnold. *Honkers and Shouters: The Golden Years of Rhythm and Blues.* Macmillan, 1978.

Smith, Jessie C. *Notable Black American Women, Books one and two.* Gale, 1991/1996.

Stamper, Powell. *The National Life Story: a History of the National Life and Accident Insurance Company of Nashville, Tennessee.* Appleton-Century-Crofts, 1968.

Steele, William O. *The Cherokee Crown of Tannassy.* John F. Blair, 1977.

Tosches, Nick. *Hellfire: The Jerry Lee Lewis Story.* Dell, 1982.

Waller, William. *Nashville in the 1890s* and *Nashville, 1900-1910.* Vanderbilt University Press.

Wexler, Jerry, and David Ritz. *Rhythm and the Blues: A Life in American Music.* Knopf, 1993.

Wittke, Carl. *Tambo and Bones: A History of the American Minstrel Stage.* Duke University Press, 1930.

Wolfe, Charles K. *The Devil's Box.* Vanderbilt University Press, 1997. See also Morton, David C.

———. *Tennessee Strings: The Story of Country Music in Tennessee.* UT Press, 1977.

Index

Photo and Illustration Sources

Almo Sounds Inc. 121 (photo by John Patrick Salisbury); **Asylum Records** 119; James Barringer 185; Richard Blaustein/Archives of Appalachia/East Tennessee State University Archives 168–169; Blue Ridge Heritage Archive of Ferrum College 34; Baxter Buck 197; Tim Campbell 160; Center for Popular Music, Middle Tennessee State University 88, 209 (2); Country Music Foundation 19, 91, 100, 111, 128; Jim Cole/Mississippi Valley Collection 75, 147; Steve Cropper 132, 138–139; Libby Davidson 42; Jim Dickinson 65; Colin Escott/Showtime Music Archive 141, 230, 235 (photo by Masel Priesman); Bob Fulcher 49; Landon & Ruby Hampton 257; Hatch Showprint 38, 114, 165, 202; Josefish/LEX 78; Ron Keith/Warner Alliance 98; Erica Lansner 58, 142, 154; Les Leverett 24–25, 31, 32, 162–163, 188, 200, 201; Kip Lornell 95; Claire Lynch 102; MCA Records 107; Fred McClellan 41; Jim McGuire/Sony Music Corporation 149; Alan Messer/Rounder Records 106; New York Public Library 151; Scott O'Malley & Associates 190; Bud Phillips 171; Lynn Porterfield/Artstar 69; Ebet Roberts 71; Schomburg Center for Research in Black Culture 73; Jack Spencer 17; Vanguard Records 156; Voo Doo Rocket, Inc. 197; Perry Walker 5, 6–7, 14, 16, 27, 28, 43, 45, 52–53, 80, 166, 173, 180, 181, 217, 243, 248, 251, 256; Claire Wasserman 221; Ernest Withers/Panopticon 82–83, 112–113, 237, 249; Peter Zimmerman 11, 59, 87, 105; Florence Zinman 50, 224, 241.

Although every attempt has been made to obtain copyright clearance on all images contained herein, copyright holders who have been omitted should please contact Miller Freeman Books so that the situation may be rectified in further editions.

MIS/74/01